CW01329399

REVIEWING SHAKESPEARE

Ranging from David Garrick's Macbeth in the 1740s to the World Shakespeare Festival in London 2012, this is the first book to provide in-depth analysis of the history and practice of Shakespearean theatre reviewing. *Reviewing Shakespeare* describes the changing priorities and interpretive habits of theatre critics as they have both responded to and provoked innovations in Shakespearean performance culture over the last three centuries. It analyses the conditions – theatrical, journalistic, social and personal – in which Shakespearean reception has taken place, presenting original readings of the works of key critics (Shaw, Beerbohm, Agate, Tynan), while also tracking broader historical shifts in the relationship between reviewers and performance. Prescott explores the key function of the 'night-watch constable' in patrolling the boundaries of legitimate Shakespearean performance and offers a compelling account of the many ways in which newspaper reviews are uniquely fruitful documents for anyone interested in Shakespeare and the theatre.

PAUL PRESCOTT is Associate Professor of English at the University of Warwick, a Trustee of the British Shakespeare Association and a teaching associate of the Royal Shakespeare Company. He has published widely on theatre history, contemporary performance and creative pedagogy, and is currently completing a short biography of Sam Wanamaker, founder of Shakespeare's Globe. His work has appeared in publications including *The New Cambridge Companion to Shakespeare*, *The Blackwell Companion to Shakespeare and Performance* and *Shakespeare Survey*. He is the co-founder of www.yearofshakespeare.com and www.reviewingshakespeare.com.

REVIEWING SHAKESPEARE

Journalism and Performance from the Eighteenth Century to the Present

PAUL PRESCOTT

CAMBRIDGE
UNIVERSITY PRESS

University Printing House, Cambridge CB2 8BS, United Kingdom

Published in the United States of America by Cambridge University Press, New York

Cambridge University Press is part of the University of Cambridge.

It furthers the University's mission by disseminating knowledge in the pursuit of education, learning and research at the highest international levels of excellence.

www.cambridge.org
Information on this title: www.cambridge.org/9781107021495

© Paul Prescott 2013

This publication is in copyright. Subject to statutory exception and to the provisions of relevant collective licensing agreements, no reproduction of any part may take place without the written permission of Cambridge University Press.

First published 2013

Printed in the United Kingdom by CPI Group Ltd, Croydon CR0 4YY

A catalogue record for this publication is available from the British Library

Library of Congress Cataloguing in Publication data
Prescott, Paul, 1974–
Reviewing Shakespeare : journalism and performance from the eighteenth century to the present / Paul Prescott.
  pages cm
Includes bibliographical references and index.
ISBN 978-1-107-02149-5 (hardback)
1. Shakespeare, William, 1564–1616 – Criticism and interpretation – History.
2. Shakespeare, William, 1564–1616 – Dramatic production.
3. Shakespeare, William, 1564–1616 – Influence. 4. Theater – Reviews. I. Title.
  PR3091.P74 2013
  822.3′3 – dc23   2013013780

ISBN 978-1-107-02149-5 Hardback

Cambridge University Press has no responsibility for the persistence or accuracy of URLs for external or third-party internet websites referred to in this publication, and does not guarantee that any content on such websites is, or will remain, accurate or appropriate.

*For my parents,
Philippa and William Prescott*

Contents

Acknowledgements		*page* ix
1	An introduction to the night-watch constable	1
	Performance, print, memory: three preludes	1
	Eunuchs in a harem: the cultural reputation of the critic	6
	Night-watch constables, men of letters and domineering pedants	10
	Critical conditions	17
	Re-viewing the Shakespearean reviewer: precedents	20
	Reviewing Shakespeare: the argument	24
2	Tradition and the individual talent: reviewing the Macbeth actor *c.*1740s–1890s	31
	Macbeth and the ghost of success	32
	'Are you a man?' Macbeth, King David and the Irish Jew	36
	Heroic assassin or common stabber? Class, masculinity and courage	43
	Mid century Macbeths: rivalry and rioting	47
	A domestic coward: Irving's Macbeth and the masculine estimate of man	50
	'Lay on': the Macbeth actor exits fighting	54
3	New Journalism, New Critics *c.*1890–1910	57
	'The climax and masterpiece of literary Jacobinism': the introduction of the signed article	58
	'Gentlemen, I am about to speak of myself *à propos* of Shakespeare': the critic and the play of personality	67
	'The best part of the circus': Shaw as New Critic	72
	'The plays as Shakespeare wrote them': Shaw and authenticity	77
	'He would buy me in the market like a rabbit': Shaw and incorruptibility	82
	'The hack work of genius': Beerbohm and Shakespeare in the *Saturday Review*	84
4	The reviewer in transition *c.*1920–1960	94
	Prologue: another Shaw?	94
	'That modern nuisance': Agate, the producer and the death of the actor	97

Unchanging Cockaigne: Agate and the recuperation of tradition	105
'Post-mortem on the egoist': style, paternity and the dynamics of succession	112
He That Plays the King: enter Tynan, stage right	116
'When comes there such another?' Tynan, Olivier and Macbeth	119
Re-enter Tynan, stage left: anti-heroic Shakespeare and the possibility of radicalism	126
Conclusion: Roundheads and Cavaliers	131

5 New contexts, new crises (1997–2012): reviewing from the opening of Shakespeare's Globe to the World Shakespeare Festival 2012 — 133

'When comes there such another?' Tynan and belatedness	136
Matters of size and status: reviewing and post-Fleet Street journalism	139
A community of the same? The cultural biography of contemporary reviewers	143
Speak, memory: a misfortune of *Macbeth*s 1995–6	145
Inheriting the Globe: the reception of Shakespearean audience and authenticity in contemporary reviewing	154
Damn Yankees: reviewing the Shakespearean audience	156
'Arsenal/Tottenham': reviewing the Shakespearean space	163
'Dear Mr Billington': the audience writes back	171
The World Shakespeare Festival 2012: coverage, comment and the framer framed	177
'Back to British business as usual': race, nation and regime change in *Henry V* at the Globe and *Julius Caesar* in Stratford	183
Epilogue: guarding the guardians, changing the guard	190

Notes	196
Works cited	199
Index	212

Acknowledgements

This book began its life at the Shakespeare Institute, Stratford-upon-Avon, and owes much to the company and advice of students and staff at that very special place. John Jowett and Russell Jackson offered typically acute comments on first drafts of early chapters. I also owe a great debt of gratitude to Peter Holland for setting the ball rolling and for being such a kind, clever and inspiring mentor.

In the years since I have benefited from dozens of conferences, seminars, panels and discussions – formal and otherwise – with too many friends, students and colleagues to do justice to here. But I am very grateful for assistance from librarians at the Shakespeare Institute (especially James Shaw and Kate Welch), the Bodleian, the British Library and the University of Warwick. Warm thanks to Andrew Dickson, Terence Hawkes, David Roberts, and Gary Taylor for input and advice at key stages; to Paul Edmondson, Peter J. Smith and Stanley Wells, for reading and generously commenting on late drafts of the manuscript. Special thanks to Michael Billington, Michael Coveney, Charles Spencer and the late John Gross for sharing their experiences and thoughts in interview. Earlier versions of parts of Chapters 2 and 5 have previously appeared in *Shakespeare Survey 58* and the Blackwell *Companion to Shakespeare and Performance* (ed. Barbara Hodgdon and W.B. Worthen).

At the business end of the publishing process, I am immensely grateful to Mary Stewart Burgher and Lydia Wanstall for giving so freely of their time and expertise in helping to proof final drafts; Chris Jackson was also an exemplary copy-editor. All errors and infelicities are my own. At Cambridge University Press, Rebecca Taylor, Joanna Breeze and Anna Lowe have all been models of care and efficiency. And I am delighted to join a generation of Shakespeareans in thanking Sarah Stanton for everything she does, for individual authors and for the profession as a whole.

It is hard to imagine a greater or a happier debt than the one I owe to my parents, without whom it is pretty safe to say this book would not have been written. I therefore dedicate this to them on the joyous occasion – 31 August 2013 – of their golden wedding anniversary.

CHAPTER ONE

An introduction to the night-watch constable

Performance, print, memory: three preludes

17 May 1833: George Douchez, Esq., physician, contemplates the corpse of Edmund Kean. Setting about the melancholy task of dissecting the great actor, he notes 'a heart excessively loaded with fat', a 'considerably emaciated' face and neck, and a brain whose substance is 'softer than usual'. Suddenly these neutral, detached observations give way to a heightened moment of appreciation: 'Body well formed, and the external form of the thorax and the abdomen so beautifully developed as to serve as one of the finest models that could possibly be presented to the eye of the sculptor or painter' (Hillebrand 1966: 371–2). Sixteen years earlier, on 27 October 1817, *The Times* had carried a review of Kean's performance as Othello, a notice that had concluded with a comparable admiration for the detail and overall effect on the spectator of Kean's physique: 'The convulsed motions of the hands, and the involuntary swellings of the veins of the forehead in some of the most painful situations, should not only suggest topics of critical panegyric, but might furnish studies to the painter or anatomist' (Hazlitt 1930–4: XVIII 263).

That two different but related forms of memorialisation should fasten on the pictorial quality of an actor's body is perhaps unsurprising. Yet what may shift the relationship from coincidence to quotation is the fact that the theatre reviewer, William Hazlitt, felt so pleased with his initial review that he republished it, almost verbatim, on two further occasions. In 1820, in a series of essays for the *London Magazine*, Hazlitt (1930–4: XVIII 302) recycled the piece in the pseudo-anonymous guise of 'the words of a contemporary journal, a short time back'. Then, after an eight-year absence from theatre criticism, he again reproduced the review in 1828 in a nostalgic piece for *The Examiner*, the only variant being that he – for some reason – altered the final words from 'painter or anatomist' to 'painter or sculptor' (394). 'Sculptor or painter' were the two professions that would spring to Douchez's mind five years later as he reviewed Kean's corpse.

12 June 1906: Drury Lane theatre hosts a jubilee celebration for Ellen Terry. The actress's fiftieth year on the stage prompts a remarkable display of affection on both sides of the proscenium. In a varied programme, performers as diverse as Eleonora Duse, Enrico Caruso, Johnston Forbes-Robertson, Benoît Coquelin and Herbert Beerbohm Tree either accompanied the dedicatee in abbreviated scenes or else offered solo turns in her honour. The matinee began shortly after midday, continued for six hours, and would have lasted longer had Terry not been required to act that evening as Lady Cicely Waynflete in a production of George Bernard Shaw's *Captain Brassbound's Conversion*. Drury Lane was the perfect symbolic setting for this exercise in nostalgia; in her address to the audience, Terry thanked Mr Collins, 'who has lent this great theatre with its inspiring memories' (Agate 1946: 144), memories that, despite repeated destruction and reconstruction, stretched back to 1663. The theatre of Edmund Kean and W.C. Macready also had more recent memories for those present: a newspaper reported that at the conclusion of the proceedings 'The audience sang "Auld Lang Syne" just as it did at Sir Henry Irving's final appearance at the same theatre just a year ago' (145). After the song, the audience slowly, reluctantly dispersed. The performance was over, but the process of remembering had just begun: 'the jaded pittites blinked as they emerged into daylight and bought evening papers that they might read about it all before going to bed' (145). Gripped by an instant nostalgia for what they had witnessed, the pittites (and presumably other sections of the audience) resorted to print media to prolong the experience a little further. When they woke up next day they might have consulted the morning papers, which had a 'more leisured say' on the event and the ability to reprint and comment on 'the speeches which were delivered late in the afternoon' of the jubilee (143).

I do not know who wrote the above press account of the jaded pittites. It was one of fifteen hundred press cuttings related to the London theatre in the period 1897–1906 sent by parcel to *Sunday Times* critic and publishing machine James Agate in May 1946. The names of the papers had been deleted by the original collector and Agate 'refrain[ed] from guesswork' (Agate 1946: xi). This parcel supplemented another package of newspaper reviews anonymously sent to Agate in 1940, and, in June 1946, forty years after Ellen Terry's jubilee, Agate edited the two donations into a book, *Those Were the Nights*. The book was aimed at 'readers who', like Terry's pittites, 'would call back yesterday' (1). Three years earlier, Agate had produced a similar anthology of reviews, *These Were Actors*, based on press cuttings bequeathed to him by Clement Scott, the most influential critic of the late nineteenth century.

12 September 2012: the morning after press night for Michael Attenborough's production of *King Lear* starring Jonathan Pryce at the Almeida Theatre, London. Charles Spencer began his *Daily Telegraph* review: 'Back in 1980, Jonathan Pryce caused a sensation with his performance as Hamlet, the hoop through which every aspiring classical actor must jump. Those who saw it will never forget the extraordinary scene in which he seemed to become physically possessed by the ghost of his dead father' (Spencer 2012). Spencer's image of the hoop-jumping actor silently quotes Max Beerbohm's review of Sarah Bernhardt's Hamlet of 1899 in which Beerbohm lamented: 'In England, as I suggested some time ago, "Hamlet" has long ceased to be treated as a play. It has become simply a hoop through which every eminent actor must, sooner or later, jump. The eminent actor may not have any natural impulse to jump through it, but that does not matter' (Beerbohm 1953: 36). Beerbohm's review is itself quotational: in this case a self-reference to one of the first pieces he wrote for the *Saturday Review* in which he complained that watching over-produced plays – such as Shakespeare's – was a haunted experience: the memory of previous Macbeths, Hamlets, Othellos fogged up the brain, cluttered the act of reception and prompted a dreary 'kind of comparative criticism . . . The play is dead. The stage is crowded with ghosts. Every head in the audience is a heavy casket of reminiscence' (9). Spencer's review kept alive the memory not only of Pryce's Hamlet of 1980, but also of Beerbohm's criticism of 1899: his review, no less than Pryce's Hamlet, was possessed by the ghost of a dead father.

On the following morning, 13 September 2012, Michael Billington's review of *Hedda Gabler* at the Old Vic began: 'Ibsen's Hedda was once described as the hoop through which every aspiring female actor must jump; and Sheridan Smith performs the feat with commendable ease and agility' (Billington 2012a). As in Spencer, 'aspiring' has replaced Beerbohm's original 'eminent'. But who was it exactly that 'once described' the Hedda hoop? Perhaps it was Billington himself, who wrote a generation earlier in 1991: '*Hedda Gabler* is now one of the most frequently performed of all Ibsen's plays, while the title role has become the female equivalent of Hamlet, the hoop through which most ambitious actresses feel obliged to jump' (*TR* 1991: 1060). The hoop, it would appear, is on a loop.

Anyone who read Spencer and Billington's reviews online could also record their own thoughts in the comments section placed beneath the review. (They could also click on a sidebar advert run throughout September and October 2012, promoting a course of 'six in-depth masterclasses on writing theatre reviews' led by *Guardian* critics.) Beneath Spencer's review Tom Snood wondered 'Why do theatres never bung a camera in the audience so that after the run we could all see it on telly? They used to do it with Whitehall Farces I seem to recall.' Billington's nuanced and lukewarm account of *Hedda* generated more debate, the last word on which fell to the unpronounceable 'HTPBDET': 'Apart from *Judas Kiss* or *Curious Incident*, both of which I have not yet seen, this is easily the best play on stage in London at present. See it for yourself.'

* * *

Many of Shakespeare's plays end with the promise of continued conversation. For the last two and a half centuries, newspaper reviews have been a vital part of that conversation and have played a key role in the collective experience of theatregoing and theatre-talking. Of all the textual inscriptions of performance, journalistic reviews are both the most widely circulated and the most influentially constitutive of memory and value. Reviews have been the primary vehicle in which performance is described and evaluated, and through which vicarious experience, opinion and reputation are propagated. This book explores the conditions – theatrical, journalistic, personal and social – in which journalistic critics have received Shakespearean performance from the origins of newspaper reviewing in the mid eighteenth century to the present day.

The preludes above offer three Polaroids from the theatrical past and announce the key themes of this book: death and deadlines; ephemerality and permanence; memory and nostalgia; quotation and recycling; surrogation and succession; authority and legitimacy. British Shakespearean theatre reviewing – no less than the performances it chronicles – has its own traditions, conventions, habits, lineages and anxieties. It is insistently intertextual and constantly recycles past writing and past experiences ('Those who saw it will never forget') in an effort to resurrect the fallen, make visible the vanished, and endow the present with shape and meaning. Erin Diamond writes: 'While a performance embeds traces of other performances, it also produces an experience whose interpretation only partially depends on previous experience. Hence the terminology of "re" in discussion of performance, as in *re*member, *re*inscribe, *re*configure, *re*iterate, *re*store' (Diamond 1995: 2). And, one might add, rehearse, repeat, reminisce and *re*view. The extent of theatregoers' dependence on previous experience – their own and others – is greater in a crowded and high-status performance tradition such as that of Shakespearean production. As Beerbohm noted, when watching many Shakespeare plays on stage, the individual and collective head is 'a heavy casket of reminiscence', and those reminiscences can be traced not merely to prior empirical encounters with the same play or performers or theatre spaces, but also to the extent of one's exposure to the body of second-hand memories, gossip and folklore that has built up over four hundred years of theatre practice. For Beerbohm this was a melancholy prospect, but many recognise the lively play of voluntary and involuntary memory as one of the chief pleasures of repeated theatregoing. Marvin Carlson, in common with many theorists of the stage, sees in all theatre a more or less therapeutic negotiation with the fact of mortality: 'the simultaneous attraction to and fear of the dead, the need continually to rehearse and renegotiate the relationship with memory and the past, is nowhere more specifically expressed in human culture than in theatrical performance' (Carlson 2003: 167); it is inevitable then that – whatever other functions they serve – newspaper theatre reviews are these attractions and fears made print, offering widely read post-mortems on who or what appeared again last night, and whether or not or how it died. For Carlson, Herbert Blau, Joseph Roach and others, performance is always ghosted, always productive of the uncanny sensation that '*we are seeing what we saw before*' (Blau 1987: 173). Perhaps it was so when Douchez gazed down on Kean's corpse – perhaps he had seen Kean before on stage with his own eyes, or perhaps he had seen Kean in print and *in extremis* through the eyewitness accounts of William Hazlitt.

HTPBDET's parting injunction – 'See it for yourself' – has the potential to render the expert critic impotent and redundant. The general public's agency and opinion are sovereign; one can certainly be a theatregoer without reading reviews. But the reverse is entirely conceivable. Indeed, when it comes to performances that history, geography or even economics have placed beyond our spectatorship, we may be entirely dependent on the critic whose presence at the performance acts as a surrogate for our own. Reading and writing reviews puts us into relationships of informational dependency and influence, just as the above anecdotes are stories of triangulated (Kean–Hazlitt–Douchez) or squared (Beerbohm–Spencer–Billington–Pryce) kinship groups, partly inflamed by what Harold Bloom (1997: 38), in another context, has called 'influenza'. We should note here that while women – such as Ellen Terry and Sheridan Smith – have often been the subjects of criticism, they have only rarely (and mostly very recently) been the authors of it; the default setting for Shakespearean reviewing is that of a male critic writing about male actors. It may therefore come as little surprise that the following pages repeat and rehearse successive moments of crisis, competition and rivalry. In doing so, they obsessively turn and return to *Macbeth*, that drama of anxious and competitive masculinity, of success, surcease and succession. In that play's violent struggles, performance anxieties and multiple hauntings I see a vivid premonition of the structures of reception and the fraught psychology of Shakespearean theatre reviewing.

* * *

This is the first book-length study of the relationship between journalist reviewers and Shakespearean performance. That no one has thought to write a book about this before perhaps indicates the low esteem in which scholars have held journalists and journalistic criticism. In the following section of this introduction I describe the cultural reputation of newspaper criticism as a secondary, parasitic pursuit conducted in the compromising context of journalism. Through a comparison with the history of English literary criticism and with the relatively recent figure of the academic Shakespeare reviewer, I then define the distinctive qualities and conditions of journalistic reviewing and its insecure status as a profession. Next I survey the precedents for this book, the articles on Shakespearean reviewing and the books on theatre criticism that have attempted to take seriously the various relationships between performance, journalistic practice, reviewers and the shifting but ever-powerful figure of Shakespeare. Finally, I discuss the problems posed by writing a history of Shakespearean theatre reviewing, before setting out the parameters and argument of this study.

Eunuchs in a harem: the cultural reputation of the critic

In *Love's Labour's Lost*, the hitherto cynical bachelor Berowne has fallen hopelessly in love, against his vows, with one of the ladies who attend on the visiting French Princess. He marvels at the metamorphosis:

> And I, forsooth, in love – I that have been love's whip,
> A very beadle to a humorous sigh,
> A critic, nay, a night-watch constable,
> A domineering pedant o'er the boy [Cupid],
> Than whom no mortal so magnificent.   (3.1.169–73)

This contest between the Critic and Love later springs to Berowne's mind when he overhears all three of his friends reveal their own secret desires for the remaining members of the Gallic contraband. Stepping forth to 'whip hypocrisy', he hypocritically laments *their* undignified transformations: seeing them love-sick, he says, is like watching wise

Solomon dance a jig, or 'critic Timon laugh at idle toys!' (4.3.168). These two related references mark the only times in all his plays that Shakespeare used the word 'critic'. It is synonymous with a range of institutional killjoys: the parish officer or 'beadle' who whips offenders, the 'night-watch constable' who catches them and the 'domineering pedant' from whose instruction they have clearly failed to benefit: all agents of law enforcement, justice and corrective instruction, all sworn enemies to love, freedom and libido. References elsewhere to the figure of the 'Critick' (whether of literature, society or the drama) in early modern English plays, poems and pamphlets describe a figure who is carping, currish, choleric, sharp-sighted, narrow-eyed, stubborn, severe, musty-visaged and foul-mouthed. These largely negative, even repellent, connotations are still familiar. The role of the critic is still popularly perceived to be one of a fault-finder, a traffic warden of the emotions, a fly in the soup at life's feast.

Playwrights and audiences have always found it pleasurable and therapeutic to traduce the integrity and competence of the night-watch constable. In Sheridan's *The Critic* (1779), Puff, albeit endearingly, represents the corruptibility of the emergent trade. Shaw frames *Fanny's First Play* (1911) with the arrival and departure of four critics whose acuity ranges from the gentle insights of Trotter (modelled, with the critic's blessing, on A.B. Walkley) to the hackery of Flawner Bannal, 'an unemployable of the business class picking up a living by an obtuse courage which gives him cheerfulness', who has 'a slight turn for writing, and ... a comfortable ignorance and lack of intuition which hides from him all the dangers and disgraces that keep men of finer perception in check' (Shaw [1911] 1934: 655). But the nadir of the critic's cultural reputation is soundly plumbed in Beckett's *Waiting for Godot*, in which Didi and Gogo's game of mutual abuse descends the chain of being:

> VLADIMIR: Moron!
> ESTRAGON: Vermin!
> VLADIMIR: Abortion!
> ESTRAGON: Morpion!
> VLADIMIR: Sewer-rat!
> ESTRAGON: Curate!
> VLADIMIR: Cretin!
> ESTRAGON: [*With finality.*] Crrritic!
> VLADIMIR: Oh!
> [*He wilts, vanquished, and turns away.*]
> (Beckett 1986: 70)

In at least two instances, contempt for theatre critics has led to elaborate fantasies of criticide. In Tom Stoppard's *The Real Inspector Hound* (1968), the metatheatrical and the metacritical collide as we oversee two critics, Birdboot and Moon, watching a new whodunit and subsequently overhear them reviewing each other's reviews. In a surreal finale, the egregiously pompous pair become trapped in the inner fiction of the whodunit and are promptly murdered. Moon and his deputy, Higgs, are dispatched by the paper's third-string critic, Puckeridge, who ends the play well positioned to achieve every critic's dream of seeing his 'entire review in neon' (Stoppard 1968: 15) outside a theatre.

The deaths at the climax of Stoppard's play are frugal when compared with the multiple critical casualties of the Hammer Horror movie *Theatre of Blood* (1973), later entertainingly adapted for the stage by Lee Simpson and Phelim McDermott for Improbable at the National Theatre in 2005. The Shakespearean actor-manager, Edward Lionheart, has faked his own suicide after repeatedly being denied the Critics' Circle award for best actor. His revenge against the reviewers who have variously slated, mocked or slept through his leads is to dispatch each of them in a Shakespearean manner: Hector Snipe is butchered by 'myrmidons' and his corpse horse-dragged through a fellow critic's funeral; Larding is drowned in a butt of malmsey; a female critic is electrocuted at the hairdressers in a nod to the inflammatory end of Joan la Pucelle; while act four of *The Merchant of Venice* is rewritten ('you'll find we've made some alterations to the text – and one rather large cut') to allow Lionheart's Shylock to remove his pound of flesh. This is snuff Shakespeare. Far too few films can boast of lines like: 'Four of my colleagues have been murdered and their deaths relate directly to your father's last repertory season.'

The Real Inspector Hound and *Theatre of Blood* take to a playfully logical extreme the widely held perception that theatre reviewers are jealous parasites on the body of art, and that no creative person would mourn their loss. Many actors and directors, for example, are apt to stress the impertinent superfluity of criticism by claiming never to read their reviews. With some alteration to diction, this interchange from the opening scene of *The Critic* can still be heard in the green rooms of the contemporary theatre:

DANGLE: Well, Sir Fretful, I wish you may be able to get rid as easily of the newspaper criticisms as you do of ours.
SIR FRETFUL: The newspapers! Sir, they are the most villainous – licentious – abominable – infernal – Not that I ever read them – no – I make it a rule never to look into a newspaper. (Sheridan [1779] 1940: 24)

And here is that great (spoof) classical actor Nicholas Craig, writing about critics in his revealing memoir, *I, An Actor*:

> It has always been my very strictest rule never *ever* to look at reviews. Not even a peek. My newsagent is bound on pain of lingering death not to come within a hundred miles of me after one of my first nights. Inevitably, friends will read out particularly flattering bits on the phone but I never take any notice, and it has never occurred to me, for instance, to have these excerpts enlarged then take them into the bathroom, cover them with marshmallows and roll naked on them until I'm exhausted. (Craig 1989: 43–4)

At the heart of this studied indifference to critics is an anxiety about their influence, a submerged recognition that the value of performance is mediated, first and foremost, in newspaper columns, and that the performer's fame – immediate and lasting – heavily depends on the written word. As Brecht said of theatre critics: 'What they say about my plays doesn't matter, my plays will survive the critics, but what they say about my productions matters very much because what they write is all that posterity will know of the subject' (quoted in E. Bentley 415).

Perhaps unsurprisingly then, analogies for the critic's function have persistently sought to deny criticism's validity and potency. When playwright Christopher Hampton was once asked what he thought of theatre critics, he replied that one might as well 'ask the lamp post what it feels about dogs' (Stefanova 2000: 82). In another gesture to the scatological, Robert Gore-Langton, the *Sunday Express*'s critic in the late 1990s, described reviewers as people who are 'paid through the nose to talk out of their arses' (Stefanova 2000: 83). But perhaps the analogy that portrays critics at their most superfluous and stunted was that of the Irish playwright Brendan Behan. Critics are like eunuchs in a harem, he claimed: 'they see it done every day but can't do it themselves' (Stefanova 2000: 83). In a more plangent key, George Steiner (1967: 21) reinforced the analogy between criticism and impotence: 'when he looks back, the critic sees a eunuch's shadow'. Walter Raleigh, while writing primarily about literary criticism at the dawn of the twentieth century, encapsulated in a letter the worst-case scenario for critics of any art form. Expanding on his earlier claim that 'the eunuch was the first modern critic', he wrote:

> I can't help feeling that critical admiration for what another man has written is an emotion for spinsters. Shakes. didn't want it. Jerome K. Jerome is in some ways a far decenter writer than Brunetière or Saintsbury or any of the professed critics. He goes and begets a brat for himself, and doesn't pule about other people's amours. If I write an autobiography it shall be called 'Confessions of a Pimp'. (Quoted in Baldick 1983: 78–9)

English literary criticism has generally been more confident of its aims and functions than either Steiner or Raleigh's melancholy and macho analogies of emasculation would suggest. Chris Baldick's account of *The Social Mission of English Criticism 1848–1932*, for example, chronicles the often staggering claims to cultural authority made by and on behalf of the literary critic. Criticism, from Matthew Arnold to the Leavises, was proposed as a culture-saving activity of the civilised mind, a high calling with significant social implications. If so-called Great Literature was the panacea to a number of societal ailments (class division, the decline of religious feeling, industrialisation, rampant commercialism), the critic's duty was to administer the dose and make sure the sick and the needy received the right prescription. Delivering the dose became easier as the act of literary criticism was institutionalised, whether in Civil Service exams or in the widespread emergence of English studies in universities. No such ambitious legacy or process of institutionalisation can be found in the history of journalistic theatre reviewing. The harems in which Raleigh pimped his trade were the actually rather respectable milieus of the lecture hall and the college tutorial – not to mention between the redoubtable covers of the *Men of Letters* series. The harem of the theatre reviewer is that promiscuous space, the newspaper column. If literature is a vocation, journalism is merely a career, and the newspaper reviewer, embroiled in the dirt, deadlines and commercialism of Grub Street, cannot hope for the disinterested authority of the Arnoldian literary critic. It is hard to imagine any literary critic, on the record at least, defining his occupation as one of getting paid through the nose to talk out of his arse.

Night-watch constables, men of letters and domineering pedants

To tease out the peculiar identity of the night-watch constable it is instructive to compare him to two close relatives: the literary critic and the academic performance critic, each of whom might be regarded as a subspecies of Berowne's 'domineering pedant'.

Theatre reviewing evolved in London in the mid eighteenth century for a number of reasons, not least of which was that theatre had reached the fruitful condition of being both sufficiently socially acceptable to discuss in bourgeois company and also a source of apparently endless controversy: 'acceptable controversy' – or 'news'. In a relatively small theatrical economy such as London in the 1740s, one could easily see everything. What one should feel and *say* about what one saw was much less clear. Historically, the church or the court had set standards of taste and interpretation, but, in the ever-expanding public sphere of clubs and coffee houses and the proliferating pages of new journals and periodicals of the Enlightenment city, a consensus emerged that judgement might be the affair of the individual – the lay authority, as it were – but that this individual's opinion was most meaningfully forged in the company of other equally enlightened amateurs. The first theatre journalists existed both to reflect and to provoke these conversations about art. One of the greatest critics in the first century of theatre reviewing, William Hazlitt, began his *A View of the English Stage* (1818): 'A good play, well acted, passes away a whole evening delightfully at a certain period of life, agreeably at all times; we read the account the next morning with pleasure, and it generally furnishes our leading topic of conversation for the afternoon' (Hazlitt 1930–4: V 173). Journalistic theatre reviewing has undergone change and sometimes convulsion in the last two and a half centuries, but some of its core functions – to respond to performance immediately, to keep people talking about theatre, and so to circulate pleasure – still obtain today.

Histories of literary criticism generally agree that the location and function of criticism changed radically in the late nineteenth century. As Hugh Grady writes:

> Literary criticism . . . passed out of the sphere of public discourse properly speaking, becoming instead a knowledge/power of new bureaucratic institutions. The modern, academic form of literary criticism developed in the late Victorian period as part of the transformation of the capitalist system from its entrepreneurial to its current corporate form and became something far from its earlier and heroic incarnation. The sea-change that Shakespearian criticism underwent from the nineteenth to the twentieth century is overwhelmingly the result of the transference of discourse on Shakespeare to a new bureaucratic setting (the modern University) and to a new class of authors (academic professionals). (Grady 1991: 28)

Grady's exemplary account of Shakespearean criticism as practised within that modern academic sphere is predicated on the 'close sociological resemblances' between scientists and literary critics in the twentieth century. These resemblances, he argues, make Thomas Kuhn's notion of the 'paradigm shift' applicable to literary criticism, with such shifts resulting from the 'general dynamics of a specialized and institutionalized community engaged in a common knowledge programme in the post-Enlightenment West' (Grady 1991: 23).

While theatrical and literary criticism may have common roots in the public sphere and in journalism in particular, their histories diverge with the rise of English studies. As literary criticism became a professionalised, knowledge–power discipline, theatre criticism remained firmly in (what was left of) the public sphere and underwent no comparable revolutionary redefinition or relocation. Its attempts at redefinition (as I later argue with reference to George Bernard Shaw and Max Beerbohm) had consequences for the practice of theatre criticism, but fall a long way short of the literary critic's paradigmatic shift from freelance amateur to institutionalised academic. Theatre criticism, in short, resisted professionalisation.

Reviewers have always been 'professional' in the sense of being financially rewarded for their writing – that uneasy conjunction of cash and criticism that has so often led to charges of bias, puffery and corruption. But theatre reviewing has never been a profession in the more theorised sense described by Magali Sarfatti Larson in *The Rise of Professionalism*. For Larson, a profession is an organised body of practitioners offering a defined and privileged skill or discipline to society. The skill is defined on 'a cognitive basis'; that is, the kind and extent of knowledge offered by the professional. Furthermore, the skill is privileged by restricting entry into the profession through cognitive and social trials. The would-be professional is required to negotiate the 'proved institutional mechanisms' for manufacturing exclusiveness: 'the license, the qualifying examination, the diploma, and formal training in a common curriculum' (Larson 1977: 15). This credentialising system is contingent on a more or less defined body of knowledge that can be standardised, quantified and examined. Larson argues that the most effective cognitive basis for 'a monopoly of competence' is one in which the knowledge required:

> must be specific enough to impart distinctiveness to the professional 'commodity'; it must be formalized or codified enough to allow standardization of the 'product' – which means, ultimately, standardization of the producers. And yet it must not be so clearly codified that it does not allow a principle of exclusion to operate: where everyone can claim to be an expert, there is no expertise. (Larson 1977: 31)

The histories of two professional associations – the Society of Dramatic Critics (formed 1907) and the Critics' Circle (1913) – show the extent to which theatre criticism fails to conform to this model. The Society petered out relatively quickly, only to be reincarnated more successfully as the Circle. According to the 'Suggested Rules' submitted at the first general meeting, the objective of the Society of Dramatic Critics was to exist 'for social and professional purposes, to facilitate the exchange of views on the material and intellectual aspects of the calling of dramatic criticism, and generally to promote the interests of that calling' (Society of Dramatic Critics 1907: 3). The principles of admission to the Society were broad: 'Persons who are, or have, been [sic] regularly employed in London in writing dramatic criticism, and critical writers on theatrical subjects, shall be eligible for membership' (4). (Broad, if metrocentric: 'Provincial Dramatic Critics may be admitted as Associate Members at the discretion of the Council' (5).)

The key objective of both associations was to legitimate, regulate and professionalise the activity of theatre reviewing. The rules of membership – the principles of exclusion and inclusion – are central to the associations' authorising identity. In 1923 the Critics' Circle celebrated its tenth anniversary by publishing the first edition of the *Critics' Circular*. This 'official organ', published at irregular intervals over the next forty years, is an important site for an understanding of the curious, liminal nature of the profession. The pages of the *Critics' Circular* tell two stories: the first of an affable, pass-the-port, monthly luncheon routine, the second of an association almost invariably on the verge of an identity crisis. The first issue sounded the key note: here Bernard Weller discussed the Circle's membership rules and urged reform of the principle that 'any writer, as soon as he joins the staff of a journal as a dramatic or a musical critic is *ipso facto* eligible for election' to the Circle. He continued:

> This [inclusive] theory – perhaps unconsciously – is borrowed from trade unionism, which works on these lines. But professional unionism is, without implying any sort of snobbishness, not quite the same thing as trade unionism. In a professional man, especially in one accredited by an official body, competence is looked for, and also a proper attachment to his profession in an economic way. In both these respects, unfortunately, the mere appointment of any one critic to a paper is, to say the least, inconclusive. There seem to be strange ideas about what constitutes a critic, particularly a dramatic critic. Given a sense of humour and a nimble pen and not much else is thought to matter. Never mind if the writer is entirely unversed in a highly technical craft, never mind if by temperament he is wholly unfitted for any such vocation, provided he is facile and amusing from the point of view of the newspaper reader. (Weller 1923: 5)

Compactly expressed, these are the anxieties of the eunuch in the harem. In Weller's account tensions abound between low and high culture, between trade and profession. Larson argues that the creation of professional markets depended on control being established first '"at the point of production": the providers of services had to be controlled in order to standardize and thus identify the "commodity" they provided' (Weller 1923: 15). Weller's problem is that the Critics' Circle, as a pseudo-legitimating cadre, has no power at that point of production. Access to the trade/profession is entirely dependent on newspaper editors and requires no standardised test of competence. The resultant commodity, theatre criticism, thus has a dubious cognitive basis. Weller insists that real criticism is not mere frivolity, but then offers an account of the ideal critic's constitution that mingles the pseudo-scientific ('highly technical') and the mystifyingly subjective ('temperament'). How does one measure and regulate 'temperament'?

The difficulty of defining theatre criticism as a profession resurfaces time and again throughout the Circle's history. From the wealth of discussion and debate, I offer three representative examples from the pages of the *Critics' Circular*.

1. At the Second International Congress of Critics held in Salzburg, August 1927, reviewers from fourteen countries faced constitutional questions. As L. Dunton Green (1927: 2) reported, 'considerable time at the first two meetings and part of the third and fourth were [sic] spent in framing a proper definition of the critic eligible for membership of Associations already existing or to be created'. After some clearly wearying debates, the Congress settled on the following resolution:

   > Associations should adopt the principle of admitting only members who ordinarily write for Newspapers and Periodicals for remuneration, who are in possession of the necessary technical equipment and have proved themselves to be both independent and unimpeachable. (2)

   Green's report is unfortunately, if inevitably, silent on the question of what that 'necessary technical equipment' might consist.

2. Editorialising in May 1931, the Circle's president, Sydney W. Carroll, listed the 'Grievances and Disabilities in Criticism' of the day. First was 'the lack of the right degree of respect and prestige on the part of almost everybody, including critics themselves, for the term "critic"' (Carroll 1931: 1). This lack of prestige should be linked to Carroll's fourth and fifth grievances:

   > 4. Lack of real professional status in critics due to the absence of any standard of qualifications for the work.
   >
   > 5. The irresponsible appointment by Editors of unqualified people to the task of criticism. (1)

   But how, those editors might have responded, were 'unqualified' critics to be denied access to the profession given the lack of a consensus on the criteria for qualification?

3. Debate at the Circle's Annual General Meeting in June 1942 centred on the uncertain nature of the association. According to the minutes, W.A. Darlington claimed:

> We operate the Circle on two levels. On the one level we are a kind of Academy and on the other a kind of trade union. These two functions are in one fundamental respect incompatible. If you are an artist you are elected to an Academy because you are a pretty good artist. A trade union must be an incentive at once for everybody. (Darlington 1942: 15)

Dilys Powell concurred that 'the prestige of the Circle is in a very bad way. In fact we are in the position of a trade union which has not the right to strike, and have not the prestige on a truly critical level which an academy would have' (Darlington 1942: 15). Powell's solution was to restrict membership; she specifically argued that critics who wrote for trade papers should be excluded from the Circle. Calls for restriction must have reached something of a critical mass by 1957, when it was decided that membership of the Circle should be by invitation only.

The Circle's shift in self-image – from 'trade union' to 'academy' – that marked the fiftieth anniversary of the founding of the Society of Dramatic Critics could not obscure the fact that the 'calling' of dramatic criticism continued to lack a competence test or any standardising procedures that might elevate it to the status of a 'profession' as defined by Larson. By the mid twentieth century the literary critic had fully evolved from the nomadic and elusive figure of the nineteenth-century 'man of letters' to the specialised and institutionalised academic, often an instructor of the pseudo-empirical and testable methods of 'practical criticism'. Theatre critics had an increasingly exclusive club in which to air their grievances, but their professional status, and thus their claim to prestige, remained tenuous.

If the Critics' Circle has historically sought (and not entirely successfully) to define itself as a Navarrian 'little academe' (*Love's Labour's Lost* 1.1.13), what of the actual academy, and in particular those institutionalised literary critics who began to intrude onto the beat of the night-watch constable?

Academic reviewing of Shakespearean performance is a much more recent phenomenon than newspaper reviewing. It emerged not from the Enlightenment public sphere but from the largely private and specialised spheres of universities, university presses and disciplinary trade magazines (a.k.a. academic journals) of the mid twentieth century. Such important annuals as *Shakespeare Survey* (founded 1948) and journals such as

Shakespeare Quarterly (1950), *Cahiers Élisabéthains* (1972) and *Shakespeare Bulletin* (1982) have regularly committed substantial space to articles on and reviews of performance. Many of these have benefited not only from the scholarly writer's expertise, wit and thoughtfulness, but also from these critics' ability to see the production more than once, to extend their analysis to several times the length of a newspaper review, and to redraft the writing until it has acquired optimum elegance, force and coherence. As the contents of Stanley Wells's anthology of criticism *Shakespeare in the Theatre* (1997) suggest, these *parvenu* pedants have been responsible for some of the most outstanding criticism of the last sixty years and have provided criticism often quite distinct from that of the newspaper constabulary that has faithfully kept its night-watch since the eighteenth century.

The difference between the two modes of criticism is hardly accidental. Indeed, it might be argued that the academic review was conceived as an antidote to the journalistic notice. What Cary Mazer wrote of the *Shakespeare Quarterly* guidelines of the 1970s holds largely true for academic reviewing at any point in the last half century: 'The principal goal has been to invert the priorities which have been the norm in theatre reviewing throughout the last two and a half centuries of popular commercial journalism. Reviews, the scholarly community insists, should be historical documents first, and consumer reports only afterwards, if at all' (Mazer 1985: 653). Pausing here is worthwhile. The logic that has traditionally distinguished journalistic from academic reviewing runs something like this: if journalists write quickly for large audiences, academics write slowly for small audiences. If journalists have the potential to exert a strong influence on contemporary theatregoing and production, academics have tended to eliminate the risk of any such influence by: (a) publishing their reviews some weeks or even months after the show has opened or, sometimes, closed; (b) avoiding crassly evaluative, consumer-oriented criticism as far as humanly possible; and (c) not taking any cash for their work, thus preempting accusations of bias or puffery. If journalists are pundits, tipsters and weather-vanes, academics are experts, historians and memorialists. If night-watch constables treat theatre as news, domineering pedants treat it as history.

There are exceptions to the strong contrasts drawn above. Academic reviewers in journals such as the *Times Literary Supplement*, for example, are no strangers to deadlines or fees. But it is nevertheless fair to say that the anti-journalistic foundational principles of academic Shakespearean reviewing have until recently gone largely unquestioned. The relatively small, often internationally dispersed, readership of Shakespeare journals, combined with the frequent time lag between the dates of performance and of review publication, ensures that the criticism has few commercial implications and is instead more obviously committed to memorialisation than journalistic reviews. Comparing the respective aims, reading strategies, and functions of academic and journalistic Shakespeare reviewing in greater detail than I can here would no doubt be instructive. Such a comparison would, however, benefit from having a sense of what could tentatively be called the dominant traditions of British Shakespearean reviewing, of the publications and the critics who have reached the widest audience and the reading strategies they have employed to turn performance into print. This book is therefore overwhelmingly concerned with the night-watch constables of Grub Street, Fleet Street and Canary Wharf.

Critical conditions

When Iago described himself as 'nothing if not critical' (2.1.122) he was perhaps drawing on the dual contemporary sense of the word as defined a year or so earlier by Bartas (1605) as: 'Critik. and Critical, sharpe Censurers also dangerous dayes for health obserued by Phisitions'. This definition reminds one that 'critic' and 'crisis' are etymologically related, finding common ancestry in the Greek *krinein*, 'to separate, decide, judge', from the root *krei-* 'to sieve, discriminate, distinguish'. The *krisis* is a turning-point in a disease, the day or days on which a doctor will be able to make a reliable prognosis; thus the critic is not only a sharp censurer, but also the physician observing dangerous days.

The differences between journalistic theatre reviewing and the work of literary critics or scholarly reviewers extend beyond their relative statuses as professions. The history and discursive conditions of journalistic theatre criticism make it in effect a very different genre from literary or academic criticism. Journalists have historically conducted their business in an atmosphere in which crisis and competition are normative. The Civil War 'newsbooks' that in many ways anticipated the modern newspaper of the eighteenth century were inevitably partisan in their support for either King or Parliament, and their power and popularity grew even as their 'reputation for fairness and balance declined' (Conboy 2010: 26). Another crisis of succession would prompt the next important phase in the history of British journalism. As Bob Clarke has noted: 'The consequences of the defeat of the divine right of Kings in the Glorious Revolution and the break in the hereditary succession would be that the fate of Kings and their governments would depend on their ability to command opinion, and opinion could only be sustained by persuasion' (Clarke 2010: 46).

The press represented the primary vehicle for such persuasion. In the first half of the eighteenth century, the development of the press was inextricable from the emergence of the party system in politics and the growing need to ventilate, interrogate or lambast, according to taste, the opinions of the Whig or Tory faction. Such divisions were always liable to influence every aspect of the newspapers' coverage: when the Theatre Licensing Act of 1737 closed all legitimate theatres except Drury Lane and Covent Garden, 'the newspapers, which were in many cases organs for party political opinion, arrayed themselves on either side of the controversy' (Gray 1931: 84). One of the core functions of an urban press is to help curate its readers' leisure time and through advertising – direct or subliminal – to suggest where else, having purchased a newspaper or journal, they might spend what remains of their disposable income. This is part of the process Habermas describes as the 'deconsecration' of art: as works of art became publicly available and accessible and moved beyond being merely components of the church's or the court's 'publicity of representation', they required their new audience to cultivate the habit of lay judgement:

> The private people for whom the cultural product became available as a commodity profaned it inasmuch as they had to determine its meaning on their own (by way of rational communication with one another), verbalize it, and thus state explicitly what precisely in its implicitness for so long could assert its authority. (Habermas [1962] 1992: 37)

But that 'rational communication with one another' often took place via the irrational and tendentious platform of the press.

A second distinguishing feature of journalistic theatre criticism is that it is governed by a set of restrictions. Reviews are constricted in length and by time (a deadline of anywhere between forty-five minutes and, at most, one week). Unlike the literary critic, the reviewer also has an obligation to a predetermined subject: the act of criticism is thus further restricted to the subject of a recently witnessed theatrical performance. (Theatre criticism often strays from its ostensible subject and is apt at any moment to turn into anecdote, gossip, day-dream or polemic, but the critic who merely wrote on whim with no connection to recent performance would be either sacked or promoted to columnist.) These restrictive conditions are epitomised in the opening sentence of George Henry Lewes's 1853 review of Charles Kean's *Macbeth*: 'I should like to write an essay on *Macbeth*, but journalistic necessities compel me to confine myself to the two leading characters, and of them to speak only in hints' (Lowe and Archer 1896: 232). By subsequent standards, Lewes had acres of print. Even so, his experience was one of frustrated incompletion, of not having the space in which to express fully his opinions. Chris Baldick (1983: 110) writes of T.S. Eliot's reviewing that 'as an occasional reviewer of books, Eliot had neither the leisure nor the license to spell out the connections between his social and literary doctrines at any length'. Baldick, in writing metacriticism, therefore understandably spends more time analysing *The Sacred Wood*, where Eliot had both leisure and licence to articulate his socio-literary beliefs, than he does reading between the lines of Eliot's book reviews. In theatre reviews, such connections between the critic's aesthetic and political views are frequently submerged, seen in flashes, spoken of 'only in hints'.

Temporally, no less than spatially, the review text is a hostage to its conditions of production. Reviews are abandoned: unlike Wilde's Miss Prism, I use the word not in the sense of 'lost or mislaid', but in the sense of relinquished or surrendered. Take the example of Michael Billington's *Guardian* review of Michael Bogdanov's 1978 Royal Shakespeare Company (RSC) production of *The Taming of the Shrew*. Billington's piece concluded thus:

> There is, however, a larger question at stake than the merits or otherwise of this particular production. It is whether there is any reason to revive a play that seems totally offensive to our age and our society. My own feeling is that it should be put firmly and squarely back on the shelf. (Billington 1993: 124)

But this socio-political point (echoing Shaw's verdict on the play in the 1890s) was not to be re-emphasised or developed in Billington's subsequent reviews of *Shrew* productions. In interview, Billington revealed that the conditions under which he had written the review led to an *ad hoc* ending that essentially misrepresented his opinion:

> I was reviewing on the night, in a hotel bedroom in Stratford, scribbling furiously, deadline eleven o'clock, trying to find a computing centre, and came up with this [closing statement] . . . it was a sort of resonant conclusion, and I suppose I was hoping that it might stimulate a little debate. Then I found when they next revived *Shrew* this line was included in the programme, as some *ex cathedra* statement. Of course, I don't believe this [that *Shrew* should be shelved]. (Billington 2000a)

As George Eliot noted: 'We must have mercy on critics who are obliged to make a figure in printed pages. They must by all means say striking things' (quoted in Collini 1988: 151).

The combined restrictions of space, time and subject matter mark theatre criticism as a fundamentally different activity from literary criticism. Without leisure, licence or length, it is difficult for a cultural activity to define itself. Histories of literary criticism seek to isolate foundational or transformational moments, paradigm shifts and vital interventions in which the subject rethought and redefined its own function. Baldick can write, for example, that Matthew Arnold's 'The Study of Poetry' (1880) 'marks a transformation in English criticism, from the defence of poetry to a bold offensive against poetry's potential competitors' (Baldick 1983: 19, 18) and that Arnold himself 'is rightly acknowledged as the founder of a distinctly "modern" movement in English literary criticism' (Baldick 1983: 19, 18). Making an analogous claim for any single text or critic in the history of theatre criticism would be very hard. Foundational figures have been identified by critics themselves: William Hazlitt said that Leigh Hunt was the critic 'who first gave the true *pine-apple* flavour to theatrical criticism, making it a pleasant mixture of sharp and sweet' (1930–4: XVIII 381), while Bernard Shaw claimed that his influential antithesis, Clement Scott, was 'the first of the great dramatic reporters' (1932: II 139). But it is clear that, although both Hunt and Scott had more or less coherent, more or less developed theories of dramatic criticism, neither initiated or bequeathed anything like a movement. Although I make the case in Chapter 3 for viewing some critics of the 1890s as self-consciously situating themselves within the New Journalistic or 'Impressionist' movements, the conditions of theatre criticism are generally not propitious for the formation of distinct schools of criticism, the histories of which might be cleanly distinguished and delineated.

* * *

These issues of professionalism, the conditions of the review genre and the notion of critical movements are further addressed at the close of this introduction, where I elaborate on their implications for the historical study of Shakespearean reviewing. With the above description of the critic's cultural reputation, nebulous professionalism and constricted conditions of production, I hope to have given some flavour (pine-apple or otherwise) of the hurried, embattled, continually crisis-ridden, quasi-legitimate and semi-professional position from which reviewers have negotiated the various crises of Shakespearean authority explored in the following chapters.

Re-viewing the Shakespearean reviewer: precedents

To date, only a handful of books take as their subject either the act of reviewing or the work of an individual theatre critic. (This excludes anthologies of theatre criticism.) None of these is dedicated to a specific exploration of Shakespearean theatre reviewing. Charles Gray's *Theatrical Criticism in London to 1795* (1931) remains the only study of length to place the act of theatrical reception in a journalistic context through a thorough survey of theatre-related writing in the expanding news and periodical presses of the eighteenth century. No one has yet undertaken the formidable task of applying Gray's approach to the history of theatrical criticism of the nineteenth and twentieth centuries. Four books focus on the second half of the twentieth century. Irving Wardle's *Theatre Criticism* (1992) offers a potted history of the profession (its early stages largely dependent on Gray) and valuably draws on the writer's experience as a practising critic to meditate on the forms and functions of contemporary theatre reviewing. Theatre reviewing in the period following *Look Back in Anger* is the subject of Gareth and Barbara Lloyd Evans's *Plays in Review 1956–1980: British Drama and the Critics* (1985). Although the book is largely a review anthology, reprinting the responses of national newspaper critics to new plays of the period, the authors also offer a long introduction that combines a critique of falling standards of criticism with a lament for 'a society now short of public orthodox religious observances' in which 'secular, personal, permissive expediencies' dictate behaviour (Lloyd Evans 1985: 45–6). Dominic Shellard's *Harold Hobson: Witness and Judge* (1995) was the first scholarly book-length attempt 'to consider the complete *oeuvre* of a single critic' and made the important point that:

> Historians working in any other field question the reliability of their source material before they begin to formulate academic judgements, but few drama specialists consider whether a theatre critic's views have been shaped by political, economic or editorial influences, let alone personal, religious or emotional sensibilities, or even the nature of the publication that they write for (daily, Sunday, weekly?) and the constrictions of the space that their editors permit them. (Shellard 1995: 7)

Economic and editorial influences are central to John E. Booth's *The Critic, Power and the Performing Arts* (1991), a study of arts reviewing in America based on interviews with critics, practitioners, newspaper editors and media executives. Booth's work offers an instructive socio-educational profile of American critics (typically white male graduates in their forties; Booth 1991: 62), as well as drawing attention to the chain of dependency between criticism, newspapers and advertising, lucidly arguing that 'survival for the industry depends on advertising, and advertising depends on raising circulation. The arts are not considered important in increasing circulation and consequently do not command major attention on most newspapers' (80). This, of course, overlaps with Noam Chomsky's more generalised critique of the subjugation of a desirably 'independent' journalism to one constricted by the fear of alienating potential advertisers: 'like other corporations, [newspapers] have a product to sell and a market they want to sell it to: the product is audiences, and the market is advertisers. So the economic structure of a newspaper is that it sells readers to other businesses' (Chomsky 2002: 14).

Articles rather than books have paid most attention to the interaction between theatre critics and specifically Shakespearean performance. From the late 1960s to the early 1980s, a number of essays sought to analyse either a single reviewer's relationship to Shakespeare or the newspaper reception of a given actor or production. Thus, Stanley Wells has written of Shakespeare in the theatre criticism of Max Beerbohm (Wells 1976), Leigh Hunt (Wells 1980) and William Hazlitt (Wells 1982), and Russell Jackson has explored the work of J.F. Nisbet (Jackson 1978), Henry Morley (Jackson 1985) and the relationship between Shaw, Augustin Daly and Ada Rehan (Jackson 1994). Taking the actor-centred approach to reception, Marteen Van Dijk (1982) has examined relations between Charles Philip Kemble and the press, and M. Glen Wilson (1975) has argued that memory of Charles Kean is largely misfounded on the pro-Macready slant of contemporary journalism. Wilson makes explicit the sometimes unwritten claim of all studies of reviewer reception: 'Until we know the identity of the reviewer, his critical biases and private motivations, his personal relationships with theatrical figures, and the ideological commitments and the audience of his publication, the value of a given theatrical notice as historical evidence cannot be determined' (M. G. Wilson 1975: 95). When newspaper reviews are read strictly as a means of reaching the 'reality' of a performance, they will often frustrate the theatre historian. When they are read as evidence of much wider theatrical-cultural phenomena, however, they are invaluable sources. Read as a guide to what actor X did in a certain role on a certain evening, reviews have a limited value; as guides to the ways in which audiences of the past have read performance, have found meaning in theatre and have negotiated the worth of Shakespeare, reviews are enormously fruitful documents. A shift of emphasis from the former to the latter could be described as a move from production to reception. In his article 'Theatre Audiences and the Reading of Performance', Marvin Carlson advocated just such a shift:

> Since theatre analysis in the past has emphasized the study of the text and of the performance over the study of reception, it has given almost no attention

> to those elements of the event structure aside from text and performance or of the larger social milieu, which may be as important to the formation of the reading of the experience as anything actually presented on the stage. (Carlson 1989: 90)

Carlson (1989: 94) cites such elements as publicity, programmes and reviews as vital in mediating between performance and spectator, 'suggesting to the latter possible strategies and mechanisms to be employed in reading performance'. Adapting the reader-response theories of Wolfgang Iser, Hans Robert Jauss, Umberto Eco and Stanley Fish, Carlson argues that these theorists' concerns with institutional structures and communities of readership are if anything more relevant to theatre, where 'communities, by the active choice of assembling to attend plays, are more apparent as groups to themselves and to others than are the more abstract literary communities' (85). He concludes the article by reiterating the need to attend to how audiences actively make meaning:

> A clearer understanding of how spectators today and at other historical periods have learned and applied the rules of the game they play with the performance event in the theatre will provide us with a far richer and more interesting picture of that complex event than has the traditional model which treated the spectator as an essentially passive recipient of the stage's projected stimuli. (Carlson 1989: 97)

Carlson's call for theatre historians to attend to the communal structure of performance reception has been repeatedly answered since the late 1980s. Many of these readings have sought to move, in Barbara Hodgdon's words, 'beyond text-centered analyses to situate spectators and their reading strategies as the primary objects of investigation' (Hodgdon 1988: 171). In her exploration of the London reception of Robert Lepage's *A Midsummer Night's Dream*, Hodgdon argues that it is possible to read the discourses of national newspaper critics as not only 'a struggle over the meaning of theatrical signs but as symptomatic of current cultural anxieties about gender, race, and nationality' (173). The revelation of these often subtextual anxieties is central to many studies. Celia R. Daileader (2000: 179), for example, argues in her discussion of the career of the British black actor Ray Fearon that, in their responses to his performances in *The White Devil* and *Othello*, 'critics unconsciously replicated the texts' racialized language', and that sexual and racial stereotypes typically underscore the reception of any black classical actor. Carol Chillington Rutter is also interested in the ways that white culture uses Shakespearean performance to achieve particular white cultural work. She argues, for example, that the reception of Glen Byam

Shaw's *Antony and Cleopatra* offers a 'snapshot of cultural discourse in 1953 Britain', particularly Kenneth Tynan's review of the production, in which 'racism, nationalism, misogyny and paternalism map transparently on to each other' (Rutter 2001: 72).

The most popular focus for recent review-readings has been the reception of female gender and sexuality. That this has become such a productive area of study may have much to do with the asymmetrical relationship between the actress and a reviewing community that has always been predominantly male. Laurie E. Osborne examines both textual and pictorial representations of Viola and Olivia in the nineteenth century, and finds in Leigh Hunt's review of Maria Tree's Viola a 'displacement of concerns about performance onto concerns about female propriety and appearance' (Osborne 1996: 133). Sarah Werner likewise argues that the reviewer reception of Gale Edwards's 1995 RSC *Taming of the Shrew* was 'shaped by masculinist assumptions' and that critics typically 'mixed their own anxieties about gender roles with their beliefs about how Shakespeare should be staged' (Werner 2001: 89, 87).

All these studies have expanded the sense of the remits of performance criticism and theatre history; all have been inspirational precedents for the case studies offered in this book.

Reviewing Shakespeare: the argument

The range of potential primary sources for this book is vast, no less than every review written of a Shakespearean performance in Britain over the last two and a half centuries. With so much material, a process of radical selection is inevitable. This, in practice, has meant an overwhelming attention to the cultural products of the capital: London performances (with occasional forays to Stratford-upon-Avon) as reviewed in London newspapers and periodicals. This admittedly restricted focus is not based on the assumption that Shakespearean reviewing in the regions or indeed in other countries is any less important or interesting than that which takes place in London. Cross-country and cross-cultural comparisons have been made in some recent collections, and I hope theatre historians will pursue them in the future (see Edmondson et al. 2010; Prescott et al. 2012).

In writing of the clash of performance principles that occurred when Konstantin Stanislavsky and Edward Gordon Craig co-produced *Hamlet* in 1911, Dennis Kennedy (1993: 57) claims that the conflict between 'the champion of the interior actor' and 'the advocate of the *Übermarionette*... provides us with a paradigm, in question form, about how to produce Shakespeare: play the characters or play the themes?' A similar question confronts the historian of theatre criticism: should one structure the exploration around a succession of individual critics or look beyond the individual practitioner for broader, more impersonal trends? Wells's, Jackson's and Shellard's studies, for example, take the former, individual-based approach; the work of Hodgdon, Werner and Daileader takes the latter, which treats reception as more the product of a community of reviewers. As both approaches seem to me productive, this book plays both the characters and the themes. The central two chapters focus on the Shakespearean reviewing of individual critics (George Bernard Shaw, Max Beerbohm, James Agate and Kenneth Tynan), but are framed by chapters that use critical communities as the structuring principle of exploration.

I approach theatre criticism as a representative journalistic discourse, a discourse that, as Brian McNair and other media sociologists have argued, 'is not, and never can be, neutral and objective, but is fundamentally interpretative, embodying the dominant values and explanatory frameworks of the society within which it is produced' (McNair 1994: 39). The 'propaganda model' of understanding the media advanced by Chomsky and Herman in *Manufacturing Consent* is not a 'theory', according to Chomsky, rather 'a kind of truism – it just says that you'd expect institutions to work in their own interests, because if they didn't they wouldn't be able to function for very long' (Chomsky 2002: 14–15). The arts pages in which theatre reviews appear may not be the key sites for the manufacture of consent; editorials and leaders notwithstanding, the front and back pages of a newspaper are arguably its most important. (Chomsky would argue that the traditional back page privileging of sporting coverage does as much as anything else in 'diverting the general population from things that really matter' (100).) Nevertheless, in the choice of what they cover and how they allow their writers to discuss it, arts editors make political decisions. Brian McNair writes:

> the media play an important role in the 'labelling' of radical political action as deviant. When political groups (or other types of association, such as trade unions) go beyond the limits of normal parliamentary action (participating in demonstrations and strikes, for example) the media intervene to label these activities as deviant or illegitimate, marginalising them and diverting public attention away from the root causes of social conflict towards its epiphenomenal forms. (McNair 1994: 32)

T.A. Van Dijk (1988: 182) concurs that 'the structures of news reports at many levels condition the readers to develop dominant interpretive frameworks rather than alternative ones'. This book explores the labelling process and the propagation of dominant interpretive frameworks in Shakespearean critical reception. In doing so, it follows Pierre Bourdieu's argument that 'taste' – that apparently most subjective, natural and innocent experience of the world and of art – is in fact a social and political marker that classifies the classifier (Bourdieu [1979] 1986: 6). To exercise one's taste for high art forms presents different challenges from those of participating in lower cultural forms such as sport and television: 'to participate in high art is to forgo the direct and unmediated perception of the artwork itself. The principal consequence is the dependence of one's own judgment of artistic quality on the judgments of others' (Shrum 1996: 9). After the dumbshow in *Hamlet*, a Prologue steps forward to introduce the play proper; Ophelia wonders 'Will a [he] tell us what this show meant?' (3.2.136). In the case of the consumption and evaluation of high art, there is a smack of Ophelia in all of us. 'The higher a work is in the cultural hierarchy, the more important is discourse about the object to its status' (Shrum 1996: 26). Given the high cultural standing of Shakespeare, it is to be expected that in the reception of Shakespearean performance far more is at stake than the desirability or otherwise of 'purely aesthetic' considerations. Rather, the right to be reported and remembered as a legitimate Shakespearean performer depends on the ability to satisfy the dominant values of reviewers, whether these values concern masculinity and class (Chapter 2), authority and authenticity (Chapters 3 and 5), the politics of the theatrical economy (Chapter 4), or the incursions of foreign and low cultures into the sacred sphere of British high culture (Chapters 4 and 5).

Writing any form of history involves a recognition that the historian creates as much as grasps the meaning of the past and that the resulting narrative is only one of many stories that might be told about the subject. Richard J. Evans summarises the historian's quandary:

> We all pull out from the seamless web of past events a tiny selection which we then present in our historical account. Nobody has ever disputed this. The dispute arises when some theorists believe that the selection is largely determined by the narratives and structures which occur in the past itself, and those who think it is imposed by the historian. (R.J. Evans 1997: 142)

The historical account of Shakespearean reviewing offered in this book does not pretend to be wholly 'determined by the narratives and structures which occur in the past itself'. Nor does it make any claims to being comprehensive. Rather, I have chosen to describe the relationship between Shakespearean performance and journalistic reviewing at four stages in the history of reception. I argue throughout that the night-watch constable's key function has been to patrol the boundaries of legitimate interpretation by adjudicating what 'Shakespeare' as embodied in performance is permitted to signify.

Chapter 2 examines reviewer responses to six major productions of *Macbeth* from Garrick (1744) to Irving (1889) and describes the ethos of competition that structured them. The chapter identifies comparative criticism, in which individual actors are placed in a system of rivalry and their interpretations deemed legitimate or otherwise, as a transhistorical feature of Shakespeare reviewing that is especially prevalent in the long era of the actor-manager. (I return to the reception of *Macbeth* as a touchstone of reviewing practice in Chapters 4 and 5.) Chapter 3 begins, chronologically, where the first chapter ended, in Henry Irving's London. I argue that late Victorian society witnessed a journalistic revolution that had profound implications for the status of the reviewer and the practice of theatre criticism. Focusing on the work of Shaw and Beerbohm in the *Saturday Review*, I discuss the effects of the New Journalism on Shakespearean reception, and in particular the ways in which such emergent phenomena as the signed article and the cult of personality encouraged critics (pre-eminently Shaw and Beerbohm) to compete with and seek to undermine Shakespearean authority, whether of the actor-manager, William Poel's authenticity movement or the playwright himself.

Chapter 4 reads the Shakespearean reviews of James Agate and Kenneth Tynan as ambivalent responses to shifts in early to mid twentieth-century performance. While noting Agate and Tynan's indebtedness to the New Critics of the 1890s, I argue that both critics had to negotiate the tensions of their distinct historical moment, that of the transition from an actor-managerial to a producer-director's theatre. I describe how Agate sought to efface the advent of the producer by insisting on the primacy of the lead actor in Shakespearean production, thus reinforcing the dominant tradition of interpretation described in Chapter 2. The second part of the chapter discusses Tynan's early espousal of the hierarchic principle in classical theatre, his subsequent adoption of the idea of the ensemble, and the ways in which these incompatible desires resurface in his relationship with Shakespeare, Bertolt Brecht and Laurence Olivier. Chapter 5 describes the influence of Kenneth Tynan on reviewers, their anxiety about the diminished status of the reviewer in the mass media at the turn of the twentieth century and their dominant interpretive strategies when confronted with Shakespearean production, as evidenced in their response to the opening seasons of Shakespeare's Globe, to a cluster of *Macbeth*s in the mid 1990s and to the productions that comprised the World Shakespeare Festival of 2012.

Throughout this study, I am interested in the decisive role journalistic evaluation plays in the process that Joseph Roach has called 'substitution-as-public test' (Roach 2000: 35). In this test, a candidate is auditioned for a role, a role that is typically synonymous with a previous, usually deceased, artist or other symbolic public personality. The role itself entails 'the cultural work of carrying the burden of a public's ideal self-conception' (35). In his essay 'The Performance', Roach uses the theory of substitution to describe the way in which actors 'attempted' parts on the Restoration stage, while in his *Cities of the Dead*, substitution describes a far more complex, ethnographically diverse set of performances. In adapting Roach's theory to Shakespearean stage history, I suggest that the role is defined as one of unassailable Shakespearean authority, and that the cultural work of the successful candidate is to be the living substitute of the absent original. Thus I see the history of the Macbeth actor's reception as a series of public auditions for the right to embody Shakespearean authority. Likewise I read the reviews of Agate and Tynan as animated by an anxiety about substitution, a fear that the rise of the director and the ensemble was usurping the traditional authority of the actor.

In contemporary reviewing, I argue that the crisis of substitution is once again evident in responses to Shakespeare's Globe, that facsimilar, substitutional space that has consistently frustrated critics' notions of Shakespearean legitimacy. Furthermore, the idea of substitution-as-public test is highly relevant to the history of newspaper reviewing. In the long twentieth century described in Chapters 3, 4 and 5, I argue that critics, as public performers, have been acutely aware of their position as successors in a critical tradition. Theatre, the most ephemeral of the arts, is in particular need of a sense of tradition and continuity, of some way of staying the moment. While constructing and reinforcing traditions of performance, reviewers have also self-consciously engaged with traditions of criticism. In Beerbohm's substitution for Shaw as critic of the *Saturday Review*, in the marketing of Tynan as Shaw's successor, and in the current anxieties that no comparably influential reviewer has replaced Tynan and that, indeed, the authority of the critic might be usurped by that of the reader or 'citizen journalist', one sees the stresses of that tradition, the substitutional pressure placed on the night-watch constable.

The Society of Women Journalists was founded in 1895, but female critics appear only in the final chapter of this book. The substitutional rituals and concerns described above have predominantly concerned men: male reviewers, male actors, male directors. If one accepts that rivalry, competition and violence are traditionally 'masculine' traits, there is something inherently masculine and homosocial about the *conditions* of performance and reception. Bruce Smith (2000: 60), in summarising the various types of masculine role in the Shakespeare canon, finds one factor common to them all: 'masculine identity of whatever kind is something men give to each other'. Smith is talking about the attribution of identity between dramatic characters in the fictional world of each play, but his observation is equally valid for the relationship between actor and critic, and critic and critic. Theatrical reviewing is a vital cultural activity that is performed almost exclusively by men. Currently British national newspapers employ only a handful of first-string female critics; to the best of my knowledge, there were no long-serving or significant female theatre reviewers in the eighteenth and nineteenth centuries and for most of the twentieth. When an actor plays a Shakespearean lead, he unavoidably enters into a system of rivalry. If the play is one of the most frequently revived in the canon, this familiar canonicity creates competition, allowing – even necessitating – an evaluative process that is always longitudinal, and often synchronic. And the adjudicators of this competition between men have traditionally been men. But, as we have seen, these male adjudicators have often suffered a rhetorical emasculation – they are eunuchs in the harem or midwives to someone else's brats. From the early eighteenth century a 'hack' might refer to a prostitute as well as a biddable scribbler, and the 'power without responsibility' that critics are sometimes said to wield is, as in Stanley Baldwin's notorious comparison, 'the prerogative of the harlot throughout the ages'. (Never mind that the subjects of Baldwin's ire, Lords Beaverbrook and Rothermere, were not acting like female prostitutes, but rather like male press barons.) The ensuing battles over Shakespeare should therefore be seen partly in the context of the anxious manhoods of performers and critics alike in the competitive, capitalist micro-economies of theatre and the press.

* * *

In his Preface to *A View of the English Stage*, William Hazlitt quoted Rochefoucault's assertion that the reason lovers are so fond of one another's company is that it enables them to be always talking about themselves. Hazlitt added:

> The same reason almost might be given for the interest we feel in talking about plays and players; they are 'the brief chronicles of the time', the epitome of human life and manners. While we are talking about them, we are thinking about ourselves. (Hazlitt 1930–4: V 173)

Roughly a century later, Arthur Bingham Walkley, paraphrasing Anatole France, made the same point with great clarity: 'In order to be frank, the critic ought to say; Gentlemen, I am about to speak of myself *à propos* of Shakespeare' (Walkley 1903: 52). A central contention of this book is that when theatre reviewers describe and evaluate Shakespearean performance they unavoidably offer descriptions and evaluations of themselves and the societies in which they write. When, like the newspaper-buying audience of Ellen Terry's jubilee, one wants to bring back the yesterday of performance, one cannot know too much about the material, personal and ideological conditions in which performance became print.

CHAPTER TWO

Tradition and the individual talent
Reviewing the Macbeth actor c.1740s–1890s

This study of the reception of the Macbeth actor serves as an exposition of some dominant themes in Shakespearean reviewing. While the remainder of this book focuses more narrowly on specific and defined periods, this chapter takes a selectively diachronic approach in order to establish a background of evaluative habits and trends to the long twentieth century that forms the main focus of this study. Certain keynote themes emerge: the importance of the wider cultural context in reading reviews; the centrality of a competitive, canonical tradition in Shakespearean reviewing; the multifarious influences on the way Shakespearean performance is recorded and remembered; and the undercurrent of national and gender assumptions that runs throughout Shakespearean reception. Each of these themes recurs, with minor or major variations, throughout the ensuing chapters.

I begin with Garrick in the 1740s for two reasons. First, Garrick's *Macbeth* marks a crucial moment in the performance history of that play, a moment, at least rhetorically, when performance returned to Shakespeare's text after the seventy two year reign of Davenant's adaptation. As Stephen Orgel (2002: 246) writes, 'Garrick's assertion, the invocation of the author to confer authority on the production, marks a significant moment in both theatrical and textual history.' Second, and more important, theatrical (as contrasted with dramatic) criticism began to be widely practised in newspapers, journals and periodicals only in the second quarter of the eighteenth century. 'By the 1720s', David Thomas and Arnold Hare (1989: 199–200) write, 'an increasing number of newspapers and journals were published in London, but theatre performances were rarely discussed. Normally, critical commentary in the press was reserved for those occasions when plays provoked a heated aesthetic or political debate' – plays such as Steele's *The Conscious Lovers* (1722) or Gay's *The Beggar's Opera* (1728). However, as George Winchester Stone (1957: ccii) notes, 'with Garrick's debut in 1741, a burst of theatrical criticism began, which maintained a steady increase in interest until his departure from the stage in 1776'. As well as journalistic reviews, this chapter refers to the wider spectrum of texts that surround performance: memoirs, biographies, diaries, literary criticism and letters, in addition to the increasingly theatre-oriented output of newspapers and journals. By this means I hope to provide a broader context in which to place individual acts of Shakespearean reception, and specifically that of the Macbeth actor.

Macbeth and the ghost of success

The reputations of performers and performances have a marked tendency to ossify. In the performance history section of his Cambridge edition of *Macbeth*, A.R. Braunmuller (1997: 64) writes: 'David Garrick's performances as Macbeth were supported by those of Hannah Pritchard as Lady Macbeth – he effectively abandoned the rôle after her retirement – and he remains perhaps the only English actor to have conquered the part.' There is some virtue in that 'perhaps', but, as if to substantiate his claim, Braunmuller continues:

> Almost two centuries later [after Garrick], a distinguished critic succinctly praised and faulted Laurence Olivier by comparing him to Garrick: 'Since it would seem that with the exception of Garrick a great Macbeth has never been in the calendar, it is reasonable to expect that the new one should be lacking in adequacy.' (Braunmuller 1997: 64)

The distinguished critic was James Agate responding to Olivier's performance in 1937, and Braunmuller's citation affords a good example of how habits of thought are reinforced through intertextual reiteration. The authority of Agate's verdict and its value as evidence are apparently unassailable, despite the fact that what Agate (like Braunmuller) knows of Garrick's Macbeth is only and can only be via the body of texts the performance generated.

Braunmuller's rhetoric of exclusivity, of highly selective canonisation, is common to discussions of *Macbeth* in performance.[1] Nicholas Brooke (1990: 44) writes in his 1990 Oxford Shakespeare introduction that 'few leading actors have ever been distinctively identified with the role', while, speaking for many journalistic critics of the play, Kenneth Tynan (1961a: 98) stated flatly in 1955 that 'nobody has ever succeeded as Macbeth', although Tynan was (as shown in Chapter 4) revising that opinion in the light of Laurence Olivier's performance.

The idea that Macbeth is a nearly unplayable role, one that few, if any, actors have conquered, can be found in reviews and other responses to performance from Garrick's time to the present day. It has become almost a subdivision of the theatrical folklore that holds the play to be cursed in performance. More than any comparably important part in the canon, Macbeth has frequently been perceived to be beyond the scope of whichever actor is attempting the role. Theatre history is littered with the corpses of flop Macbeths: Charles Macklin, Kean (father and son), Henry Irving, Ralph Richardson and, more recently, Peter O'Toole, Derek Jacobi, Alan Howard, Mark Rylance: the line may well 'stretch out to th'crack of doom' (4.1.133). It is hard to imagine any critic writing that Olivier was the only English actor to have conquered Hamlet. Harder still, given the macho atmosphere of the statement, to imagine 'Peggy Ashcroft was the only English actress to conquer Rosalind'. Yet Braunmuller's verdict has further implications for Shakespearean performance criticism than simply what it reveals about widespread perceptions of Macbeth. This verdict is not, of course, based on the critic's own experience, but an opinion derived wholly from contemporary accounts of Garrick's performance, the textual traces his acting left behind. These traces may unanimously speak of Garrick's greatness, but what did it mean to be a great Macbeth in the mid eighteenth century?

The placing of Garrick as the successful original performer who was succeeded only by failures offers a lapsarian narrative of performance. Herbert Blau's pregnant observation 'where memory is, theatre is' (Blau 1990: 382), might here be reconfigured: where theatre is, selective memory is. Selective memory, as Joseph Roach writes in *Cities of the Dead*:

> requires public enactments of forgetting, either to blur the obvious discontinuities, misalliances, and ruptures or, more desperately, to exaggerate them in order to mystify a previous Golden Age, now lapsed . . . I believe that the process of trying out various candidates in different situations – the doomed search for originals by continuously auditioning stand-ins – is the most important of the many meanings that users intend when they say the word *performance*. (Roach 1996: 3)

According to Roach's book, this auditioning of stand-ins, a process he names 'surrogation', is employed to explain a range of circum-Atlantic performances in which competing histories are remembered, forgotten or transfigured. But the public auditioning of stand-ins finds a more literal application in Shakespearean performance history, in which candidates sequentially or simultaneously undertake ostensibly the same role in the attempt to efface the memory of previous actors and, ideally, to acquire a possessive synonymity with the part. One thinks immediately – such is the power of second-hand memories – of Betterton's Hamlet, Siddons's Lady Macbeth, Kean's Richard III and so on. Most relevant here is Roach's discussion of the installation of Thomas Betterton as a cultural icon, and the links between Shakespearean tradition, cultural memory and the structures of competition between the living and the dead that organise our responses to canonical performance. Roach writes:

> In a culture where memory has become saturated with written communication distributed and recorded by print, canon formation serves the function that 'ancestor worship' once did. Like voodoo and hoodoo, the English classics help control the dead to serve the interests of the living. The public performance of canonical works ritualizes these devotions under the guise of the aesthetic, reconfiguring the spirit world into a secular mystery consistent with the physical and mental segregation of the dead. In this reinvention of ritual, performers become the caretakers of memory. (Roach 1996: 77)

This has clear implications for any study of Shakespearean performance and reception, particularly of the pre-twentieth-century theatre. Entry into the Valhalla of collective memory depended to a large degree on the outcome of competitions between actors and theatres. The trying-out of various candidates in the same role over a *longue durée* is central to canon formation, as is the notion of success or failure in that role as defined against past practice. In 1898 Max Beerbohm wrote of seeing a succession of actors in the same role that in such circumstances 'The play is dead. The stage is crowded with ghosts. Every head in the auditorium is a heavy casket of reminiscence. Play they never so wisely, the players cannot lay those circumambient ghosts nor charm those well-packed caskets to emptiness' (Beerbohm 1953: 9). Roach (1996: 78) argues, in strikingly similar fashion, that even after death, actors' roles 'gather in the memory of audiences, like ghosts, as each new interpretation of a role sustains or upsets expectations derived from the previous ones'. This theatrical competition between youth and age, the dead and the living, new role-playing and old, seems particularly pertinent to *Macbeth*, a play which can be read as an Oedipal fantasy of surrogation. As Marvin Rosenberg (1982: 31) writes, 'the youth versus age *agon* is acted out doubly: Macbeth against older Duncan, then Malcolm against older Macbeth who would destroy – does destroy – threatening younger men children, until one destroys him'. It is also a play in which the stage is inhabited by the living and the dead, where the latter erupt into the present. Macbeth can no more vanquish the circumambient Banquo than the Macbeth actor can put to rest the cumulative memories of past interpretation. 'The time has been / That, when the brains were out, the man would die, / And there an end. But now they rise again' (3.4.77–9). I place the reception of the Macbeth actor in the context of this spectral structure of reception, a structure that has served as a paradigm of theatrical reception throughout reviewing history.

The way in which any given Shakespeare play fits into this structure of competitive reception is contingent on a number of interrelated factors, chief among which is the frequency with which the play is revived. As a general rule, the likelihood of frequent revival in the pre-twentieth-century theatre depended on three main factors: first, the economy of the play's roles – in effect, where the play falls (or was perceived to fall) on the continuum between star vehicle and ensemble piece. Within the actor-managerial ethos, those plays without a clear casting appeal to the lead actor were obviously far less liable to be produced.[2] Second, revival was more likely if the play offered (or could be adapted to offer) the opportunity for theatrical spectacle, could serve as a pretext to exhibit the latest developments in theatre technology. Third, frequent revival was only plausible if the play's moral and political concerns spoke to (or, once again, could be made to speak to) the concerns of the present.

The predication of Shakespearean production on the performance of the outstanding individual (frequently the actor-manager) is not, of course, an exclusively pre-twentieth-century phenomenon. *Hamlet* or *Lear*, for example, are still usually revived only if the director can find an actor who is exciting or prestigious enough to stimulate anticipatory interest in an overcrowded market. Yet it is also clear that, owing to a number of historical developments (for example, the rise of the director, the introduction of state subsidies, the emigration of many lead actors from theatre to film and television), power in the theatrical economy is no longer the preserve of individual actor-managers, so the dominant structures for reception have adjusted accordingly (see Chapter 4).

In surveying the reception of the Macbeth actor from Garrick to Irving I aim not only to describe an important interpretive pattern of pre-twentieth-century reception, but also to challenge one of the habits of thought through which one experiences past (and present) Shakespearean performance. The habit of thought is canonical and competitive, and its rhetoric is one of success/conquest and failure/defeat. I want to complicate this depiction of past performance by drawing attention to the various colourful influences on the way the Shakespearean actor was received, specifically the extent to which the protagonist's and actor's masculinity was a source of concern for reviewers and repeatedly inflected their evaluation (and thus the memory) of each performance.

The last three decades have witnessed an increase in studies of masculinity, most, across a spectrum of disciplines, stressing the social and historical construction of manhood. Anthropologist David D. Gilmore, for example, argues in *Manhood in the Making* that being a man is more than a function of biology and is an acquisition rather than a birthright in most known cultures. Despite significant differences in economic structure, history and custom, 'most societies hold consensual ideals – guiding or admonitory images – for conventional masculinity and femininity by which individuals are judged worthy members of one or the other sex and are evaluated more generally as moral actors' (Gilmore 1990: 10). Lady Macbeth clearly invokes and manipulates these consensual ideals of manhood in her attempts to prompt her husband to act. As social constructions of the feminine traditionally centre on ornamentation and passivity, it would be culturally unthinkable for Macbeth to reverse the argument that precedes Duncan's murder: 'You're a woman, why don't you do it?' is a non sequitur: 'An authentic femininity rarely involves tests or proofs of action, or confrontations with dangerous foes: win-or-lose contests dramatically played out on the public stage' (12). Gilmore's language (actors, dramatically, public stage) reminds one that the site for these tests of masculinity is inherently theatrical, that doing all that becomes a man is a dramaturgical accomplishment.

In this exploration of the performance and reception of six major Macbeths, I follow Laurie E. Osborne in her argument that 'acknowledging the differences between text and performance requires that we attend to the rhetoric as well as the context of the textual attempts to capture performance' (Osborne 1996: 142). In the period under discussion, authority, legitimacy, canonisation and competition, manliness, violence and nationalism all featured in the rhetoric and context of the textual responses to the Macbeth actor. Awareness of the presence of these preoccupations in the textual traces of performance should complicate the notion of success or failure in a Shakespearean role.

'Are you a man?' Macbeth, King David and the Irish Jew

David Garrick was 27 and only three years into his London career when he decided to produce and star in a *Macbeth* that would (after decades of Davenant) substantially return to Shakespeare's text, although with certain crucial emendations and additions. His uncertainty of success, of passing the rite of passage, is testified by his pre-performance publication of a pamphlet, the short title of which was *An Essay on Acting*. Such an intervention is indicative of the importance of widely circulated texts in the battle over theatrical authority and legitimacy. According to his first biographer, Arthur Murphy, 'a paper war . . . begun by the small wits' commenced the moment Garrick announced his intention to play the part. Murphy wrote: '[Garrick] knew that his manner of representing Macbeth would be essentially different from that of all the actors who had played it for twenty or thirty years before; and he was therefore determined to attack himself ironically to blunt, if not prevent, the remarks of others' (Murphy 1801: I 198). Garrick's performance and its textual pre-representation mark an important moment in the philosophy of lead performance. To offer a self-consciously new interpretation of a canonical role runs the risk of alienating an audience devoted to a genealogical tradition of interpretation. The mentality of this tradition in the early eighteenth century is best expressed in John Downes's *Roscius Anglicanus* (1708), where, in two instances, the authority of Betterton's performance is traced to Shakespearean instruction. Pre- and post-interregnum theatrical culture are umbilically linked in a fantasy of continuity that effaces the rupture of the Civil War:

> The Tragedy of *Hamlet*; *Hamlet* being Perform'd by Mr. *Betterton*, Sir *William* (having seen Mr. *Taylor* of the *Black-Fryars* Company Act it, who being Instructed by the Author Mr. *Shakespear*) taught Mr. *Betterton* in every Particle of it; which by his exact Performance of it, gain'd him Esteem and Reputation, Superlative to all other Plays.[3] (Downes [1708] 1987: 51–2)

Garrick's bold gesture was to sacrifice the authority of this performance tradition and instead to present his own authority as deriving, *despite* the intervening successions of *Macbeth*s, from Shakespeare, and specifically from his text. The playbills announced that the production would be 'As written by Shakespeare', in implicit contradistinction to those based on Davenant's adaptation. But, as Stephen Orgel (2002: 246) points out, 'the original text, in fact, was only marginally more satisfactory to Garrick's sense of the play than it had been to Davenant's. Why then the claim of authenticity?' Chiefly, I would argue, the claim of textual authenticity was offered to justify, to a potentially hostile community of interpreters, Garrick's divergence from performance tradition and to locate the privileged origins of his originality.

The circulation of *An Essay on Acting* was likewise a pre-validating move. Garrick's pamphlet, anonymously put out and written in the persona of a fantastically demanding critic, was an attempt to win the first battle of what might be a long campaign. In persona, he objected to the propriety of such a physically underwhelming actor presuming to play the 6-foot

Scottish warrior, suggesting that Fleance might be a more appropriate part for the diminutive Garrick. (In performance, Garrick would cut the scene in which Macbeth is said to feel his title 'Hang loose about him, like a giant's robe / Upon a dwarfish thief' (5.2.21–2); 'dwarfish thief' was not an image Garrick, anxious of physicality and legitimacy, wanted to implant in his audience's imagination.) Clearly Garrick was acknowledging a cultural conception of Macbeth's physicality. Representing manhood – particularly courageous, heroic manhood – is an aesthetic problem.[4] As William Ian Miller (2000: 189) writes in *The Mystery of Courage*, 'we have no secure cultural rules of thumb about the shape and size of female courage', yet men's bodies are consistently read for their predictive value. This issue of Macbeth's physicality resurfaces in comparisons of Kemble and Kean's bodies and their relative appropriateness for the role. Garrick's comparison between the actor's body and that of the boy-character Fleance is humorously hyperbolic, but underscores performance anxieties: 'Are you a man?' indeed.

A number of theatrical historians have recognised that Garrick altered Macbeth/*Macbeth* to suit the tastes of his time, encapsulated in his friend Samuel Johnson's essay on the character which foregrounds 'the excellence and dignity of courage, a glittering idea which has dazzled mankind from age to age' (Johnson 1908: 170). The privileged guiding image of masculinity in mid eighteenth-century England was the man of sensibility, and Garrick assiduously recast Macbeth into this refined mould. Thomas Davies, who wrote that 'the genius of Garrick could alone comprehend and execute the complicated passions of Macbeth' (T. Davies [1784] 1971: 83), is an indicative guide to what was found valuable in Garrick's performance:

> In drawing the principal character of the play, the author has deviated somewhat from history; but, by abating the fierceness of Macbeth's disposition, he has rendered him a fuller subject for the drama. The rational and several delight, which the spectator feels from the representation of this piece, proceeds, in a great measure from the sensibility of the murderer, from his remorse and agonies, and from the torments he suffers in the midst of his successful villany. (T. Davies [1784] 1971: 92)

The ostentatious manifestation of remorse was a vital preoccupation of mid to late eighteenth-century criticism of dramatic villains. Davies claimed that Shakespeare abated the violence of Macbeth's disposition in converting chronicle to play; Garrick's reworking of Shakespeare in turn mellowed the melancholy murderer still further. The critic can more easily locate the play's meaning and value in the remorse of the protagonist if certain atrocities are airbrushed. Garrick, for example, removed most of Lady Macduff's scene with her son, including his murder. Furthermore, he appended a dying speech for Macbeth, an unhappy pastiche of Faustus's last gasps, that sought to emulate the conventional and terrifying morality of Marlowe's play. As Francis Gentleman noted in Bell's edition of 1773:

> If deaths upon the stage are justifiable, none can be more so than that of *Macbeth*. *Shakespeare's* idea of having his head brought on by *Macduff*, is either ludicrous or horrid, therefore commendably changed to visible punishment – a dying speech, and a very good one, has been furnished by Mr. *Garrick*, to give the actor more éclat. (Quoted in Garrick 1981: 72n)

The on-stage death of the hero not only provides a moment of brilliant ostentation, of heightened display, but also – as A.C. Bradley would later argue after Hegel – aims to elicit from the audience 'a rush of passionate admiration, and a glory of the greatness of the soul' (Bradley 1909: 77).

Garrick's surgery on *Macbeth* thus produced a protagonist whose masculinity was less transgressive of contemporary decorum than Shakespeare's might have been. Dominated mentally and physically (if Johann Zoffany's portraits of the pair are accurate) by his wife, Macbeth was largely divested of responsibility for instigating evil. In a culture that privileged reaction over action (Donohue 1970: 222), it was appropriate, if not desirable, for Macbeth to reiterate ideals of masculine nobility through the expression of sensitive remorse. At the lines 'Prithee, peace. / I dare do all that may become a man; / Who dares do more is none' (1.7.45–7), *The Universal Museum* reported: 'The audience saluted him with a clap; which I could not help being much pleased with, as it not only showed a good judgement to applaud so fine a sentiment but at the same time a refin'd humanity' (9 January 1762; Tardiff 1993: 20). In this fashion Garrick 'conquered' Macbeth.

By the time Charles Macklin played Macbeth at Covent Garden in 1773, Garrick's performance in the part had achieved the status of a benchmark against which all competitors would be judged. Francis Gentleman's passage on *Macbeth* in his *Dramatic Censor*, which was published anonymously in 1770, represents this communal standard. In Gentleman's opinion, there was 'not one personage to be found in English drama, which [sic] more strongly impresses an audience, which requires more judgment and greater powers to do it justice' (Gentleman [1770] 1969: 1 107), and this power to do justice to the role lay exclusively with Garrick. The performances of James Quin, Thomas Sheridan, Spranger Barry, William Powell, Charles

Holland and William 'Gentleman' Smith were all dismissed as multiply flawed (109–11), with Garrick alone an '*immortal*' (108) and 'matchless genius' (109), endowed with the capacity to represent Macbeth. Macklin, like the would-be heirs to King David, the surrogate Macbeths in Gentleman's account, would now have to face a constituency of audiences and critics devoted to a canonical reading of the part. Roach writes:

> Because collective memory works selectively, imaginatively, and often perversely, surrogation rarely if ever succeeds. The process requires many trials and at least as many errors. The fit cannot be exact. The intended substitute either cannot fulfill expectations, creating a deficit, or actually exceeds them, creating a surplus. Then too the surrogate-elect may prove to be a divisive choice, one around whom factions polarize, or the prospective nominee may tap deep motives of prejudice and fear, so that even before the fact the unspoken possibility of his or her candidacy incites phobic anxiety. (Roach 1996: 2)

Garrick had last played the role four years before, in 1769, and it was now deemed to be the property of William 'Gentleman' Smith. This moniker resulted from Smith's affluent descent from a father who was a wholesale grocer and tea importer in the City of London, his attendance at Eton, his marriage to the sister of the Earl of Sandwich and his lofty boast that he had never stooped to wearing a stage beard or disappearing through a trap-door. In a profession with historically tenuous ties to good breeding, Smith was no doubt keen to stress his social legitimacy. When Macklin announced his intention to play Macbeth, squib warfare commenced with partisans of 'Gentleman' and 'King David' pitching in with predictive criticisms of the projected performance. Such an energetic polarisation and factionalism is entirely consonant with Roach's description of the atmosphere of attempted surrogation. The particular antagonism of Garrick's supporters was based on long memories; it was thirty years since Garrick and Macklin's friendship had come to an acrimonious end when Garrick had broken an actors' strike at Drury Lane, and the theatre management subsequently refused to have Macklin back (Benedetti 2001: 75). Macklin's defection to Covent Garden had then been followed by a series of head-to-head artistic clashes, such as the two houses' competing *Romeo and Juliet*s in the 1750 season. A retrospective account in a 1779 issue of the *Gentleman's Magazine* described this in typically agonistic and macho terms:

> Mr. Garrick, not intimidated by the strength of the opposition, took the field on the 5th of Sept. with an occasional Prologue spoken by himself; which was answered by another delivered by Mr. Barry [at Covent Garden]... Those

were only preludes to the trial of strength which was soon to follow... Both houses began [performances of *Romeo and Juliet*] on the first of October; and continued to perform it for 12 successive nights; when Covent Garden gave up the contention; and its rival kept the field one night more, with the credit of holding out longer than its opponent. (*Gentleman's Magazine*, 49 (1779), 172–3; reprinted in Adler 1997: II 172–3)

Perhaps in an attempt to avoid a repetition of the attritional contest twenty-three years before, Macklin, after the opening night of his *Macbeth*, attempted to defuse the competitive atmosphere of Shakespearean acting and reception by writing that he wished '*only to please*, not to *conquer* [that verb again] or *defeat*' (*The Morning Chronicle*, 27 October 1773). It was to no avail. In Garrick's *Essay on Acting*, the actor had attached the disingenuous epigraph 'Macbeth hath murdered Garrick'. Garrick's supporters, three decades later, cracked an intertextual joke at Macklin's expense: 'In act the second, scene the first, Shakespeare has made Macbeth murder Duncan; now Mr. Macklin, being determined to copy from no man, reversed this incident and in the very first act, scene the second, murdered Macbeth' (*London Evening Post*, 23–6 October 1773; quoted in Appleton 1961: 180). A rash of nasty impromptus spread through the newspapers, many satirising Macklin's presumption in attempting Macbeth, some on racial grounds: 'I learned tonight what ne'er before I knew,/That a Scotch monarch's like an Irish Jew' (quoted in Appleton 1961: 180). The *London Chronicle* (26–8 October 1773) carried the following stanza:

> 'Tis somewhere old *Dryden* has said or has sung,
> That *Vergil* with Majesty tosses his dung,
> And now if alive, he might sing or might say
> That with dignity *Garrick cuts throats* in a play:
> But Macklin appears so ungrateful a wretch
> His murders are done in the stile of Jack Ketch.
> (Quoted in Bartholomeusz 1969: 80)

'Jack Ketch' was the traditional name for any hangman, but the writer of the *Chronicle* verses may well have had the original Ketch in mind, a hangman of the 1670s and 1680s who had a reputation for both savagery and colossal incompetence. Were an actor to cut throats (or at least order for them to be cut), he should do it with Garrick's customary elegance.

After a series of physical skirmishes during and after Macklin's first two performances, the atmosphere became so riotous in the theatre that the management cancelled the run after the fourth night. Before what was to be his final performance as Macbeth, Macklin appeared before the audience 'with a sheaf of newsclippings in his hand', the paper bullets that had rained down on the very idea of his performance. He accused the actors Reddish and Sparks from Drury Lane of planning a hostile coalition against him, but affidavits sworn under oath by both men the next day 'brought the dispute to such a head in the newspaper[s] that a riot occurred the night of 18 Nov., when Macklin did Shylock (since [theatre manager George] Colman would not risk *Macbeth* after 13 Nov.) and announcement was made by Colman that Macklin had been dismissed' (Stone 1957: III 1757). The tussle for canonicity, for the right to be thought of and remembered as a great Macbeth, was as much a question of off-stage events as of anything Macklin did during his performance.

Any reflection on the relationship between Garrick, Macklin and the role of Macbeth must also take into account the broader climate of theatrical criticism in the mid to late eighteenth century. The periodical and newspaper press that adjudicated the claims of rival Shakespearean actors (and thus bequeathed the memory of performance) was not in any sense disinterested. Rather, it was fully instrumental in what Marc Baer (1992: 57) has called 'the habit of contention', both manufacturing and reporting the long series of disputes between managers, actors, politicians and the public. Bonnel Thornton neatly summarised the distortions consequent to this politics of performance in the *Connoisseur* in 1754: 'Parties and private cabals have often formed to thwart the progress of merit, or to espouse ignorance and dullness: for it is not wonderful, that the Parliament of Criticism, like all others, should be liable to corruption' (quoted in Gray 1931: 25). The inextricability of parliamentary and theatrical politics is apparent throughout the eighteenth and nineteenth centuries, from the opening night of Addison's *Cato* (1713), in which Tories and Whigs turned the event into an evening of political competition, to the OP (Old Price) riots of 1809, in which support of or opposition to price increases at Covent Garden were indexed to political affiliation. (The riots first broke out, incidentally but not atypically, during a performance of *Macbeth*.) The Theatre Licensing Act (1737) exacerbated the factionalism apparent at *Cato* by closing all theatres save the royal patentees, Drury Lane and Covent Garden, thus ensuring that the two houses would 'from ancient grudge break to new mutiny'. By the 1790s, for example, as Marc Baer and Jonathan Bate (1989) have argued, political ideology strongly dictated theatrical alliance; Covent Garden was considered establishment and pro-Pitt, while Drury Lane had crucial links to the opposition, not least through its owner, Sheridan, who was a leading Whig MP. Given that most newspapers and periodicals were ideologically committed to – and often financially supported by – either the government or the opposition, such alliances thickly muddy the evidential waters for the theatre historian.

Great caution should be exercised in using contemporary reviews as evidence for artistic superiority or inferiority. Garrick's relationship with newspapers and journalists was anything but aloof. Charles Gray's *Theatrical Criticism in London to 1795* offers this summary of the probability of systematic bias:

> It had been known about town many years earlier [before 1770] that Garrick owned stock in two or three newspapers and was on very friendly terms with the editors of those and other papers ... it is fairly clear that Garrick watched very closely over the nurture of his reputation by the press. He was quick to resent attack and was active in attempts to persuade men to praise him. Although he claims never except in one instance to have written his own 'puffs', there is some evidence that he was at least furthering his business interests in the competition of the theatres by writing up the performances in which he was interested. And furthermore his widow, many years after his death, told Edmund Kean that David always wrote his own criticisms ... it must be said that there appears to have been some foundation for even so egregious an exaggeration. (Gray 1931: 201)

To be remembered as the conqueror of a part, the actor must first conquer the press. Garrick's attempts to stifle dissent and to mute adverse criticism were probably aimed solely at preserving his reputation of preeminence in the mid to late eighteenth century. In persuading the Parliament of Criticism repeatedly to vote in his favour, Garrick was also ensuring his exalted position in the afterlife of theatrical memory.

Heroic assassin or common stabber? Class, masculinity and courage

In his biography of John Philip Kemble, James Boaden summarised the acting and interpretive choices that Macbeth was seen to demand of the actor in the late eighteenth and early nineteenth centuries:

> Does the actor ... exhibit to us the noble nature absolutely sunk and depraved by the act, or a base one losing its very cunning in the fear of deduction? Is he a hero, who descends to become an assassin, or a common stabber, who rises to become a royal murderer? (Quoted in Donohue 1967–8: 71)

Whilst this binary far from exhausts the interpretive options of the role, it reveals an important paradigm of contemporary critical attitudes. As with all binaries, a hierarchy is implied. Boaden's questions are rhetorical, not open-ended, and the privileged reading of the part, as it had been since Garrick, is that of 'the noble nature sunk and depraved by the act'. However he finishes the play, Macbeth begins it as a heroic example of ideal manhood. Boaden's opposites (noble/base, hero/common stabber, descends/rises) also have clear class connotations. Whether intentionally or not, he was encapsulating the interpretive and professional rivalry of the two great Macbeths of his era: his subject, Kemble, and the actor who would eventually rise to displace him in popular esteem, an upstart crow if ever there was one, Edmund Kean. The first encounter between the two rivals took place during a performance of *Macbeth*. Kemble chose the play as the first drama to be staged at the newly reconstructed Covent Garden in April 1794. Unfortunately for him, the seven-year-old Edmund Carey (as Kean was then known) had been cast as one of a bevy of goblin-cum-spirits whose presence was intended to lend a haunting preternaturalism to Macbeth's confrontation with the weird sisters (4.1). At the moment when Kemble, as Macbeth, entered the cavern, Kean 'either accidentally or intentionally made a forward step which he was unable to recover' (Molloy 1888: 13). In an attempt to get back in line, Kean somehow contrived to knock over his neighbour, who, domino-like, felled *his* neighbour, and so on, 'until the whole wicked company lay prostrate' (13) and irreparably compromised the integrity of the scene. The gods were standing up for bastards; Edmund the base topped the legitimate Kemble in a lampoon premonition of their future rivalry.[5]

Kemble played Macbeth opposite his sister, Sarah Siddons, for over thirty years (1785–1816), and, Coleridge's complaint that 'these were not the Macbeths of Shakespeare' notwithstanding, the pair achieved a level of widespread critical approbation rare in the reception history of the play. When Kean opened his Macbeth in late 1814, he was challenging an established, already canonised production. In that year he had already excelled in playing a pair of Shakespearean misfits: Shylock, the part in which he made his London debut, and that other great outsider, Richard III. The qualities that had distinguished those performances – pace, energy, an unorthodox physicality – were now singled out as inappropriate for Macbeth. The issue of how an abstract principle can be embodied in the male physique resurfaced in performance reception. We have seen how Garrick worried that his small stature might count against him; for Kean, size did matter. Kemble was a taller and broader man than his new rival, and, according to contemporary cultural meanings ascribed to that brand of male physicality, Kemble's body was more predictive of such qualities as dignity and courage. A clear idea of these cultural meanings can be gleaned from Leigh Hunt's review (written in 1819) of Macready as Coriolanus:

> As far also as height and figure go, he will have no rival in the part: for though it is curious enough that heroes and great political chiefs have for the most part been short rather than tall (as in the instances of Alexander, Agesilaus, Caesar, Charles the 5th, Frederick the 2nd, and Bonaparte), yet this is not the poetical or sculptural ideal of a hero. (Hunt 1949: 244)

The reception of Kean's Macbeth (as well as his Coriolanus) was influenced by his incompatibility with such a codified ideal. In *The Life of Edmund Kean*, Bryan Waller Proctor ([1935] 1969: II 106) admitted that Kean's 'small stature and incessant activity were the causes, perhaps, of his being generally less imposing than Mr. Kemble, who threw into the character [Macbeth] a more than regal dignity'. As Bourdieu ([1979] 1986: 176) writes in *Distinction*, the class speech opposition between 'popular outspokenness and the highly censored language of the bourgeois' is replicated at the level of bodily behaviour: 'The same economy of means is found in body language: here too, agitation and haste, grimaces and gesticulation are opposed to slowness – "the slow gestures, the slow glance" of nobility, according to Nietzsche – to the restraint and impassivity which signify elevation' (Bourdieu [1979] 1986: 177). The theatre critic of *The Examiner*, watching Kean in his third year as Macbeth, exemplified the socially constructed disjunction between agitation and elevation in his complaint that Kean's 'mouthing and mastication, in the quieter scenes, are as little contemplative, as his general appearance is heroic' (Tardiff 1993: 89). (A more recent example of what could be called an homunculist critique of Kean's physicality can be found in Peter Thomson's enjoyable essay on Kemble and Kean: 'however vehement his gestures of defiance were, on stage or off it, he [Kean] was a little man, on stage or off it, when the chips were really down' (2000: 126).) Macbeth was one of the few Shakespearean roles in which Kean suffered in comparison with Kemble; for Hazlitt, as for many reviewers, Kean was too close to the 'common stabber' Boaden described – too far from the ideal of the high-born hero presented by Kemble.

An off-stage contest of interpretations clearly delineated Kemble's conception of the role. In his essay 'Macbeth and King Richard the Third: an Essay, in Answer to Remarks on Some Characters of Shakespeare' (1817), a vastly expanded version of his much earlier pamphlet 'Macbeth Reconsidered' (1786), Kemble sought to defend Macbeth's manhood against two previous critiques. Thomas Whately made his 'Remarks' on Shakespeare's characters in 1770, but they had to wait until 1785 to be published, and a further four decades to receive Kemble's final 'Answer'. What appears to have really provoked Kemble was the more recent recycling of Whately's arguments in Steevens's 1803 edition of Shakespeare's complete works. Whately, in making the by then conventional comparison of the characters of Richard and Macbeth, had argued that the latter was distinguished by a 'natural timidity', 'an acquired, though not a constitutional, courage' (Whately [1785] 1997: 50). (Questions of 'principled' and 'natural' courage and the degree to which a Shakespearean character possesses either were also central to that milestone of character criticism, Maurice Morgann's 'Essay on the Dramatic Character of Sir John Falstaff' (1777).) Macbeth's ideas, Whately claimed, 'never rise above manliness of character, and he continually asserts his right to that character; which he would not do, if he did not take to himself a merit in supporting it' (Whately [1785] 1997: 50); Richard, on the other hand, 'never thinks of behaving like a man, or is proud of doing so, for he cannot behave otherwise' (52). In this reading, Macbeth's consciousness of the gap between inherent and acquired manhood and his awareness that, in contrast to the uncomplicated Richard, he is capable of not behaving like a man, mark his masculinity as assailable and problematic.

Kemble would have none of this. His lengthy defence of Macbeth's manhood involved detailed denials of Whately and Steevens's charges of timidity and cowardice. Kemble pointed to Banquo and Duncan's exchange near the opening of the play in which they extol Macbeth 'precisely for his being pre-eminently endowed with that very courage, which they [Whately and Steevens] have the temerity to deny him' (Kemble [1817] 1997: 36). Kemble's insistence on Macbeth's 'constitutional courage' (120) is obsessively reiterated and, as with all obsessions, could shade into inadvertent comedy. For Kemble, even Macbeth's ordering of Fleance's murder was not a cowardly act: 'Macbeth meditates the death of Fleance on motives unmixed with cowardice; for, allowing, for one moment, that he personally feared the father, it is absolutely impossible that he could have any *personal* fear of the son, who had not yet passed the term of boyhood' (58–9). Indeed, such is Macbeth's fearlessness and bloody resolution, that Kemble took issue with the then current emendation of the line 'unseam'd him from the nave to th' chops' (1.2.22) in which 'nape' had been substituted for 'nave'. Decapitation, however, was not sufficiently assertive for the intrepid hero Kemble believed Shakespeare to have presented. Arguing that the upward motion was entirely congruent with military reality, Kemble cited in a footnote the example of Charles Ewart, a sergeant in the Scots Greys, who had 'bravely brought off a French eagle in the glorious battle won by the immortal Duke of Wellington at Waterloo'. Ewart, appropriately a Scottish warrior, reported that, on being attacked by a lancer, he had then sword-thrusted his assailant 'from the chin upwards, which went through his teeth' (Kemble [1817] 1997: 17–18).[6] Kemble's essay began with an allusion to Anglo-French critical 'skirmishes' over Shakespeare, in particular Voltaire's 'paper bullets of the brain' (5); in his invocation of Waterloo in defence of Macbeth's warrior status, Kemble reinforced the links between nation, manhood and theatrical legitimacy.

Mid century Macbeths: rivalry and rioting

An entry from the diary of William Charles Macready, 26 April 1841:

> I have improved Macbeth. The general tone of the character was lofty, manly, or indeed as it should be, heroic, that of one living to command. The whole view of the character was constantly in sight: the grief, the care, the doubt was not that of a weak person, but of a strong mind and of a strong man. (Macready 1875: II 178)

Macready was evidently pleased with these improvements because he felt that they pushed him closer to an ideally assertive Macbeth; in this account, heroism is unthinkable without manliness or social and mental elevation. Macbeth was Macready's favourite Shakespearean lead, and he played it for over three decades (1820–51) in front of a largely enthusiastic public but a succession of hostile critics. In another diary entry he records: 'I had taken a newspaper from Calcraft's table that gave me very moderate praise for Macbeth, observing that though good, it was not so good as Kean's, which was a total failure' (Macready 1912: I 112). Professional vanity may be behind the description of 'total failure'; Kean was evidently widely praised for some moments in his interpretation. Yet Macready's blanket dismissal is symptomatic of how the passage of time can simplify artistic reputation, of how balanced contemporary response can harden into unbalanced history.

'Manly', 'heroic', 'not that of a weak person, but of a strong mind and a strong man': was Macready protesting too much in his self-congratulatory diary entry? Macready's Macbeth was widely criticised, in fact, for its *lack* of manliness, for its passivity and moral cowardice. The *Spectator* wrote that 'Lady Macbeth always appeals to the bravery and manhood of her husband. These personal characteristics require to be made prominent to give due effect to the struggle between courage and conscience'; Macready, conversely, not only 'made Macbeth too passive an instrument of destiny, but degrades him into an ignoble craven, and an object of contempt rather than of pity' (9 April 1842; Tardiff 1993: 101). In a review written to commemorate what was to be Macready's last performance in the role, the critic of the *London Illustrated News* wrote:

> We are of those who always saw a radical defect in the stage representations of this hero, and who require the nobility of character and the courage to be exhibited which Shakspeare [sic] predicates of him in the earlier scenes of the play... We therefore protest altogether against that prostration of soul and body with which Mr. Macready and others invest Macbeth throughout the first two acts of the play. It is a profane mistake, reducing the 'noble, brave' and 'peerless' ideal of Shakspeare to the level of a melo-dramatic murderer. It is too late now to call on Mr. Macready to amend his conception; but we record ours for the benefit of his successors. (13 October 1849; Tardiff 1993: 102)

Kenneth Tynan (1961a: 135) once described theatre reviews as 'letters addressed to the future', and this Victorian critic is clearly familiar with the notion that reviews have an afterlife that can shape cultural memory. In his criticism of Macready's interpretation, the critic begins by locating himself in a disgruntled community; nobility and courage are, as they have been since Garrick, the collective yardsticks of performance. Yet, as with much adverse response to the Macbeth actor throughout the play's theatrical history, the critic's ideal is based on a highly selective reading of the text. Many things are said of Macbeth in the play – by his wife, his admirers and his enemies – and it is revealing to see which of these epithets are typically deployed as yardsticks against which to measure (and more often with which to beat) the Macbeth actor. In reviews dating from Garrick to the present day, certain descriptions are repeatedly invoked as standards of measurement: 'noble', 'brave', 'Bellona's bridegroom', 'the milk of human kindness' (if the actor is too full of it – a curious case of the critic as Lady Macbeth, reproaching the Macbeth actor for an excess of passivity). All of these descriptions occur in the play's opening scenes before the murder of Duncan. I have found only one review reference, however, to the following exchange:

> MACDUFF: Not in the legions
> Of horrid hell can come a devil more damned
> In evils to top Macbeth.
> MALCOLM: I grant him bloody,
> Luxurious, avaricious, false, deceitful,
> Sudden, malicious, smacking of every sin
> That has a name. (4.3.56–61)

This could hardly have described the Macbeths of either Garrick or Kemble, who were critically rewarded for the excision of these traits. On the other hand, when Kean, Macready (unintentionally) and Irving (intentionally) embodied these adjectives, they were censured for infidelity, for profane misunderstandings of Shakespeare's character. A more recent 'failure', Michael Redgrave, attributed critical dissatisfaction with the part in performance to a discrepancy between word and action:

> If Antony [in *Antony and Cleopatra*] is a difficult part, how much more difficult, and notoriously so, is Macbeth. Here again, the audience arrives at the theatre with highly-coloured but vague expectations of this Scottish chieftain, this murderer; and here again we find that Macbeth is described as noble and valiant and during the whole play we see him do nothing that is either noble or valiant. This part is indeed what we may well call a teaser and it is notable that no actor has, as it were, claimed Macbeth as his own. (Redgrave 1954: 138)

Redgrave's account painfully recognises that the difficulty of the part inheres not only in the text, but also in the circumstances of reception. He complains of the way in which 'all these great parts have enlarged themselves in people's imaginations far beyond the bounds of the text' (Redgrave 1954: 138). But it is also the case that within the bounds of the text – especially in the exchange between Malcolm and Macduff quoted above – lies a Macbeth whose reported nobility and valour are severely compromised, and whose catalogue of vices has been largely ignored by actors and critics wedded to a certain heroic conception of the role.

Macready's Macbeth offers one further example of the interface between performance, reception and masculinity. The newspaper on Calcraft's table placed Macready in diachronic competition with a deceased actor. In the late 1840s, however, a more immediate and palpably dramatic rivalry formed between Macbeths. When the American actor Edwin Forrest toured the UK in 1845 he was dismayed by elements in the audience who expressed a very vocal dissatisfaction with his talents. As was the case when Macklin's Macbeth was booed, this hostility was assumed to be the result of audience loyalty to another actor, and Forrest apparently suspected that Macready was in some way responsible. When Macready embarked on an American tour in 1848 he was therefore prepared for some resistance. At first, his performances of Macbeth passed without much incident – the odd lobbed shrapnel of loose change, the occasional boo – but as the tour progressed, so did the disruptions, with ever-larger missiles projected from the auditorium across the footlights. In Cincinnati, Macready was forced to compete with the distracting on-stage presence of one half of a dead sheep. When he arrived in New York in the spring of 1849, the level of tension became so intense that, by what turned out to be the last performance, there were only seven women in the audience, a sure sign of expected violence. Rioting indeed broke out, the militia were called, and, with their backs against the wall, opened fire, killing an unknown number of the rioters – perhaps as many as thirty; it was the first time in America's history that soldiers had fired repeatedly 'at point-blank range into a civilian crowd' (Cliff 2007: 241).

Richard Nelson's fine play *Two Shakespearean Actors* (1991) dramatises the events of the Astor Place Riots by exploring the contrasts between English and American attitudes to life and art. Forrest is characterised as proto-Stanislavskian, a Method actor *avant la lettre*, while Macready represents the melodic, dignified and slightly stilted tendencies of the British theatre. The final scene of the play is a fantasia. Outside the theatre one hears raised voices and gunshots, while inside, alone at last, are the rival actors. Increasingly amicable, they compare notes on their profession, grow to admire each other's strengths and finally bond over a series of Shakespearean soliloquies. I call this scene a fantasia not only because it never happened, but also because its premise – of two actors bonding over a Shakespearean lead role – is so at odds with the reality of performance and reception in the eighteenth- and nineteenth-century theatre.

A domestic coward: Irving's Macbeth and the masculine estimate of man

Towards the end of Macready's career an important shift took place in the literary critical debate on Macbeth's character. In 1844 George Fletcher published an article in the *Westminster Review* entitled '*Macbeth*: Shakespearian Criticism and Acting', in which he became possibly the first critic to argue that Macbeth had planned to usurp and murder Duncan prior to the events dramatised in the play (Braunmuller 1997: 69n). Similar interventions followed that, perhaps overstating the case to dent an existing critical hegemony, sought to replace the man of sensibility with the selfish criminal, whilst simultaneously suggesting that Lady Macbeth was more the devoted housewife than the amoral virago of theatrical tradition. Fletcher (1847: 198) wrote of Helen Faucit's Lady, for example, that 'she was not the "fiend" that Mrs. Siddons presented to her most ardent admirers – but the far more interesting picture of a naturally generous woman, depraved by her very self-devotion to the ambitious purpose of a merely selfish man'. The most controversial Macbeth of the late nineteenth century sought to embody these new critical tendencies on the stage.

Henry Irving produced and starred in *Macbeth* in 1875, and then again in 1888–9. The first of these productions was far less successful, critically and certainly financially, than the second. Although literary critical discourse had changed in the interim, Irving was criticised in 1875 for many of the perceived shortcomings that Macready had exhibited three decades earlier. Theatre critics were still preponderantly devoted to the noble and manly reading of the part that Macready had described as the ideal 'general tone of the character'. Like Macready, and every other unsuccessful actor of Macbeth since Garrick, Irving was widely criticized for portraying ignobility, moral cowardice and villainy, even though Irving had wanted to strike a forceful keynote on his first entrance with his generals. In his study-book (the nearest thing to a prompt-book for the production) Irving had written that Macbeth should be: 'Lofty, manly, heroic. Living to command. The grief, the care, the doubt, not of a weak – but of a strong man, of a strong mind . . . A man of action – of overpowering strength and resolution' (quoted in Hughes 1981: 95). If this sounds familiar, one recalls Macready's proud diary description of the performance in which he felt he had got the measure of Macbeth: 'The general tone of the character was lofty, manly, or indeed as it should be, heroic, that of one living to command . . . the grief, the care, the doubt was not that of a weak person, but of a strong mind and of a strong man' (Macready 1875: II 178). The resemblance between the two passages is so striking that I think Irving had possibly read Macready's account and internalised or even memorised the description of this ideal strong man Macbeth. Sir Frederick Pollock published his two-volume edition of *Macready's Reminiscences, and Selections from his Diaries and Letters* in the same year as Irving's production. If this study-book entry captured the actor's aspiration, as is frequently the case in cultural production, reception clearly did not neatly mirror intention. Irving's most recent biographer summarised the response to the 1875 *Macbeth* as one in which 'some journalists praised Irving's "remorse, which looks like cowardice, perhaps, to an indolent and vulgar spectator" but the majority were vulgar enough to share Mr Punch's opinion that "the exhibition of physical terror and cowering, shrieking remorse . . . becomes repulsive"' (Hughes 1981: 101). Clement Scott thought Irving's conception of the part quite legitimate:

> A moral coward, outwardly brave if you like, but full of treachery and deceit, plotting against those who have shown him most favour, and contriving his crimes so as still to curry favour with the world – such is Macbeth. The world thinks that Macbeth must be a good fellow because he is a brave soldier; but Shakespeare – who mirrors the conscience of Macbeth – tells us what a moral coward a brave soldier can be. (Scott 1896: 74)

Despite this concession to Irving's interpretation and rejection of what 'the world thinks', Scott ultimately realigned himself with a more orthodox response to the character. Although he had praised Irving's intellect as a 'young student' of Shakespeare, he found the actor lacking the more traditional, muscular expressions of masculinity: 'no great actor has ever succeeded equally well in all the Shakespearean characters he has assumed. Many, indeed, like Mr. Irving, have not been gifted with the physical strength or robust vigour necessary to the trying demands of a tragedy like "Macbeth"' (Scott 1896: 79). The critic of the *London Illustrated News* agreed that Irving's 'style is somewhat too domestic for an heroic person of robust proportions' (2 October 1875; Tardiff 1993: 134). The Macbeth actor's body was once again the subject of the critical gaze and, on at least one occasion, ridicule. One periodical (*The Gentleman*) peddled the rumour that Irving was anxious about his physical suitability for the part, but that this fear was laid to rest when he came across the line 'Throw *physique* to the dogs' (Rosenberg 1978: 88n).

Henry James (1948: 36), who saw the show six weeks after its opening, summed it up as one that had 'produced not a little disappointment in the general public'. James, like Scott, partly admired Irving's reading of the character but faulted his execution, locating that fault chiefly in the actor's physicality and voice:

> His personal gifts – face, figure, voice, enunciation – are rather meager; his strong points are intellectual... he has thought out his part, after a fashion of his own, very carefully, and the interest of his rendering of it lies in seeing a spare, refined man, of an unhistrionic – of a rather sedentary – aspect... grappling in a deliberate and conscientious manner with a series of great tragic points. This hardly gives an impression of strength, of authority. (James 1948: 36–7)

Grappling, but not conquering. James (1948: 37), surveying Irving's negative reception, conceded, '[he] has been much criticized for his conception of his part – for making Macbeth so spiritless a plotter before his crime, and so arrant a coward afterward. But in the text, as he seeks to emphasize it, there is fair warrant for the line he follows.' Textual fidelity may be the professed yardstick for theatrical evaluation, but, as the reception history of *Macbeth* shows, other factors – not least cultural definitions of heroism and masculinity – contribute equally to the process by which a performance is evaluated and remembered.

When Irving chose to revive *Macbeth* in December 1888, he sought literary means (like Garrick before him) to render his interpretation more acceptable to the reviewing community. Unlike Garrick's pamphlet, Irving's preemptive strike was not penned by the actor and anonymously circulated; rather, it was the work of Comyns Carr, a friend of Irving's whose wife designed the astonishing dress that Ellen Terry would wear on stage and that John Singer Sargent would immortalise on canvas. Carr's pamphlet condensed arguments about the natures of the Macbeths that had been current since Fletcher in the 1840s and thus offered a literary exegesis for the reading that Irving and Terry would present at the Lyceum. Carr's pamphlet differs from Garrick's in most respects. Garrick addressed himself to critics who habitually prescribed what movements an actor should make at certain key moments, their inflexions on individual words and their appearance. Irving, ventriloquising through Carr, sought to preempt a critical mindset more preoccupied with psychological plausibility, more thoroughly attuned to the idea of the actor as a three-dimensional character critic. Revealingly, perhaps the only continuity between the two texts (written roughly a century and a half apart) is the concern – occasional in Garrick, preeminent in Carr – to address the vexed question of Macbeth's courage.

Although, as the *Athenaeum* put it, Irving's 1888 *Macbeth* was 'practically the same that thirteen years ago stirred eager controversy' (5 January 1889; Tardiff 1993: 136), the pre performance publication of Carr's monograph clearly and positively influenced critical response. Moreover, the production was a commercial hit, running for 151 nights to capacity audiences, and was revived in 1895 for an American tour. Yet for all the apparent persuasiveness of Carr's argument of the inherent villainy of Macbeth and the innocence of his wife, reviewers still resisted the central interpretations. Ellen Terry's devoted Lady was too far from Siddons for most critics' comfort: 'the notion that this spiritual and ineffable creature could prompt to murder and assist at its committal is an insult to masculine estimate of woman', complained the *Athenaeum*. But the masculine estimate of man was also at stake. According to the *Saturday Review*, Irving's interpretation was persuasive enough to have 'proved that Macbeth has been too flatteringly portrayed in the past . . . It will no longer, we think, be quite so vehemently contended that Mr. Irving's conception of Macbeth is unduly heroic.' But the reviewer continued:

> There is, on the other hand, plenty of room for the criticism that Mr. Irving's rendering of Macbeth is even more unheroic than his conception. It is impossible to deny that Macbeth is, on the whole, a poor creature. The very fact that one is compelled to insist so much on his mere physical courage is a tolerably clear indication that it is his only masculine virtue. He has no will, no nerve, no constancy of purpose, and his superstitious awe of the supernatural is excessive. (5 January 1889; Tardiff 1993: 138–9)

Irving could nevertheless have still displayed 'more dignity of demeanour, and – at any rate occasionally – more self-control and self-respect' (Tardiff 1993: 139). Although, as we shall see, Irving was relatively successful in conveying physical courage in the play's final act, his perceived deficiency in other masculine virtues proved unpalatable to many critics. His lack of the masculine traits of nerve and self-possession became a leitmotif of reception. This would seem to be anticipated by the notes Terry made on Macbeth in the two bound copies of the play Irving had specially printed for her in preparation for the production. In one of the interleaved blank pages, she wrote of Macbeth:

> A man of great *physical* courage frightened at a *mouse*. A man who talks and talks and works himself up, rather in the style of an early Victorian hysterical heroine... M must have had a neglectful mother – who never taught him the importance of self-control. He has *none*! and is obsessed by the one thought *Himself*. (Quoted in Manvell 1968: 194)

Responsibility for Duncan's murder could only credibly be attributed to Irving's Macbeth, turning him into the common stabber, the ignoble craven, the 'merely selfish man'. Marvin Rosenberg (1982: 85) writes that 'Irving's spectacular scoundrel evidently satisfied some need of the time'. Given the largely negative critical response to his performance, it might be more accurate to say that Irving's characterisation conspicuously *failed* to satisfy some need of his time.

'Lay on': the Macbeth actor exits fighting

At one moment in *Macbeth* the protagonist's masculinity is orthodox and unproblematic. After the vacillations of the opening acts, then the murderous, insomniac villainy of the insecure king, Macbeth ends the play besieged and alone on the battlements of Dunsinane. When Macduff reveals that he is not of woman born, Macbeth and the audience know that he is doomed. Nevertheless, he will not yield: 'Before my body / I throw my warlike shield. Lay on, Macduff, / And damned be him that first cries "Hold enough!"' (5.10.32–4). Our last impression of Macbeth is of a warrior, blindly courageous in the face of an unassailable fate. The fourth scene of the play has prepared us for the idea that facing death as if it were 'a careless trifle' can be the most becoming act of a man's life (1.4.8–11). For the first and last time we see Macbeth in action, and this active courage does much to redeem his vexed masculinity. Even for Thomas Whately, so critical of Macbeth's courage, the character is restored to a state of conventional and admirable masculinity at the play's conclusion: 'he summons all his fortitude; and, agreeably to the manliness of character to which he had always formed himself, behaves with more temper and spirit during the battle than he had before' (Whately [1785] 1997: 73).

It therefore seems more than coincidental that all the actors under discussion here, from Garrick to Irving, were critically well received in their death scenes. Kean's death, for example, was so impressive as to alter perception of his stature: 'In the bustle of the fight, as may naturally be supposed Mr. KEAN becomes the very "giant of the scene"', wrote G.J. DeWilde in *The Drama* (March 1824; Tardiff 1993: 90). John Forster wrote of Macready: 'But, unquestionably, Mr. Macready's greatest achievement in this tragedy is the fifth act... Nothing can probably be grander than his manner of returning, with that regal stride after he has received his mortal thrust, to fall again on Macduff's sword' (Lowe and Archer 1896: 7). Henry Irving's final act also seemed to compensate some reviewers for his performance's overall lack of masculine virtue. Clement Scott wrote of the 1875 production:

> Amidst all the varied pictures of this striking tragedy none will be better remembered than that of Macbeth, hunted down at last, and hacking with desperate energy at the firm sword of Macduff, with his suit of mail disordered, and his grizzled hair streaming in the wind. (Scott 1896: 77–8)

Frederick Wedmore in *Academy* found similar power in the conclusion of the 1888 production: 'the play's end, as Mr. Irving interprets it, is of superb effectiveness, to summon our admiration for the courage... of its main character' (Tardiff 1993: 144). Then there is Terry's account of the final moments in the last act after the battle: 'He looked like a great famished wolf, weak with the weakness of an exhausted giant, spent with exertions ten times as great as those of giants of coarser fibre, and stouter build' (Terry 1933: 232–3). In the examples of Kean and Irving, the actor's body is presented as morphing, superheroically, from the mediocre to the gigantic. These and other responses celebrate the performance of great physical courage, *tableaux vivants* of conventional masculinity. Even after

Garrick's death speech, or variation thereof, was cut from performance, almost nothing became the Macbeth actor's stage-life like the leaving of it.

Macbeth, like all Shakespeare's protagonists, places a number of demands – physical, emotional and intellectual – on the actor. Yet an actor has a far greater statistical likelihood of flopping if he is playing Macbeth than if he is playing equally taxing roles such as Hamlet, Richard III or Lear. The cultural subtexts of reviews make it clear that critics have placed other demands on the actor, demands arising as much from perceptions of manhood as from any desire for textual fidelity. The 'difficulty' of the part does not inhere exclusively in Shakespeare's (and Middleton's) text, but is partly the result of far broader societal conceptions of what is acceptable or laudable in human, here specifically male, behaviour.

In *Cultural Selection*, Gary Taylor (1996: 11) writes of how 'the living are measured by a standard set by the remembered achievements of the dead. Every maker is shaped and judged by the comparison with the memory of famous earlier makers.' In reading traces of the theatrical past, we must be sensitive to the circumstances – material and ideological – in which these memories are imprinted. In the case of *Macbeth*, this means considering the cultural pressures of masculinity, both as a performative ideal for dramatic character and as a system of thought embedded in the act of reviewer reception. Later chapters in this book return to the reception of *Macbeth* and the Macbeth actor as evaluated in the reviews both of an individual critic (Kenneth Tynan) and a community of interpreters (the national newspaper reviewers of the mid 1990s). The following chapter, however, begins where this chapter ends: in a London theatre scene dominated by Henry Irving and the Lyceum.

CHAPTER THREE

New Journalism, New Critics c.1890–1910

The London theatre underwent a sea-change in the closing years of the nineteenth century. Myths of origin are inherently controversial, but when William Archer (1891: 664) wrote that 'the 7th June, 1889, the date of the production of *A Doll's House* at the Novelty Theatre, was unquestionably the birthday of the new movement', he was understandably attempting to fix the coordinates of a theatrical landscape that was in a tremendous state of flux. In *Resistible Theatres*, John Stokes (1972: 3) identifies the closing decades of the nineteenth century as a time 'when theatre and theatre business began to assume a new and central position in the public consciousness – a shift that was, for obvious reasons, parallel to and even dependent upon the rise of popular journalism'. With respect to theatre criticism, that indecision between 'parallel to' and 'even dependent upon' hints at the difficulty of disentangling the relationship between theatre practice and journalism. Intuitively, the newspaper page would be expected to mirror the contemporary stage, but frequently in the history of the theatre, critics have acted as more or less unacknowledged legislators of the stage, guiding it to its future by reflecting its present shortcomings. This is especially true of a period in which many important critics found themselves in a partisan community, split between supporters and detractors of the New Drama. What all critics shared, however, was a place in an arena of cultural production and a profession that were evolving as rapidly, if not more so, than the theatre to which it responded.

The first half of this chapter describes the changes in journalistic practice in the last two decades of the nineteenth century and their profound implications for the function and the status of the theatre critic. This description focuses on a set of related developments: the widespread introduction of the signed article, the increasing respectability of journalism as a profession, the cult of the critic's individuality, the twin imperatives of independence of thought and incorruptibility, and the authority of the reviewer as a qualified judge of the competing claims to authority on the contemporary stage. If one accepts Robert D. Hume's claim that 'the contexts of original composition and reception are unrecapturable in their original totality and complexity' (Hume 1999: 84), a process of selection is inevitable. The second half of this chapter places the Shakespearean criticisms of two prominent reviewers – George Bernard Shaw and Max Beerbohm – within the context of the New Journalism. Most of the reviews discussed were written between 1895 and 1905: the lifespan of Poel's Elizabethan Stage Society, the gap between Irving's knighthood and his death, and the period in which the *Saturday Review* published all of Shaw's and over half of Beerbohm's theatrical criticism.

'The climax and masterpiece of literary Jacobinism': the introduction of the signed article

The shift from anonymity to identification and attribution is one of the most profound changes in the history of the newspaper and periodical. The implications for the function and afterlife of the dramatic critic are widespread and far-reaching. Within artistic coteries and journalistic circles, it is questionable how much the dramatic critic had ever enjoyed complete anonymity – managements might typically have a fair chance of matching names and faces to the obfuscating bylines attached to reviews. Within a claustrophobic and incestuous community, the preservation of the anonymity of a high-profile personality such as a critic would be surprising. Indeed, in the mid nineteenth century it was possible, as John Hollingshead proved in 1867 in a new journal, *Broadway*, to expose the identities of the leading London dramatic critics (Kent 1980: 32).

Yet for the average reader of a newspaper or periodical, the critic's identity was, for most of the nineteenth century, a topic of speculation rather than certainty. The model of anonymity had historically subsumed the individual journalistic voice within the corporate identity of the newspaper: in the ideally homogeneous publication, whether the text one was reading had one author or one hundred would be impossible to decipher from internal evidence alone. Special contributions from individuals might be highlighted if the report were to come from abroad or was an early example of investigative journalism. In the first case, the byline might read 'From Our Own Correspondent', marking the journalist as physically independent of the newspaper office, but professionally its property. In the case of investigations into workhouse conditions or baby farming, such as those Frederick Greenwood commissioned for the *Pall Mall Gazette* in the late 1860s, the nonchalant and unhelpful byline 'Amateur Casual' hid the identity of the journalist – who became something of a hero to readers and fellow professionals alike. Theatre critics might sign themselves as 'From Our Stall' (as W.S. Gilbert did for *Fun*), 'Quasimodo' (Cecil Howard in the *Sunday Times*), 'Vivian' (George H. Lewes in *The Leader*), or 'Theatrical Lounger' or 'Hugo Vamp', depending on inclination (Thomas W. Robertson in the *Illustrated Times*). This may not have been 'the free circulation, the free manipulation, the free decomposition and recomposition of fiction' or nonfiction that Foucault posited as his utopian vision of anonymous and autonomous textuality – newspapers, after all, cost money, and some form of socio-political identity was inherent in every publication. Widespread anonymity, however, hindered if not prevented the general reader in knowing at any point to whose voice they were listening.

The appending of a proper name to the review text radically alters the reading experience, the nature and ethics of the text, and the status of the journalist. As the century wore on, and especially from the 1880s after the advent of the New Journalism, signed articles became increasingly common, especially outside the editorial pages. This shift from anonymity to attribution was not exactly synchronous between the periodical and the newspaper. As Laurel Brake (1988: 9) writes, 'It may be suggested that while [in the 1880s] the periodical press was moving, with reservations, toward signature and fragmented authority, the newspaper press came to occupy the middle ground between blanket anonymity and the vulgarity of named contributors.' For theatre criticism, however, periodicals and newspapers did not uniformly adopt the signed article in the late nineteenth century. As late as 1931, Sydney Carroll (1931: 1) could list as one of the 'grievances' of modern reviewing 'the habit most papers have of publishing criticism anonymously or as coming from the paper instead of allowing the critic to attach his name to each contribution'. Nevertheless, the newspaper reader of the 1890s was in the unprecedented position of receiving the work of such prominent reviewers as Shaw, Beerbohm, Archer and Scott as the result of identifiable people. For the first time, the review space became a site for foregrounded individuality, for an expression of the author's self that may or may not be consonant with the tone and the opinions of the rest of the publication – a point to which I return with specific reference to the writing of Shaw and Beerbohm.

For Shaw, looking back in 1898 on the journalistic shifts of the previous two decades, the signed article appeared as the logical conclusion of a complex of developments in newspaper content and form. In the last review proper he wrote for the *Saturday Review*, Shaw attacked H.D. Traill, co-author of an apparently dire Lyceum piece, *The Medicine Man*, and formerly an 'academic literary gentleman' who had shamelessly used the press to puff his own publications. Shaw implied that Traill's use of reviewing for pompous self-aggrandisement was now, in 1898, an anachronism:

> Some time in the eighties London rose up in revolt against this view. The New Journalism was introduced. Lawless young men began to write and print the living English language of their own day . . . They split their infinitives, and wrote such phrases as 'a man nobody ever heard of' instead of 'a man of whom nobody had ever heard,' or, more classical still, 'a writer hitherto unknown.' Musical critics, instead of reading books about their business and elegantly regurgitating their erudition, began to listen to music and distinguish between sounds; critics of painting began to look at pictures; critics of the drama began to look at something else besides the stage; and descriptive writers actually broke into the House of Commons, elbowing the reporters into the background, and writing about political leaders as if they were play-actors. The interview, the illustration and the cross-heading, hitherto looked on as American vulgarities impossible to English literary gentlemen, invaded all our papers; and, finally, as the climax and masterpiece of literary Jacobinism, the Saturday Review appeared with a signed article in it. (Shaw 1932: III 377–8)

In Shaw's account, the innovation of authorial identity in the *Saturday* crowned a period of profound change in journalism. The introduction of youth, challenges to received notions of appropriate register, a new way of seeing and hearing in arts criticism, the theatricalisation of politics, formal and typographical experimentation under the influence of American ground-breakers such as Joseph Pulitzer and William Randolph Hearst – all these factors altered the landscape of popular journalism. Furthermore, the social perception and make-up of the journalist had altered radically in the previous two decades. In 'The Work of Art in the Age of Mechanical Reproduction', Walter Benjamin cited this era as one in which writing and authorship were democratised:

> For centuries a small number of writers were confronted by many thousands of readers. This changed toward the end of the last century. With the increasing extension of the press, which kept placing new political, religious, scientific, professional, and local organs before the readers, an increasing number of readers became writers – at first, occasional ones. It began with the daily press opening to its readers space for 'letters to the editor'. (Benjamin 1992: 225)

In the London of the 1880s and 1890s, few people exploited the new-found space of the correspondence pages as often or as entertainingly as

George Bernard Shaw (see Holroyd 1990: 213–14). Writing in 1936, Benjamin traced the fading of the distinction between author and public to the journalistic innovations of the close of the previous century. Alongside this democratisation, the profession of journalist (perhaps not coincidentally like that of the actor) doubtless acquired greater cultural currency and respect in the last quarter of the nineteenth century. The 'growing tendency for critics to be of public school and/or university background' reflected, according to Christopher Kent, both 'the growing respectability of journalism as an occupation and . . . the growing number of university graduates seeking jobs' (Kent 1980: 33). In a subsequent article, Kent and Tracy C. Davis (1986: 99) calculated that, by the end of the period 1830–1914, the 'available information on the education of the 403 critics [of all arts] identified indicates that journalism had achieved a significant degree of respectability' over the course of the Victorian and Edwardian eras. As Jane Stedman (1995: 167) argues, 'the men who wrote and reviewed plays were increasingly gentlemen working in what was not quite a gentleman's profession. The reviewer of books dealt with literature; the reviewer of plays with ephemera.' An informal but nevertheless collective campaign emerged to validate both the legitimacy of the stage, and, co-dependently, the respectability and social function of journalistic theatre criticism.

Max Beerbohm, writing in June 1902, gave a retrospective account of the legitimisation of the profession. In 'Honour Among Dramatic Critics' Beerbohm, having recently read a pamphlet from the 1870s lampooning the corruptibility of dramatic critics, noted the quaint remoteness of this theme and found it worthwhile 'to inquire how and why it is that dramatic criticism has, in so short a time, undergone so great a change, becoming so very respectable indeed' (Beerbohm 1953: 210). His inquiry concluded that, in the relationship between production and reception, art gets the critics it deserves:

> You must remember that in the seventies and early eighties English drama was almost wholly in the hands of miserable hacks whose highest accomplishment was making of adaptations from French plays. As an art, it did not exist: it was simply one of the less lucrative trades. Accordingly, the task of criticising it was tossed to the fools. In the newspaper offices any reporter was considered good enough to 'do' a new play. (Beerbohm 1953: 210)

By 1902 English drama had been 'out of the slough' for some time, and:

> now even the editors of the daily papers – some of them, at any rate – have so far moved with the times (and with the 'Times') that they prefer to have their dramatic criticism done well. Like the editors of weekly papers, they

seek a man of real ability, a man who can observe, and think, and feel, and perhaps write. (Beerbohm 1953: 211)

(Beerbohm's use of 'man' here is not an example of lazy homogenisation: in the period 1830–1914, only five female critics of any art form have been identified, and only two of these covered drama. One (Pearl Craigie) had a brief spell in *Life*, the other (Constance Margaret Scott, wife of the critic Clement Scott) had a similarly short tenure with *John Bull* magazine – see Kent 1980 and Kent and Davies 1986.) The man that editors sought, according to Beerbohm, was 'not going to devote himself wholly to dramatic criticism. He has other stakes in life or art, and it would not pay him to withdraw them':

> Thus, if one analysed a list of the intelligent dramatic critics (and this would be a fairly exhaustive list, since almost all the duffers have died out), one would find two civil servants, a barrister in good practice, two poets, an essayist, a political secretary, a caricaturist, the editor of a monthly review, several men whose main business is in reviewing books, and other men in various other callings. Indeed, I do not think there is one who is merely a dramatic critic. There are only two whom one would describe as being primarily dramatic critics. (Beerbohm 1953: 211)

Beerbohm's optimistic survey of impartiality concludes that 'the modern dramatic critics are immune from moral danger' because, unlike their predecessors of the 1870s, they have 'greater interests outside the theatre than inside it' (Beerbohm 1953: 212). The association with the professions or with high literary pursuits and the catalogue of respectable day jobs are offered as symbolic of incorruptibility and independent judgement, qualities that were seen as vital constituents of legitimate reviewing by the 1890s. The level of cultivation and eclectic professionalism among the reviewing community could imply that Wilde was not being altogether flippant or gratuitously paradoxical when he has his mouthpiece, Gilbert, opine in 'The Critic as Artist' (1890) that 'as a rule, the critics – I speak, of course, of a higher class, of those, in fact, who write for the sixpenny papers – are far more cultured than the people whose work they are called upon to review. This is, indeed, only what one would expect, for criticism demands infinitely more cultivation than creation' (Wilde [1890] 1950: 123).

An ideal of accountability and objectivity entered the profession, which, if it was not always realised, was at least a symptom of the increasing seriousness with which the function of the dramatic critic was viewed. In this atmospheric context the signed article emerged. The question of who was speaking reached the foreground of journalistic practice. Amid the ruins of the newly fragmented authority of the periodical and, to a lesser extent, of the newspaper, the so-called New Critic was born. Foucault's lines on the significance of the author's name are helpful in understanding the importance of the signed article:

> Such a name permits one to group together a certain number of texts, define them, differentiate them from and contrast them to others... The author's name serves to characterize a certain mode of being of discourse: the fact that the discourse has an author's name, that one can say 'this was written by so-and-so' or 'so-and-so is its author,' shows that this discourse is not ordinary everyday speech that merely comes and goes, not something that is immediately consumable. On the contrary, it is speech that must be received in a certain mode and that, in a given culture, must receive a certain status. (Foucault [1969] 1988: 201)

The newspaper is predicated on the ephemeral, on being the printed equivalent of everyday speech and easily consumed. T.P. O'Connor extended the consumption metaphor in his 1889 article on 'The New Journalism', which, in an appeal for boldness of presentation and clarity of meaning, distinguished between book and paper: 'The newspaper is not read in the secrecy and silence of the closet as is the book. It is picked up at a railway station, hurried over in the railway carriage, dropped incontinently when read' (O'Connor 1889: 423). The perceived sub-literariness of journalism rests largely on its status as a cultural form that 'may be seen as the commercial and ideological exploitation of the transient and the topical, a ceaseless generating of "news" and novelty' (Brake 1988: 1). The newspaper's claim to universality, permanence and timelessness – the perceived qualifications for high cultural forms – is tenuous at best. This may partly explain the widespread intellectual distrust of journalism exemplified by Matthew Arnold's notorious jeremiad against the New Journalism in May 1887, or Nietzsche's categorical 'We feel contemptuous of every kind of culture that is compatible with reading, not to speak of writing for, newspapers' (Nietzsche 1968: 80). The nineteenth-century periodical enjoyed a higher cultural status than the newspaper and, in its typical translation from single issue to multi-issue volume, partly resisted the dominant perception of journalism as 'ordinary everyday speech that comes and goes'. Yet, even when confronted with a collected series of periodicals in the high cultural form of a book, the overall effect is still one of a genre marked by heterogeneity rather than consistency, one that is incapable of the unity of tone, subject and purpose expected of art. As Margaret Beetham (1990: 25) argues, the periodical is difficult to define textually because, like the newspaper, it is the product of a corporation, not an individual: 'One way of identifying a text has traditionally been to situate it in the *oeuvre* of a particular author. However, the concept of authorship becomes problematic in relation to the periodical, where typically even one number involves several writers.' Lyn Pykett (1990: 11) poses a similar series of questions: 'If we look at one periodical, one newspaper we have to ask "What is the text in the field of periodical study? Is it the individual essay? The issue? The volume? A run defined in some other way, say by the period of a particular editorship?"' The introduction of the signed article provided at least one way of resolving these dilemmas.

The signed article, even within the wider context of consumable journalism, invited the reader to group together certain texts under the proper name of the author. In intention, the signed article was introduced to serve the ethical purpose of making the critic accountable, socially if not necessarily legally, for his or her opinions without the camouflage of the *nom de plume*. As Seán Burke (1995: 289) writes in an eloquent attempt *contra* Foucault to rehabilitate the idea of the author, 'the primary ethical function of the signature is therefore to set up a structure of resummons whereby the author may be recalled to his or her text. As with the legal signature, the textual mark is addressed to the future; to mortality and to the afterlife of the written sign.' Burke's notion of the signature as an address to the future is richly suggestive when applied to the context of late nineteenth-century theatrical journalism and reception. In the history of literature or of any other high art form, those texts or works that can be attributed clearly have a greater chance of claiming a foothold in cultural memory. Canonicity is generally uncomfortable with anonymity.

It is no coincidence that, in the period in which the signed article established itself as a common practice in theatre reviewing, the number of books published that consisted of anthologies of reviews by a single critic increased dramatically. The widespread rescue of review texts from their original, perishable locations had two key functions and effects. First, it relocated the texts in the more stable and culturally privileged form of the book. Second, anthologisation argued a consistent critical-authorial stance in the writing, one that deserved to outlive the vagaries of journalistic contingency: the newspaper, although 'born only to be buried' ('Editorial' 1898: 769) as it was, could still contain material destined for an afterlife.

The tension of this relocation from newspaper to book, from journalism to literature, is apparent in the shifting attitudes towards anthologisation held by Shaw and Beerbohm. In October 1896 Ellen Terry asked Shaw:

'what did you write in the S.R. a few weeks ago about Clementina?' (Shaw 1949a: 83). She was referring to Shaw's *Saturday Review* piece on Clement Scott's *From 'The Bells' to 'King Arthur'*, written in late May. Shaw wrote back: 'You remember the publication of Scott's criticisms of the Lyceum the other day. Well, I reviewed it: that was all. Dead and gone journalism' (84). A year before, Shaw had written to R.E. Golding-Bright that his dead-and-gone music criticism was unworthy of an anthology: 'I cannot bring myself to republish my articles. They appear very entertaining in the context of the events of the week in which they appear; but just because they are good journalism, they are bad literature' (Shaw 1956: 35). But, by 1907, and in a typically Shavian volte-face, private anxiety had turned to public bravado. In republishing a journalistic 'remnant' of 1895, 'The Sanity of Art: An Exposure of the Current Nonsense about Artists being Degenerate', Shaw had to defend the reissue of a critique of nonsense that was no longer current. Shaw claimed in his preface that only writing aimed squarely at the present, and with no eye on posterity, can last beyond the moment of composition. By this logic, 'journalism can claim to be the highest form of literature, for all the highest literature is journalism' (Shaw [1895] 1986: 311); this included the enduring works of Plato, Aristophanes, Shakespeare and Ibsen, all of whom wrote for their age and not for all time. (Shaw did not always credit Shakespeare with the journalist's knack of long-term relevance.) Shaw then castigated the many thousands of 'correct men of letters and art who spent their lives haughtily avoiding the journalist's vulgar obsession with the ephemeral', before offering this resounding apologia: 'I also am a journalist, proud of it, deliberately cutting out of my works all that is not journalism, convinced that nothing that is not journalism will live long as literature, or be of any use while it does live' (311–2).

Beerbohm could never have written, as Shaw did in this preface, 'let others cultivate what they call literature: journalism for me!' (Shaw [1895] 1986: 312). In the 'Epistle Dedicatory' to the first of two volumes of selected reviews published in a limited edition of his works in 1924, Beerbohm wrote that when people had suggested he might anthologise his reviews:

> The idea seemed to me a trifle ghastly. I have a reverence for literature. For journalism I have merely a kind regard. I had never scamped my job on 'The Saturday'; but I shrank from the notion of burrowing down among those conscientious old efforts and bringing up some of them to be read in broad daylight, by the present generation, between the covers of a book. However, when it was arranged that there should be a limited edition [the ten-volume *Collected Edition*, 1922–8] of my 'works,' I agreed that a volume or two of my dramatic criticism might be slipped into it. (Beerbohm 1953: viii)

Although there had been many precedents for review anthologies by 1924, Beerbohm's account contains a residual sense of the indecorum of confusing the categories of 'journalism' and 'literature'. An earlier version of the same dynamic can be seen in some of the more negative responses to Ben Jonson's *Workes* (1616), in particular the hostility to the playwright's unprecedented, if implicit, claim that a traditionally low cultural form, the play, could be rescued from the materially vulnerable quarto form and repackaged in the privileged and durable folio. In Beerbohm's own 'Works', and despite his misgivings, journalism was ultimately 'slipped into' literature in an apparently covert, hybridising operation. For both Shaw and Beerbohm, the decision – however reluctant – to translate journalism into the more secure, privileged format of literature has had important consequences for the conception of each writer's oeuvre.

If an era's legacy and long-term influence greatly depends on the ease with which one can access and retrieve its chronicles, the theatrical period 1880–1910 is highly memorable. In this period, in the words of a *Saturday Review* essay, reviews were prolifically 'rescued from the oblivion of various periodicals' ('The Critic's Progress' 1895: 796). If the combined bibliographies of Arnott and Robinson (1970) and John Cavanagh (1989) are anywhere near accurate, these thirty years witnessed the publication of more review anthologies than any comparable period before or after. Publications included: Mowbray Morris (*The Times*), *Essays in Theatrical Criticism* (1882); Edward Dutton Cook (*Pall Mall Gazette* and *The World*), *Nights at the Play* (1883); A.B. Walkley (*The Speaker* and others), *Playhouse Impressions* (1892); Joseph Knight (*Athenaeum*), *Theatrical Notes* (1893); Clement Scott (*Daily Telegraph* and others), *From 'The Bells' to 'King Arthur'* (1896); J.T. Grein (*La Revue d'Art Dramatique*, the *Sunday Special*, *To-morrow*), *Dramatic Criticism* (1899); and William Archer's six annuals of *The Theatrical 'World'* spanning the years 1893–8 (published 1894–9).

In the thirty years preceding 1880, only a handful of such books had been published; in the three decades after 1910, roughly the same number as in the period 1880–1910 were published, but half of these were the products of that publishing phenomenon, James Agate (see Chapter 4). In addition to book anthologies of a wide range of reviewers' work, the mid 1890s also produced other important manifestations of the critic as author, not least the joint editorial projects of William Archer and Robert William Lowe. Following the co-authorship of their critique of Irving, *The Fashionable Tragedian* (1877), Lowe had independently constructed *A Bibliographical Account of English Theatrical Literature from the Earliest Times to the Present Day* (1888), written a biography of Thomas Betterton (1891) and offered a new, annotated edition of Colley Cibber's *Apology* (1889). All of these projects were committed to a scholarly memorialisation of an ephemeral art and the textual traces it leaves behind. In the mid 1890s Lowe and Archer edited, annotated and introduced the work of four reviewers whose work, albeit haphazardly, spanned the seventy years before their own book on Irving. The publication of Leigh Hunt's *Dramatic Essays* (1894), the republication of Hazlitt's *A View of the English Stage; or, a series of dramatic criticisms* (1895) and the selection of John Forster and George Henry Lewes's *Dramatic Essays* (1896) mark an important and indicative moment in the cultural status of the reviewer. These publications are significant not only because the review texts were (in the cases of all but Hazlitt) lifted from their journalistic context and legitimised in book form for the first time, but also because the books themselves were conceived and marketed in the high cultural format of the multi-volume set. Something like an informal canon of British theatre critics was being established.

If frequency of publication were not proof enough, one can safely assume that there was a healthy market for these books, particularly when one considers that, in New York, James Huneker collected an unauthorised edition of George Bernard Shaw's *Dramatic Opinions and Essays* (1906) in which he reprinted all but thirty-eight of the reviews that would ultimately appear as two volumes in the *Collected Edition* (1931), and then a year later as the three-volume *Our Theatres in the Nineties* (1932). Shaw was reluctant, despite frequent appeals, to republish his reviews while he was still employed as a theatre critic, but the existence of Huneker's edition confirms the allure of the reviewer's name and the publishing vogue it facilitated.

'Gentlemen, I am about to speak of myself *à propos* of Shakespeare': the critic and the play of personality

If the signed article enabled the critics of the period to enter the realm of the bellettrist, it also apparently provided a strong stimulus to the newspaper and periodical market. In tandem with the increasing use of interviews and human interest stories in the New Journalism, the personality of the journalist became a marketing point. Depressed by the absence of informed, impartial debate in the lead-up to the general election of 1895, Shaw wrote in a review (ostensibly devoted to the Elizabethan Stage Society's *Twelfth Night*) that the public was bored by political discourse, because 'criticism with a foregone conclusion is a contradiction in terms; and criticism by politicians always has its conclusion foregone, because the critics are party men' (Shaw 1932: 1 184). Shaw, reiterating his own independence in theatrical politics, asked what his own criticism would be worth, 'if I had first to ascertain the politics of Sir Henry Irving, Mr Tree, Mr Alexander, Mr Wyndham, Mr Hare, and so on, and then to enthusiastically praise all the enterprises on one side, and to denounce and disparage those on the other' (1: 184–5). He went on to argue that the arts critic has greater liberty than the political leader writer and therefore holds more attraction for the general reader:

> The public, while submitting to the party manner of criticism as it submits to any other institution under which it has been reared, brightens up significantly when anyone drops that manner for a moment. It displays a personal curiosity about the art critic which the political leader writer never excites. Nobody knows or cares who writes the political articles in the Daily Telegraph. But Mr Clement Scott's name cannot be concealed. And it is so with every paper. If the name of a contributor bursts through the veil of anonymity, it is sure to be that of a writer on literature or art, never that of a reliable party leader writer... the more independent a speaker is, the more interest the public takes in him. (Shaw 1932: 1 186)

Shaw's point was prophetic. Outside the leader columns, all newspapers have now succumbed to attributive bylines, even though some remained committed to anonymity for most of the twentieth century; in *The Times*, for example, anonymity lasted until 1967. Colin Seymour-Ure (1991: 135) writes that 'in a world of TV, anonymous journalism probably could not have survived: when we see a face, we want a name'. The disappearance of anonymity 'fitted an era in which electronic media were taking over the "hot" news role and papers were selling the expertise of their staff at interpretation, comment, analysis, more than for traditional hard news' (136). Shaw's account reminds us that the selling of staff expertise 'at interpretation' not only began well before the advent of television, but also emerged specifically in arts criticism.

Nobody knew or cared who wrote the political articles for the *Daily Telegraph* because they were predictable and partisan. Anonymity in journalism had historically served as a guarantee of objectivity, but Shaw found this objectivity was specious and had no intrinsic relation to independent thought. Independence of thought, signalled by the proper name of the author, sold newspapers. Shaw saw Scott as a seminal figure in the history of theatre reviewing, the 'first of the great dramatic reporters':

> Other men may have hurried from the theatre to the newspaper to prepare, red hot, a notice of the night's performance for the morning's paper; but nobody did it before him with the knowledge that the notice was awaited

by a vast body of readers conscious of his personality and anxious to hear his opinion, and that the editor must respect it, and the sub-editor reserve space for it, as the most important feature of the paper. (Shaw 1932: II 139)

Scott's genius lay in the unfiltered projection of a febrile, genially non-intellectual personality and an utter disregard for the notion of objective criticism. 'Whoever has been through the experience of discussing criticism with a thorough, perfect, and entire Ass', wrote Shaw, 'has been told that criticism should above all things be free from personal feeling. The excellence of Mr Scott's criticisms lies in their integrity as expressions of the warmest personal feeling and nothing else' (Shaw 1932: II 139–40).

Seán Burke, in writing of the postmodern objection to authority as embodied in the signature, argues that 'the legitimate ethical objections to autonomist and universalising notions of subjectivity have been conflated with the function of the signature which in fact works contrariwise to affirm the *specificity* of subjecthood' (Burke 1995: 286). Rather than confirming the author's position within a hegemonic discourse, the signature liberates the signatory, inviting him or her to take an individuated stance against the received and the dogmatic. In journalistic criticism, this specificity was increasingly privileged in the last quarter of the nineteenth century. In 'The Critic as Artist', Wilde's Gilbert puts it succinctly: 'it is only by intensifying his own personality that the critic can interpret the personality and work of others, and the more strongly this personality enters into the interpretation, the more real the interpretation becomes, the more satisfying, the more convincing, and the more true' (Wilde [1890] 1950: 142–3). In the year of Wilde's essay, 1890, Shaw, anticipating his own later comments on Scott, had written that 'a criticism written without personal feeling is not worth reading. It is the capacity for making good or bad art a personal matter that makes a man a critic' (Shaw 1981: II 168).

Metacritical commentary in the period is highly conscious of the novelty of this approach. An anonymous article entitled 'The Critic's Progress' (1895: 796) in the *Saturday Review* of 15 June 1895 began: 'Although the modern spirit has modified almost to the extent of reconstitution every form of artistic activity, it has transformed none of them quite so radically as the art of criticism.' The New Critic's 'attitude towards art is rather analytical than militant. Instead of acting as an intermediary between the artist and the public, he is concerned mainly with the adventures of his own soul among masterpieces' (796). That closing, unattributed dictum of Anatole France also found its way into a series of lectures given by A.B. Walkley at the Royal Institution in February 1903. Walkley, following Wilde in complicating the distinction between artist and critic, argued that all literary producers 'are creators, and what they all create is aesthetic feeling. And the raw material out of which they create this is the same, namely, themselves. Criticism, like any other art – whatever else it may be – is a mode of self-expression' (Walkley 1903: 52). Over a decade earlier, Walkley had written in his review of *Rosmersholm*:

> We take a purely aesthetic delight in him [Ibsen], because he gives us new impressions. There is an impressionist in one of Mr. Henry James' novels, whose *animula vagula blandula* is summed up in this way: 'I drift, I float, my feelings direct me – if such a life as mine may be said to have a direction. Where there's anything to feel I try to be there!' Well, dramatic criticism just now is impressionist; it is drifting and floating. There is always something to feel in the playhouse, when Ibsen is being played, and we try to be there. (Walkley 1892: 54)

This review first appeared in *The Speaker*, and was later reprinted in Walkley's first anthology, *Playhouse Impressions*, a gently polemical title. In a pronouncement that encapsulated the play of personality in turn-of-the-century reviewing, Walkley told his audience at the Royal Institution: 'In order to be frank, the critic ought to say; Gentlemen, I am about to speak of myself *à propos* of Shakespeare' (Walkley 1903: 52).

Centring the value of criticism in the personality of the critic required the ambitious critic to develop the cult of his own individuality. The journalistic events leading up to the debut of Max Beerbohm's signature in the *Saturday Review* offer an outstanding case study. Throughout the mid 1890s, Beerbohm had sporadically contributed articles to the periodical, all unsigned, although his notoriety as a preeminent contributor to the *Yellow Book*s may have made his signature unnecessary. In a series of correspondences aimed at Clement Scott, Beerbohm announced his arrival on the journalistic theatre scene. In addition to being arguably the most prominent and influential theatre critic of the period, Scott had achieved celebrity through his essays, lectures and fiction, 'to say nothing of the publicity which newspapers gave his lawsuits and disputations' (Brown 1985: 172). In Beerbohm's wrangle with Scott, the linked phenomena of signature, self-publicity and theatrical metacriticism representatively coincide. In 'A Vain Child' (1896) Beerbohm had written that:

> Now, in the delusion that editors, loving the pauper, will fill his pockets, I write for a weekly paper, and call myself 'We'. But the stress of anonymity overwhelms me. I belong to the Beerbohm period. I have tumbled into the waters of the current journalism, and am glad to sign my name, MAX BEERBOHM. (Quoted in Danson 1989: 19)

Virginia Woolf (1925: 217) would later write that Beerbohm 'has brought personality into literature, not unconsciously and impurely, but so consciously and purely that we do not know whether there is any relation between Max the essayist and Mr Beerbohm the man'. The stress of anonymity, and the concurrent wish to be provoked into discarding the veil, may have motivated the campaigns Beerbohm conducted against middle-brow literary figures in his early journalism. In the *Saturday Review* of 12 September 1896 he anonymously reviewed Clement Scott's *Lays and Lyrics*, a book that had, rather curiously, been first published eight years previously and that, according to Beerbohm, established Scott as 'the poet of the Seaside' (Beerbohm 1896a: 282). After an unrestrained bout of quotation of some of Scott's most ludicrous lines, he then took the opportunity to satirise Scott's theatre criticism: 'His column in the "Daily Telegraph" seems daily to topple down under its own weight. As criticism, his work is still worse. Cooped in the gilded confinement of the stage-box, Scott's soul becomes restless and intractable. The glare of the footlights blinds his clear, poetic vision' (283). Under the guise of a benevolent campaign, Beerbohm advocated that Scott be relieved of his reviewing duties and be presented with a one-way ticket from London to Bexhill-on-Sea, 'there to work out his [poetic] genius'. The following week's correspondence page featured a letter from a supporter of Scott ('A Lover of Fair Play') complaining of 'the brutal attack'. Following the understatement 'of course, he [Scott] is not Lord Tennyson', the supporter offered the defence that Scott 'can turn out a patriotic ode with the best of them'; 'I should advise your critic to look to it when next Mr. Scott's column in the "Daily Telegraph" "topples down under its own weight" it does not fall and crush him' (315–16). In the *Saturday Review* of 26 September Beerbohm's name features not in respect to the spat with Scott, but to his incessant self-promotion. The anonymous author, arguing that the novelist Marie Corelli was guilty of disingenuously seeking media attention 'in the infinite publicity of her seclusion', wrote 'Miss Corelli concludes her letter to the "Westminster" with the usual hit at her critics and with another at Mr. Max Beerbohm, who, also intent on advertisement, replied to her in the next issue' (337).

In the edition of 10 October, under the correspondence title 'Hold, Furious Scot! [sic]', Beerbohm responded to Scott's angry complaint in *The Era* of the previous week, a complaint that centred on the cowardice of Beerbohm's anonymity in the poetry review. The chance was seized: 'Here I am, a real, live Rat; young, it may be, but quite calm; rejoicing in a Christian name and a surname (both printed below), and in a fairly keen sense of humour.' From the 'chaos of bluster' in Scott's rebuke, Beerbohm chose to deal with Scott's grievance at his assailant's anonymity:

> Well, first as to my anonymity. Out of that Mr. Scott strives to make much capital... it seems that Sydney Grundy, Robert Buchanan and George Bernard Shaw... have all attacked him in signed articles. *Argal*, they are men. My attack was unsigned. *Argal*, many very terrible things, including the certainty that I am a Rat, and that I was animated with spite and restrained by cowardice. (Beerbohm 1896b: 395)

Shaw had reviewed a book of Scott's in the *Saturday*, and 'it would have been strange if, for once, he had withheld his customary G.B.S. On the other hand, no circumstances made my signature pertinent, nor had I ever signed any of the articles which, from time to time, I have been contributing to the "Saturday Review". Why should I have signed this one?' (Beerbohm 1896b: 396). Beerbohm protested that he had never made any secret of his authorship of the article, that it was widely known in theatrical circles and had even been disclosed by a Sunday newspaper. In the following weeks, Scott-bashing was firmly in vogue in the correspondence pages of the *Saturday*. A representative reader wrote: 'I am, like many others, not sorry for your difference with Mr. Clement Scott. He presumes upon his "name" to foist rubbish upon editors and the public' ('Mr. Clement Scott's Ignorance' 1896: 444). In the battle of names, Beerbohm had successfully brought his own centre stage in denigrating that of a rival; the critical arena was now set for a new phase in 'the age of Beerbohm' and for his entrance, eighteen months later, as 'MAX', theatre critic of the *Saturday Review*.

'The best part of the circus': Shaw as New Critic

In January 1897 George Bernard Shaw, entering his second year as a theatre critic, wrote to Ellen Terry: 'The theatre is my battering ram as much as the platform or the press: that is why I drag it to the front. My capers are part of a bigger design than you think: Shakespear, for instance, is to me one of the towers of the Bastille, and down he must come' (Shaw 1949a: 136). Shaw's reviews in the *Saturday* welded the battering rams of the theatre and the press together in the assault on authority and tradition. A year later Shaw would describe the *Saturday*'s introduction of the signed article as 'the climax and masterpiece of literary Jacobinism'; Shakespeare as 'one of the towers of the Bastille' was clearly a target for the critic as Jacobin. In the appendix to *The Quintessence of Ibsenism* (1891) Shaw had argued that the critical resistance to the Norwegian playwright was based on several key factors: critics' widespread lack of theatrical qualifications; the problems that the libel laws presented to insecure critics; and the cowardice of newspaper editors in not supporting heretical opinion. 'All this', Shaw continued:

> does not mean that the entire press is hopelessly corrupt in its criticism of Art. But it certainly does mean that the odds against the independence of the Press critic are so heavy that no man can maintain it completely without a force of character and a personal authority which are rare in any profession, and which in most of them can command higher pecuniary terms and prospects than any which journalism can offer. (Shaw [1891] 1971: 362)

In the years leading up to his appointment as the *Saturday*'s critic, Shaw had vigorously constructed 'force of character and a personal authority'. In the decade before 1895, in addition to a handful of novels published, incessant public speaking and prodigious pamphleteering, Shaw had been art and music critic for both *The Star* and *The World*. In his two years at *The Star*, he found himself in the hotbed of the New Journalism. The first editor of the paper, T.P. O'Connor, with W.T. Stead of the *Pall Mall Gazette*, pioneered the movement. As Stead (1902: 478) wrote: 'He and I may fairly claim to have revolutionised English journalism... we broke the older tradition and made journalism a living thing, palpitating with actuality, in touch with life at all points.' Shaw reminisced that his sole object in joining *The Star* had been 'to foist Fabian municipal Socialism on it' (Shaw 1949b: 112), and for a time he was delighted with the paper's progressiveness, a time during which the articles got 'positively Jacobin; and the further they went the better London liked them'. In fact, the extremity of opinion in some of Shaw's articles had caused O'Connor to refuse to print Shaw for a period, until a stage-managed protest from the Fabian Society convinced him to reinstate Shaw as a contributor. When Shaw offered to succeed Belfort Bax (the co-founder of the Socialist League) as music critic, O'Connor acquiesced, perhaps grateful to relocate Shaw in a less politically contentious area of the paper.

In a trade with aspirations to codified professionalism, Shaw saw his years with *The Star* and *The World* as a period of intensive qualification. In a letter of 1894 sent to Reginald Golding-Bright, then an aspiring critic and later Shaw's agent, Shaw advised:

> Remember, to be a critic, you must be not only a bit of an expert in your subject, but you must also have literary skill, and trained critical skill, too – the power of analysis, comparison, etc. I have had to go through years of

work as a reviewer of books, a critic of pictures, a writer on political and social questions, and a musical critic in order to qualify myself for the post I now hold on the staff of *The World*. (Shaw 1956: 13)

As Corno di Bassetto, he would occasionally but pointedly vaunt his qualification to criticise drama. In March 1889 A.B. Walkley, at that time *The World*'s theatre critic, urged Shaw to see a production of *Richard III* at the Globe; Shaw wrote, 'I did go to the Globe... because a musician only has the right to criticize works like Shakespear's earlier histories and tragedies... These things cannot be spectated (Walkley signs himself Spectator): they must be heard. It is not enough to see *Richard III*: you should be able to *whistle* it' (Shaw 1961: 172, 173). In addition to the technical skills Shaw acquired in his pre-*Saturday* reviewing, his writing was also informed by the stylistics of the New Journalism. In the first edition of *The Star*, O'Connor promised 'In our reporting columns we shall do away with the hackneyed style of obsolete journalism' (quoted in Morison 1932: 289); Stead's maxim 'impersonal journalism is effete' (quoted in Brake 1988: 22) was complemented by his encouragement of arts coverage that ditched specialist terminology and made itself accessible to the general reader. The personal reaction against highly technical and obfuscating musical criticism informs much of Shaw's writing as Corno di Bassetto; as Shaw would write in his Preface to *London Music in 1888–89*, 'vulgarity is a necessary part of a complete author's equipment; and the clown is sometimes the best part of the circus... I purposely vulgarized musical criticism, which was then refined and academic to the point of being unreadable and often nonsensical' (quoted in Holroyd 1990: 232). Shaw's theatre criticism would aim for a similarly demystifying diction and sense of direct informal address. Here Shaw saw a precedent in the mid century reviews of George Henry Lewes, whose 'vulgarity and impudence', whimsicality and lack of pretension 'in some respects anticipated me' (Shaw 1932: II 161). Indeed, Shaw pointed out, in his review of Forster and Lewes's *Dramatic Essays* (1896), that William Archer's introduction to the anthology also identified the earlier critic's influence:

> [Lewes] reminds Mr William Archer of a writer called Corno di Bassetto, who was supposed – among other impostures – to have introduced this style of writing when Mr T.P. O'Connor invented the half-penny evening paper in 1888. But these articles of Lewes's are miles beyond the crudities of Di Bassetto, though the combination of a laborious criticism with a recklessly flippant manner is the same in both. (Shaw 1932: II 161-2)

Forty years after Lewes wrote for *The Leader*, journalistic conditions were more propitious for the informal (and identified) critical voice. As a *Saturday Review* article declared in 1897, 'The regular contribution of a piece of writing that shall be highly personal, chatty and wayward in its aim, [is one] that many editors have set before them' ('Review of Reviews' 1897: 279). Shaw's criticism fulfilled these editorial criteria. His market appeal is signalled by the fact that, for the first three months at least, his articles were almost exclusively the only signed pieces in the *Saturday*. On the front page contents list for 5 January 1895, amid an editorial 'Appeal to Lord Rosebery', and pieces on the recently deceased Christina Rossetti and 'The British School of Electricians', '"Slaves of the Ring," by G.B.S.' stands out as the only contribution to the periodical's thirty-two pages to bear the name of its author. Although 'Military Degradation in France', a piece about the Dreyfus affair, is subtitled '(A Personal Experience)' and written in the first person singular, it is unattributed. Over the next ten weeks, only one edition carried a name other than Shaw's. As the year progressed, more and more articles were attributed. Shaw's reviews consistently, in the three and a half years of his tenure, occupied a greater amount of space than any other contribution – typically, somewhere between three and a half to four columns (four columns being the equivalent of a double-page spread); his nearest competitor, the music critic J.F. Runciman ('J.F.R.'), would average roughly a column fewer. On occasion, Shaw enhanced his prominence in the contents list by importing a journalistic device he had learnt at *The Star*, the so-called 'talking headline'. Review titles such as 'Poor Shakespear!' (2 February *and* 6 July 1895) 'Why Not Sir Henry Irving?' (9 February 1895) 'Sardoodledom' (1 June 1895) and 'Ibsen Ahead!' (7 November 1896) call attention either to vocal inflection or critical coinage, urging the individual presence of the reviewer and the independence of the review space.

An early indication of Shaw's all-licensed independence from the periodical matter that surrounds him can be found in the *Saturday*'s editorial response to Irving's knighthood. On 1 June 1895 an editorial item (probably written by Frank Harris) welcomed the news as a 'victory over an unjust prejudice and a snobbish tradition', adding that the honour had not been bestowed before time: 'This act of justice has not been "graciously conferred": it has been resolutely demanded and enforced by an artist to whose profession it means a social charter of some value' ('Sir Henry Irving' 1895: 718). Shaw's campaign against Irving had begun in his third review for the periodical, 'King Arthur' (19 January), and found forceful expression in a piece on Irving's speech-making (9 February), in which Shaw, in a manifesto for candour and independence, wrote:

> Of all the critics who paid Mr Irving flowery little compliments on his exhibition next day, there is not one who does not know this [that his speeches are trite bunk] as well as I know it. Some day, no doubt, I, too, shall succumb to Mr Irving's charm and prestige. But for the present I prefer to say what I think. (Shaw 1932: I 35)

The force of Shaw's critical personality, and the consequent prominence of his signature, marked off his review space as a subversive area. Shaw claimed that he entered music criticism after a period of writing leaders for *The World* in which he had 'spread such terror and confusion' that his offer to relocate to the arts pages was gratefully received. Music criticism being a trade in which 'lunacy is privileged', he was 'given a column to myself precisely as I might have been given a padded room in an asylum' (Shaw 1960: 1). His column in the *Saturday* was a similarly ludic, carnivalesque location in which the inmate could bounce off the walls, freely smashing received ideas and cherished icons without the views expressed being necessarily those of the editor. And no icons were more cherished or more prominent on the theatrical landscape at the turn of the century than Irving and Shakespeare.

With hindsight, Shaw admitted that disappointment fuelled much of his animus against Irving; on first seeing Irving as Digby Grant in *The Two Roses*, Shaw 'instinctively felt that a new drama inhered in this man, though I had then no conscious notion that I was destined to write it; and I perceive now [1929] that I never forgave him for baffling the plans I made for him' (Shaw 1949a: xxiv). Alongside Shakespeare, Irving stood as a twin tower of the theatrical Bastille. Shaw's constructions and destructions of Shakespeare – by turns disingenuous, impassioned, serio-comic, adulatory and wilfully dismissive – are notoriously slippery. It is easy to sympathise with William Poel, who, on reading Shaw's review of Tree's *Much Ado About Nothing* ('On the whole a very bad play, but a very enjoyable entertainment'), lamented that 'a reader cannot always be sure of grasping the writer's exact point of view' (Shaw 1920: 14). On the one hand, one must clearly distinguish between Shaw's reactions to Lyceum Shakespeare or Daly's Shakespeare and his attitude to the works of William Shakespeare. Shaw's criticism almost invariably ridiculed the former and frequently venerated the plays themselves, as extra-theatrical entities. On the other hand, this veneration was by no means constant, and, depending on the writer's mood or topical agenda, many of Shakespeare's plays as plays were dismissed by Shaw as outmoded, barbaric, trivial and fustian. Context is everything. Michael Holroyd and Russell Jackson have placed

Shaw's criticisms in the context of his wooing of Ellen Terry and Ada Rehan – a wooing that characteristically blended the professional and the psycho-sexual. Here, I expand on the personal and professional motivations of Shaw's Shakespearean criticism, with particular reference to the journalistic context outlined in the first half of this chapter. The notion of authority is central to this context – Shaw's authority as a critic-dramatist, the cultural authority of Shakespeare and the authoritative position of Irving in the theatre of the 1890s – as are issues of self-publicity, incorruptibility and accountability.

'The plays as Shakespeare wrote them': Shaw and authenticity

A fantasy of substitution animated Shaw's writing on Shakespeare. In a letter to Ellen Terry of 28 August 1896, he advised her to make her appearance in the Lyceum's *Cymbeline* her last as a Shakespearean heroine: 'And when you have finished with Imogen, finish with Shakespear. As Carlyle said to the emigrant "Here and now, or nowhere and never, is thy America" so I say to you "Here (at Fitzroy Square) and now is thy Shakespear"' (Shaw 1949a; 39). In the same letter, Shaw recalls sightings of Terry with Irving, the second authority figure in her life: 'I once or twice have met you on Richmond Terrace or thereabouts with him, like two children in a gigantic perambulator, and have longed to seize him, throw him out, get up, take his place, and calmly tell the coachman to proceed' (40). This fantasy of replacing – professionally and emotionally – Shakespeare and Irving was encapsulated in Shaw's needy demand in a later letter: 'Oh play *me*, Ellen, *me*, ME, ME, ME, ME, ME' (163). The tenor of Shaw's review of *Cymbeline* was something of a *fait accompli*: 'The article is finished and gone irrevocably to press. A mass of pounded, smashed, lacerated fragments, with here and there a button or a splinter of bone, is all that is left of your unhappy son, of H.I., of Shakespear, of Webster, and of the Lyceum stage management' (74).

The most frequently illustrated aspect of Shaw's reviews of Shakespeare is the critic's emphasis on the text as music (see Haywood 1969 for a representative example of critical commentary). The argument that Shakespeare's plays find their power and beauty in the musical arrangements of words is a constant refrain in Shaw's reviews, as if the critic were constructing his own Wagnerian leitmotif in his critical opus. His early review of the 1889 *Richard III* set the tone with its proposal that the plays demanded a critic with a Shavian breadth of qualification: 'The ear is the sure clue to him: only a musician can understand the play of feeling which is the real rarity in his early plays' (Shaw 1932: I 24). Most references to the Shakespearean music present it as a divine score that sweeps 'the scenes up to a plane on which sense is drowned in sound' (III: 147); without the sonority, Shakespeare's plays are as bland as Da Ponte's libretto for *Don Giovanni* without Mozart's music. Shaw's first Shakespearean review, written for *Our Corner* in August 1886, struck the keynote of seduction: *Love's Labour's Lost,* 'even when it is rhymed doggrel... is full of that bewitching Shakespearean music which tempts the susceptible critic to sugar his ink and declare that Shakespear can do no wrong' (Shaw 1961: 120).

Yet Shaw's evocations of Shakespeare's musicality, as warm as they may be, are evidently a backhanded part of his strategy to topple the authoritarian tower. His criticism recurrently implies – sometimes explicitly, often covertly – that the plays are intellectually, socially and psychologically moribund, and a modern audience can or should be impressed by them only when they aspire to the condition of music. Reviewing Daly's *Much Ado*, Shaw argued that to paraphrase Shakespeare's verse is to reveal the extent to which the impact is dependent on sound rather than thought; 'paraphrase Goethe, Wagner, or Ibsen in the same way, and you will find original observation, subtle thought, wide comprehension, far-reaching intuition, and serious psychological study in them' (Shaw 1932: III 322). Of *Othello* in 1897, he wrote pithily, 'Tested by the brain, it is ridiculous: tested by the ear, it is sublime' (148). The works in general were 'as dead *dramatically* as a doornail' (Shaw 1949a: 38); Shakespeare, Shaw wrote after suffering through an evening of anniversary celebrations in April 1896, was 'for an afternoon and not for all time' (Shaw 1932: II 110).

Shaw might have turned all this into a talking headline – 'Shakespeare Not Our Contemporary!' – and one should view from this perspective Shaw's reception of William Poel's productions for the Elizabethan Stage Society. Shaw is frequently cited as a critical midwife of authenticity, a harbinger of what would later be labelled 'The Shakespeare Revolution'. Edward M. Moore (1972: 21) writes, for example, that 'Shaw's was almost the only important critical voice raised in [Poel's] favour', adding, somewhat controversially, that 'at the time Shaw's patronage was probably at least as much a handicap as a blessing'. Indeed, in mid to late twentieth-century accounts of Poel's reception, Shaw is often commended for his approval of Poel and favourably contrasted with other critics (e.g. Archer, Walkley and Beerbohm) who were suspicious of Poel's antiquarianism and merciless about his eccentricities. Moore takes these critics to task for sharing 'the same fallacy... the argument that Shakespeare would have used scenery if he could is totally irrelevant; he did not, and his plays are not meant to employ it, nor are they written so that it can be used effectively' (30). Edwin Wilson wrote in his introduction to *Shaw on Shakespeare* that Shaw was, with Poel and Granville Barker, 'one of those most responsible for a return to Elizabethan-type production with its respect for the integrity of Shakespeare' (Shaw 1961: xxii). A.C. Sprague offered a similarly conservative approval of Shaw's 'brilliant defence' of the Elizabethan Stage Society, concluding 'as with the criticism of great plays, so with their representation: a sensitive regard for the author's intention is ever to be preferred to mere impressionism or virtuosity' (Sprague 1947: 33, 37). In short, Moore, Wilson and Sprague all represent Shaw as an uncomplicated and perceptive supporter of the authenticity movement.

Two points need to be made about Shaw's public sympathy with Poel's experiments in authenticity. First, Poel's productions not only provided Shaw with ammunition against Lyceum Shakespeare, but also reinforced his surprisingly conservative construction of Shakespeare's authority. Second, his responses to Poel are complicated when placed in the context of the entire review texts and of Shaw's interventions in actual Shakespearean production.

Poel's work can be analysed as an early modernist reaction to the age of mechanical [re]production. To adapt Benjamin's essay, subsequent performances of given Shakespeare texts can be viewed as 'reproductions', and 'even the most perfect reproduction of a work of art is lacking in one element: its presence in time and space, its unique existence at the place where it happens to be' (Benjamin 1992: 214). If 'changes of ownership are subject to a tradition which must be traced from the situation of the original', Poel's productions attempted to efface centuries of changes of ownership of Shakespeare's plays, invoking 'the presence of the original' modes of production as 'the prerequisite to the concept of authenticity' (214). The Elizabethan Stage Society's one-night stands or very short runs further emphasised the feeling of the event as irreproducible, in sharp contradistinction to the often lengthy Shakespearean runs at the Lyceum:

> The unique value of the 'authentic' work of art has its basis in ritual, the location of its original use value... but the instant the criterion of authenticity ceases to be applicable to artistic production, the total function of art is reversed. Instead of being based on ritual, it begins to be based on another practice – politics. (Benjamin 1992: 217, 218)

Shaw's recurrent metacritical concern was that dramatic critics should bring to their writing an informed and passionate knowledge of the living conditions of the present, a socio-political imperative of testing stage reality against actuality. In his sixth month as the *Saturday*'s theatre critic, he wrote: 'my real aim is to widen the horizon of the critic, especially the dramatic critic', who, instead of bringing a large accumulation of stage knowledge to bear on reality, 'must bring a wide and practical knowledge of real life to bear on the stage' (Shaw 1932: I 187). He ended the first half of this piece by encouraging every dramatic critic to offer himself as a candidate in the forthcoming election of the London vestries, 'and woo his ward thoroughly, and we shall never hear another word about the "Norwegian parochialism" of Ibsen's Enemy of the People' (188). What is fascinating about this review is that, having used over half his space to discuss the imminent general election, the need for impartial debate in politics and for socially engaged theatre criticism, Shaw then arrived at the ostensible motivation for the piece: the Elizabethan Stage Society's production of *Twelfth Night* at Burlington Hall. Shaw, ignoring the principles of dramatic criticism he had just expounded, does not question the archaeological, apolitical and ritualistic functions of the performance, but is content to conclude that 'it is only by such performances that people can be convinced that Shakespear's plays lose more than they gain by modern staging' (189).

Shaw's notices of Poel's productions are generally among the least engaged and detailed of his reviews. Reviewing *The Comedy of Errors* at Gray's Inn Hall in 1896, he used the event as a springboard for a sustained comparison of the acting styles of Barry Sullivan and Irving, and their competing versions of 'the old individualistic, tyrannical conception of the great actor', developing the argument to offer Irving the injunction that 'he owes it to literature to connect his name with some greater modern dramatist than the late Wills, or Tennyson, who was not really a dramatist at all. There is a nice bishop's part in Ibsen's – but I digress' (Shaw 1932: I 273). The digressive mode is typical of Shaw's reaction to Poel. Generally the reviews function, like Shaw's insistence on the Shakespearean music, to mire Shakespeare in the pre-modern, ritualistic theatre, evacuating his plays of contemporary meaning and relevance.

If Shaw's positive reception of authenticity contradicted his campaign for politically informed reviewing, his attempted interventions in contemporary Shakespearean performance were equally discordant with the staging preferences expressed in his reviews. In his columns in the *Saturday*, Shaw repeatedly critiqued two of the most prominent features of contemporary Shakespearean production: the cutting of the texts and the lavishly pictorial *mise-en-scène*. The more text a manager suppressed and the more he essayed to enchant the audience by reckless expenditure 'on extraordinary scenic attractions', 'on incidental music, colored lights, dances, dresses, and elaborate rearrangements and dislocations of the play – the more, in fact, he departs from the old platform with its curtains and its placard inscribed "A street in Mantua", and so forth, the more hopelessly and vulgarly does he miss his mark' (Shaw 1932: I 25). In his review of Lillah McCarthy's Lady Macbeth, Shaw stated his unaffected fondness for Shakespeare's plays:

> I do not mean actor-managers' editions and revivals; I mean the plays as Shakespear wrote them, played straight through line by line and scene by scene as nearly as possible under the conditions of representation for which they were designed. (Shaw 1932: I 130)

This contrasts sharply with Shaw's advice to Ellen Terry and Johnston Forbes-Robertson in his private capacity as theatrical adviser. In his letters to Terry, written while she was preparing the part of Imogen, Shaw advised substantial cuts to the text (the conclusion of which he would later 'refinish'): 'if I were you I should cut the part so as to leave the paragon out and the woman in', adding, with characteristic pragmatism and journalistic awareness, 'and I should write to The Times explaining the lines of the operation. It would be a magnificent advertisement' (Shaw 1949a: 42). In the following year (1897), on hearing that the Lyceum was planning a *Hamlet*, he showed in another letter to Terry that his own approach to staging Shakespeare would not have been the authentic bare stage he publicly commended, but was equally as pictorial as the much-maligned actor-managerial mode of presentation, if not more so:

> Lord! how I could make that play jump along at the Lyceum if I were manager. I'd make short work of that everlasting 'room in the castle'. You should have the most beautiful old English garden to go mad in, with the flowers to pluck fresh from the bushes, and a trout stream of the streamiest and ripplingest to drown yourself in. I'd make such a scene of 'How all occasions do inform against me!' – Hamlet in his travelling furs on a heath like a polar desert, and Fortinbras and his men 'going to their graves like beds' – as should never be forgotten. (Shaw 1949a: 218)

Shaw had written Forbes-Robertson 'four pages of foolscap, closely written' (Forbes-Robertson 1925: 171), and evidently some of the suggestions were adopted: 'I gave Forbes a description of what the end ought to be like . . . As Nisbet in The Times describes the scene almost in my own terms, my idea seems to have come off' (233).

'He would buy me in the market like a rabbit': Shaw and incorruptibility

If it is 'the capacity for making good or bad art a personal matter that makes a man a critic', Shaw, as a frustrated playwright of the 1890s, could not help but take the good or bad art that dominated the London theatre more personally than most critics of the time. From the outset, he was remarkably sensitive about not only his integrity as a critic, but also his position as a critic-playwright. In November 1895 he wrote to Golding-Bright that he had made no attempt to get *The Man of Destiny* produced, 'as my position as dramatic critic makes it very difficult for me to take the initiative in any negotiation with our managers' (Shaw 1956: 37). He consequently asked his young protégé to leak the information of his having written a play to the press, in the hope that a manager might take the hint and initiate negotiations. In December 1892, before taking his post as theatre critic, Shaw had attempted to run a media campaign on behalf of the production of his first play, *Widowers' Houses*. As Holroyd puts it: 'Shaw sent up all sorts of balloons of publicity for his play, interviewing himself, reviewing reviews, filling columns of *The Era*, *The Speaker*, and *The Star* with his correspondence, and claiming for the event the uproar that contemporary notices do not substantiate' (Holroyd 1990: 281). Creating a climate conducive to his own reception – even, as Holroyd suggests, rewriting that reception as it occurred – Shaw revelled in the blaze of self-promotion. Once he had assumed the role of dramatic critic, however, such tactics would have to go underground if his columns were to maintain the degree of independence and integrity he (and others) had constructed as the ideal for dramatic criticism.

At the *Saturday* his situation seemed to be that 'lucky combination of resolute, capable, and incorruptible critic, sympathetic editor, and disinterested and courageous proprietor', the rarity of which, he wrote in the appendix to *The Quintessence of Ibsenism*, 'can hardly be appreciated by those who only know the world of journalism through its black and white veil' (Shaw [1891] 1971: 363). 'As long as I remain a dramatic critic I can neither sell plays nor take advances', he wrote to Ellen Terry (Shaw 1949a: 20), and he suspected that what interest Irving was showing in producing *The Man of Destiny* at the Lyceum in spring 1896 was an embryonic attempt at corruption: 'He would buy me in the market like a rabbit, wrap me up in brown paper and put me by on his shelf if I offered myself for sale – and how else does a critic offer himself except by writing his little play, or his adaptation or what not?' (25). He nevertheless let Irving have a copy of the manuscript, a copy left to gather dust during an excruciating period of second-hand and inarticulate negotiation. Irving finally accepted *The Man of Destiny* in late September 1896. Three months later Shaw reviewed Irving's performance in *Richard III*. In the spat that ensued that review, the structure of accountability and resummoning to the text on which the ethics of the signature are predicated found spectacular example.

If 'the signature puts in place channels of accountability, responsibility and enquiry' (Burke 1995: 290), Shaw's review of *Richard III* invited Irving to exploit those channels. How much Shaw's reviews generally meant to Irving it is impossible to judge. The evidence from the protagonists is predictably discordant. While Shaw (1949a: 75) boasted to Terry that Irving would 'get up at five in the morning to read' his *Saturday* review of *Cymbeline*, Irving claimed during the *Richard III* furore:

> I had not the privilege of reading your criticism – as you call it – of Richard. I never read a criticism of yours in my life. I have read lots of your droll, amusing, irrelevant and sometimes impertinent pages, but criticism containing judgement and sympathy I have never seen by your pen. (Quoted in Holroyd 1990: 364)

Whether he honoured Shaw's writing with the label of 'criticism' or not, Irving was evidently irritated by Shaw's attacks, and in the *Richard III* review he detected a clear imputation of on-stage drunkenness. Shaw (1932: II 290) wrote that Irving was 'occasionally a little out of temper with his own nervous condition'. 'The attempt to make a stage combat look as imposing as Hazlitt's description of the death of Edmund Kean's Richard reads, is hopeless', he added (291), perhaps a sly allusion to inebriation, given Hazlitt's famous image of Kean fighting as one who was 'drunk with wounds' (Hazlitt 1854: 165). Irving, resummoning Shaw to this review text and others like it, took action by returning another text: *The Man of Destiny*. Within two weeks of the *Richard III* review, the quarrel had become a media event.

An item in the *Daily News* claimed that Irving had sent back Shaw's script to teach the critic better manners, 'thereupon [wrote Shaw] the smartest of the New Journalism editors scents a duel, and wants me to return H.I.'s fire in his paper' (Shaw 1949a: 179). Shaw resisted the temptation in order to spare Terry's feelings. Within a fortnight, however, he decided to concoct an 'exclusive' interview with himself, which he would leak to the papers through Golding-Bright. The interview, as a relatively recent journalistic phenomenon, was the perfect vehicle for Shaw's print performances. Shaw wrote the dialogue and told Golding-Bright to 'fill in the scenery and business' (186), and the performative analogy was extended in Shaw's summary that 'the management of it being in my hands I of course play H. off the stage; but I dress him well and allow him to make a point or two' (186). Whatever concessions Shaw believed he had made in the faux interview, the campaign to have his play staged at the Lyceum had been irremediably damaged, largely owing to Shaw's insistence on the independence and incorruptibility of the review space.

'The hack work of genius': Beerbohm and Shakespeare in the *Saturday Review*

In May 1897, a year after his feud with Irving, Shaw resigned his post as theatre critic. In his final piece for the *Saturday*, a 'Valedictory' rather than a review, he signed off by introducing the name of his successor:

> The younger generation is knocking at the door; and as I open it there steps spritely in the incomparable Max. For the rest, let Max speak for himself. I am off duty for ever, and am going to sleep. G.B.S. (Shaw 1932: III 386)

As mentioned, speaking for one's self was an imperative for the theatre critic of the 1890s, and Beerbohm's uniqueness, his incomparability, made him an apposite successor to the maverick Shaw. (I follow Lawrence Danson (1989: 5) in resisting the temptation to speak of Beerbohm as 'Max' on the grounds that 'Beerbohm' signifies a tougher figure, 'an artist who deserves to be treated with critical rigour'.)

Although the 26-year-old Beerbohm brought the carefully developed cult of his own personality to the job, his first piece for the *Saturday* registers an anxiety of succession that recognises the performative dimension of the review columns: 'I am in the predicament of the minor music-hall artist sent on as an "extra-turn," tremulously facing the prolonged thunder of calls for the "star" who has just sung' (Beerbohm 1953: 1). Beerbohm might have quoted York's description and cast himself as the dejected Richard II entering after Bolingbroke's 'well-graced actor' has left the stage (5.2.24). But such a classical allusion might have undermined the essay's central point: 'Why I Ought Not to Have Become a Dramatic Critic' is a beautifully controlled exhibition of Beerbohm's under-qualification for the job. Beerbohm has 'no instinctive love of the theatre', will be unable to offer any 'freshness or cerebration', will 'not be able to branch off, like G.B.S., into discussions of ethical, theological or political questions, for on such questions I am singularly ill-informed' (Beerbohm 1953: 3). Furthermore,

Beerbohm disclaims any knowledge of the canonical texts of his profession, some of which Archer and Lowe had recently made highly accessible: 'I could not test a theory nor quote a line of Hazlitt, Lamb, Lewes and the rest, whose essays in dramatic criticism I have never read' (2). Finally, as if to clinch his singular ineptness, Beerbohm cites his 'personal acquaintance with so many players': 'one well-known player is my half-brother [Herbert Beerbohm Tree]. Who will not smile if I praise him? How could I possibly disparage him?' (3).

In the context of contemporary theatre reviewing theory, Beerbohm was slotting himself into the position of the 'impressionist' critic – a critic, by Walkley's definition, who 'has greater interest in his feelings and less confidence in his general ideas and external authority' (Walkley 1903: 117). As Beerbohm's self-introduction hints, in the absence of a political or theoretical engagement with the drama, the critic must relocate his authority in the play of personality. To quote Walkley (1903: 122) addressing the impressionist critic: 'And your "authority" with the reader? It will not be found in an external set of laws, traditions, "the rules"; it will be in the delicacy, the fineness, the distinction of your impressions' (122). Beerbohm's first Shakespearean review in the *Saturday* reveals how the critic presented his own distinctiveness in relation to the twin authorities of Shakespeare and Shaw. Beerbohm began by setting some critical distance between himself and Shaw:

> Shakespeare had his short-comings. Love of him does not blind me to his limitations and his faults of excess. But, after all, the man is dead, and I do not wish to emulate that captious and rancorous spirit – inflamed, as it often seemed to me, by an almost personal animosity – in which my predecessor persecuted him beyond the grave. (Beerbohm 1953: 8)

Yet, he continued, he would have supported Shaw's attacks had he 'imagined they would induce managers not to revive certain of Shakespeare's plays quite so frequently' (Beerbohm 1953: 8). Having implicitly contrasted the cool refinement of his stance with the inflammatory belligerence of Shaw, Beerbohm nevertheless went on to offer a response to the contemporary Shakespearean theatre every bit as radical as Shaw's. Exhausted by the overfamiliarity of mainstream Shakespeare and bored with the inevitability of comparative criticism, Beerbohm suggested that the only way to preserve the affective power of Shakespeare's plays for future generations was to institute, with immediate effect, a stage ban of thirty years. Through such a moratorium, Beerbohm hoped that the plays would eventually, sometime around 1927, become something more than a tired assemblage of 'so many parts and so many scenes, so many tests and traps for eminent mimes' (9).

When he eventually treated the production that prompted the review – the Forbes-Robertson *Macbeth* – Beerbohm introduced a new twist to his negotiation of critical authority. One of the most distinctive modes of Beerbohm's writing was impersonation. In 'Why I Ought Not', Beerbohm had denied all knowledge of previous critics and other historical theatrical authorities. His readers must have been surprised when, in order to prove that contemporary critics were mistaken in treating Mrs Patrick Campbell's Lady as 'something peculiar to the spirit of this generation' (10), Beerbohm cited historical accounts by Aubrey and Pepys of previous, equally subtle Lady Macbeths. Pepys, for instance, wrote of Mrs Knipp in the part:

> Methought Mrs Knipp did never play so fine, specially in the matter of the two daggers, yet without brawl or overmuch tragick gesture, the which is most wearisome... She was most comickal and natural when she walks forth sleeping (the which I can testify, for Mrs Pepys also walks sleeping at some times), and did most ingeniously mimick the manner of women who walk thus. (Beerbohm 1953: 10)

Both the Aubrey and Pepys quotations were pastiches by Beerbohm himself. Stanley Wells (1976: 136) claims that the spoof was so straight-faced that it 'may easily go undetected', yet William Archer resummoned 'Max' to his text in the following week's edition of *The World*. On 15 October (two weeks after the *Macbeth* review) Beerbohm (1969: 62) wrote that he was sorry to learn that Archer had 'been fretting about me and my method of criticism. He complains publicly of me that I am in the habit of "fabricating authorities" and "fabricating opinions"'. Archer also took exception to Beerbohm's advocacy of a Shakespearean stage ban. In his response, Beerbohm elaborated his theory of the adverse effect of repetition on 'aesthetic receptivity', mischievously endorsing Archer's call for a state theatre in which '*Hamlet*, &c.' could be played incessantly as 'a simple means of sickening everyone of *Hamlet*, &c., so thoroughly that my "close time" for those plays would very soon become a necessity and a fact' (64).

In the following month, November 1898, Beerbohm, perhaps mindful of the public questioning of his critical authority, chose not to review his half-brother's production of *The Musketeers* at Her Majesty's. His substitute, Robert Ross (signing himself simply 'R'), wrote:

> A first night at Her Majesty's Theatre is quite as much a social as a dramatic event of importance, and perhaps for this reason the contributor of dramatic criticism to the 'Saturday Review' preferred to appear on the occasion of the

production of Mr. Sydney Grundy's version of the elder Dumas's famous novel, in another character than that of a critic. (Ross 1896: 631)

The alibi of a cultivated socialite is a plausible one, but Beerbohm was more probably being seen to be having ethical qualms. These did not last, however, and thenceforth he frequently reviewed his half-brother's productions, with the proviso that he would never comment directly on his relative's performance. Of Beerbohm Tree's Malvolio, he wrote that the actor approached the role as that of an intrinsically absurd 'egomaniac': 'So much for Mr Tree's conception of the part. As for his execution of it, I think I can safely say . . . but I must not break a certain self-imposed rule with which my readers are already familiar' (Beerbohm 1969: 350). Beerbohm, indeed, could not 'safely say' anything as explicit as an outright appreciation of his half-brother's acting, but often glowingly reviewed his stage-management and productions.

Beerbohm's review of Tree's *King John* is one of his most experimental and technically innovative, and marks a response to two contemporary critical issues. Beerbohm described a succession of vivid stage moments, building a sequence of snapshots through which to convey the plot and the values of the production. He evoked the staging in the historic present tense – not inappropriately, given the combination of modern stage management and an antiquarian aesthetic that characterised the production:

> It is the dusk of dawn in the orchard of Swinstead Abbey, and through the apple-trees the monks hurry noiselessly to the chapel. The dying king is borne out in a chair. He is murmuring snatches of a song. The chair is set down and with weak hands he motions away his bearers. (Beerbohm 1969: 192)

At the end of the description, Beerbohm commented, 'I have written down these disjointed sentences, less in order to enable my readers to imagine the production at Her Majesty's Theatre than to preserve my own impressions' (Beerbohm 1969: 192). In 'the delicacy, the fineness, the distinction' of his impressions, Beerbohm would seem to be aligning himself once again with the impressionist school of criticism. Yet there is another more or less submerged dynamic in this review, that of impartiality. Remarkably, nowhere in the course of the review does Beerbohm refer to any actors by name. Having been bored by the play on the page, he expressed a 'great debt of gratitude to the management' that had brought it alive theatrically, but once again declined to name the producer. He concluded: 'I can say without partiality, and with complete sincerity, that I have never seen a production in which the note of beauty was so surely and incessantly struck as in this production of *King John*' (193) – 'partiality' and 'sincerity' being, at this point, the two most contentious aspects of Beerbohm's critical reputation. Beerbohm promised to write about the actual performance 'as soon as there are not so many other plays clamouring to be noticed', although he never made good this promise. Generally Beerbohm showed little embarrassment at the fact that 'Fate has prejudiced me in Mr. Tree's favour' (231), but his *King John* review is a fascinating indication of how he might have found a critical method to pre-empt accusations of partiality.

If Beerbohm's attitude to the authority figures of contemporary actor-management – to Irving, his half-brother and to Forbes-Robertson – was one of straightforward appreciation, his relationship to the plays and authority of Shakespeare was much more complicated. Despite the initial disassociation with Shaw's demonstrative anti-Shakespeareanism, Beerbohm's construction and representation of Shakespeare were consistently as radical as his predecessor's.

In 'Shakespeare in Max Beerbohm's Theatre Criticism', Stanley Wells (1976: 136) comments that Beerbohm was so 'unappreciative' of some of Shakespeare's plays that 'I prefer to pass over his remarks as rapidly as possible'. Beerbohm had claimed in his first Shakespeare review in the *Saturday* that he had no interest in emulating Shaw's dyspeptic, 'captious' anti-Shakespeareanism; yet the Shavian note is sounded frequently in later reviews, albeit in the more languid Beerbohmian key. 'Throughout the fabric of his work', Beerbohm (1969: 342–3) wrote of Shakespeare in 1901, 'you will find much that is tawdry, irrational, otiose – much that is, however shy you may be of admitting that it is, tedious'. As a 'discriminating admirer' (247) of the plays, Beerbohm set himself against the 'sacred and all engrossing mission . . . to propagate the worship of Shakespeare' (245) that he discerned in Benson's repertory company and Poel's neo-Elizabethanism. His favourite plays – *Hamlet, A Midsummer Night's Dream, As You Like It* – were performed too often for his palate to remain receptive; his least favourite plays, he consistently argued, should not be performed at all, whether by pictorial stage managements (of whom he approved) or by reconstructionists (of whom he didn't). A major thrust of the argument was that Shakespeare was neither serious nor discriminatory enough in his selection and treatment of sources. Wells cross-references Beerbohm's critique to the argument that Bridges, Stoll and Schücking would make in various forms in subsequent years, what could be labelled the 'dyer's hand theory', that Shakespeare is bad when he sinks to the level of the groundling's expectations (a theory that resurfaces in the reception of Shakespeare's Globe, discussed in Chapter 5). Beerbohm's criticism of Shakespeare was, if anything, more serious. 'It is no excuse', Beerbohm (1969: 342) wrote, 'for him [Shakespeare] to say that the Elizabethan public wanted him to confine himself to the stupid stories with which it was familiar, and that, unless he obeyed it, he could never have caught its ear. For a second-rate dramatist that excuse were valid enough. But Shakespeare was not a second-rate dramatist.' The two words Beerbohm used most commonly in his critiques of Shakespeare were 'tedious' and 'hack'. *The Merry Wives of Windsor* is 'the wretchedest bit of hack-work ever done by a great writer' (473); 'plays like *Twelfth Night*, which consist mainly of hack-work, should be interpreted with real charm and ability, or not interpreted at all' (347); such plays as *Henry V* and *The Taming of the Shrew* are 'the hack-work of genius' (340). Even the composition of Beerbohm's favourite, *A Midsummer Night's Dream*, is figured under the journalistic conditions of hire and salary: it 'is the most impressive of all Shakespeare's works, because it was idly done, because it was a mere overflow of genius, a parergon thrown off by Shakespeare as lightly as a modern author would write an article on International Copyright for an American magazine' (230).

In a neat inversion of status, Shakespeare is presented as the figure that Beerbohm feared he had himself become: the artist spoiled by a combination of laziness and commercialism. The reluctant 'creature of magazines and newspapers' (Danson 1989: 18), he worried that his carefully nurtured image of the dandy bellettrist was suffering through his journalism. 'The Editor of this paper has come to me as Romeo came to the apothecary, and what he wants I give him for the apothecary's reason' (Beerbohm 1953: 4), he wrote in his first *Saturday* article. (Beerbohm's caricature of the transaction is reprinted as the frontispiece to *More Theatres*.) Edmund Gosse, who had styled himself Beerbohm's mentor, accused him (in a letter Cecil alludes to but does not date) of writing 'so badly' and 'so insincerely' in his *Saturday* columns. Beerbohm responded that his reproach 'makes me feel that such literary talent as I had must have been gradually debased and blunted by the hebdomadal habit' (Cecil 1964: 194). Without pushing the projection too far, an anxiety about the integrity of commercial writing clearly influenced Beerbohm's critique of Shakespeare. In the choice of the word 'hack', with its unavoidable journalistic connotations of degradation and prostitution, Beerbohm was, in Walkley's formulation, speaking of himself '*à propos* of Shakespeare'.

Shaw oscillated wildly in his evaluation of the aesthetic value of Shakespeare's plays, yet his responses to the plays as staged authentically were fixed and positive. For the reasons I have described, Shaw welcomed a version of Shakespeare-worship that sought to reground the authority of performance within the aura of authenticity. In this respect, Beerbohm's response to Poel reveals that his attitude to the authority of Shakespeare was if anything more iconoclastic than his predecessor's. When *The Importance of Being Earnest* was revived in 1902, seven years after its premiere, Beerbohm (1953: 189) wrote that '[a] classic must be guarded jealously. Nothing should be added to, or detracted from, a classic. In the revival at St. James', I noted several faults of textual omission... Mr. Wilde was a master in selection of words, and his words must not be amended.' Yet Beerbohm never invoked this standard of textual integrity and fidelity for Shakespearean performance. As an ardent modernist, Beerbohm saw little or no value in pretending modern staging techniques did not exist, or that Shakespeare's plays benefited from shedding the picturesque accretions such techniques enabled. Shakespeare's 'good' plays, he wrote in a review in 1901, 'deserve a great outlay of money and taste', yet 'are (if you do not know them too well) delightful under any conditions'. Shakespeare's 'bad' plays, however, 'can be made tolerable only by beautiful production and performance. If the production and the performance be beautiful enough, they become delightful' (Beerbohm 1969: 340). Beerbohm disliked *Twelfth Night*, so it is not surprising he greeted Poel's attempt to present it without 'a great outlay of money and taste' unsympathetically. Describing the Elizabethan Stage Society's activities as 'owlish' – 'implying a certain rather morbid and inhuman solemnity and a detachment from the light of day' – Beerbohm argued that the 1903 *Twelfth Night* was instruction without delight, and that authenticity depended on a far more violent suspension of the spectator's belief than the pictorial spectacular:

> Shakespeare wrote at a time when the science of scenic production was in its infancy, and he himself, as he has told us, was conscious and resentful of its limitations. We have developed that science, and it is only when Shakespeare's plays are produced with due regard to that development that they seem to us works of living art. Doubtless, the Elizabethan audience was not, like the quicker-witted poet, conscious of the defects in the Elizabethan productions. But we, in the twentieth century, cannot project – or rather retroject – ourselves into their state of receptivity. We cannot forget what we have learned. (Beerbohm 1953: 258)

That last point would resurface in the reception of Shakespeare's Globe at the other end of the twentieth century. Beerbohm took greatest exception not to Poel's own motivations – which he treated as harmless and gently eccentric – but to the rhetoric of authenticity that found expression in programme notes and newspaper pieces:

> It seems absurd that we should have to make a stand in the matter. Yet it is a fact that the mode of the Elizabethan Stage Society is by some authoritative persons pretended to be the one and only dignified mode of presenting Shakespeare's plays – to be a mode in comparison with which ours is tawdry and Philistine and wicked. (Beerbohm 1953: 259)

Beerbohm had wittily granted, in a review of Poel's Q1 *Hamlet*, that the Elizabethan Stage Society's expressly 'educational' aims were realised to the extent that Poel succeeded in 'teaching us to pity the poor Elizabethans and be thankful for the realism of the modern theatre' (Beerbohm 1953: 64). In more serious mood, however, the critic resented the implication that the authentic movement occupied a socio-aesthetic high ground at which it was impertinent or heretical to lob critical grenades.

* * *

In early 1899, following the publication of *The Perfect Wagnerite*, Shaw found himself criticised in the very pages that used to publish his own upbraidings. On 4 February J.F. Runciman, the music critic of the *Saturday Review*, accused Shaw of being 'hopelessly wrong' in interpreting the Ring cycle as Fabian tract. The strength of his objections notwithstanding, Runciman concluded of his former colleague: 'Mr. Shaw, in spite of his error, is still the best critic of the school which superseded the Old one' (Runciman 1899: 140). Shaw, ever spoiling for a public altercation, wrote back the following week: 'Why does J.F.R. turn from his warfare with the Old Critics to make a parricidal onslaught on me, the father of the New Criticism?' He went on to accuse Runciman of waxing lyrical over such retrograde ideas as Beauty, 'through the familiar art cant of Maida Vale, unspeakably unworthy of J.F.R.' (Shaw 1899: 177). By the close of the nineteenth century the campaign against the 'art cant of Maida Vale' had solidified sufficiently to be given a title: the New Criticism. And Shaw, from the position of journalistic retirement, looked on the brood of New Critics as his offspring. It is an indication of the increasing seriousness of the profession that the years following Shaw's retirement witnessed the foundation of the Society of Dramatic Critics (1907) and the Critics' Circle (1913). As described above (in Chapter 1), the Society faded quickly and the Circle has, throughout its history, had great difficulty in determining the grounds for the critic's real professional status. Nevertheless, the foundation of both associations bears testimony to the desire of Shaw and his near-contemporaries for greater critical legitimacy and a new sense of corporate identity.

I have argued that the form and function of theatre criticism changed profoundly in the last quarter of the nineteenth century, and that these changes should inform any reading of the priorities, methods and style of theatrical reception in general and of Shakespearean reception in particular. From 1880 to 1914 the readership of newspapers roughly quadrupled (Williams 1961: 204), and this enlarged audience consumed a new type of journalism, one predicated on such diverse imperatives as entertainment, impartiality, ease of consumption, celebrity and controversy. The demand for individuality of perspective and anti-orthodox thought was demonstrated and fulfilled in the Shakespearean reviews of George Bernard Shaw and Max Beerbohm. Clement Scott, the most outstanding example of the orthodox critic, wrote (in a Maida Valeian mode) that he looked to Shakespeare for 'that idealism, and imagination, and tenderness, and human nature, without which art cannot exist and the stage is useless' (Scott 1899: I 491). Scott exemplified the uncomplicated attitude to authority – whether of Shakespeare or Irving – that would be severely challenged by the exponents of the New Criticism. Shaw and Beerbohm's Shakespearean reviews show a complex of contextual influences at play: the ethics of the signature, the play of personality, the cult of the author-critic, the competing demands of personal agenda and public impartiality, and the more general negotiation of authority – the authority of the critic, of the actor-manager and of Shakespeare.

Stephen Sondheim's musical *The Frogs* (1974) replaces Aristophanes' contest between Euripides and Aeschylus with one between Shaw and Shakespeare. In a lively, ill-tempered debate, Shakespeare quotes his most mellifluous lines to a jealous and pathologically deconstructive Shaw. The agon is brought to a definitive conclusion with Shakespeare's beautiful rendition of 'Fear No More'. Shakespeare is announced the winner and is rewarded with safe passage from Hades back to earth. As he and Dionysus embark (the musical was written to be performed in a swimming pool), Shaw, 'his animal cries... heard throughout the myrtle grove', is dragged away to some distant corner of Hades (Sondheim et al. 1985: 206). Shaw had himself staged this contest twice before, first in his *Saturday Review* columns, and second in *Shakes Versus Shav*, a puppet play written in 1949, the year before his death. In Shaw's dramatic valediction, Shakes returns from the grave:

> Hither I raging come
> An infamous imposter to chastise,
> Who in an ecstasy of self-conceit
> Shortens my name to Shakes, and dares pretend
> Here to reincarnate my very self,
> And in your stately playhouse to set up
> A festival, and plant a mulberry
> In most presumptuous mockery of mine,
> Tell me, ye citizens of Malvern,
> Where I may find this caitiff.   (Shaw 1961: 276)

Shaw's fantasy of substitution, of competing with and ultimately replacing, Shakespeare is enacted in *Shakes Versus Shav*. The 'jealous Bard' (Shaw 1961: 279) fails to vanquish the upstart reincarnation through argument, but a moment of opportunistic stage-craft brings the piece (and Shaw's dramatic oeuvre) to a conclusion:

> SHAV. . . . We both are mortal. For a moment suffer
> My glimmering light to shine.
> *A light appears between them.*
> SHAKES. Out, out, brief candle! [*He puffs it out*].
> *Darkness. The play ends.*   (Shaw 1961: 279)

If the following interchange from a BBC quiz show in the early twenty-first century is anything to go by, the fantasy of substitution, the competition between reviewer and national playwright first begun by Shaw in the 1890s, may have had a lasting effect on the collective psyche:

EAMONN HOLMES: What's the name of the playwright commonly known by the initials G.B.S.?
CONTESTANT: William Shakespeare. ('Dumb Britain' 2002: 8)

CHAPTER FOUR

The reviewer in transition c.1920–1960

Prologue: another Shaw?

Before the artistic showdown between Shakespeare and Shaw in *The Frogs*, it is decided that each contestant should have a second. These deputies are asked to provide a critical reference for the prizefighter:

SHAKESPEARE SECOND: Shakespeare, we owe everything to him. Samuel Johnson.
SHAW SECOND: Shaw is unique. Kenneth Tynan.
SHAW: Who?
DIONYSOS: The creator of 'Oh, Calcutta'. (Sondheim et al. 1985: 194)

The idea of Kenneth Tynan as Shaw's deputy stretches back to the very beginning of Tynan's career. 'Shaw is unique', Tynan (1961a: 152) wrote in 1956: 'An Irish aunt so gorgeously drunk with wit is something English literature will never see again. But there is fruit for the symbolist in the fact that, prolific as he was, he left no children.' If the children did not exist, they would have to be invented. Tynan's first wife, Elaine Dundy, remembers a series of publicity campaigns run by the *Evening Standard* in the early 1950s to promote its new dramatic critic, chiefly advertising placards that 'blazed with the provocative, if perplexing, question: "Another Shaw?"' (140).

It could be argued that if Tynan resembled any of the New Critics at this point it was Beerbohm. Like the (nominally) incomparable Max, Tynan stepped spritely onto the critical scene at an improbably young age, and with an adopted pose that was 'very fin de siècle, Yellow Book, Oxford flamboyant' (Dundy 2001: 109). But the comparison with Shaw, it must have been decided, would sell more newspapers. It may also be significant that Tynan began to write for the *Standard* in May 1951, only six months after Shaw's death, when the idea of succession – even reincarnation ('Another Shaw') – had a particular appeal to a bereaved public. Both the *Express* and the *Standard* began to run ads with such excited headlines as:

> Not since the time of young George Bernard Shaw has there been a theatre critic like Kenneth Tynan... he is the voice and spirit of youth... he has delighted theatregoers and infuriated those producers who have come under his lash. He has done a brilliant series of articles which will begin today in the *Evening Standard*. (Dundy 2001: 140–1)

These advertisements are intriguing: Shaw was hardly a 'young' sensation as a theatre critic. Although he had been a relatively young music critic, Shaw was 38 when he began publishing theatre criticism in the *Saturday Review*. Either Dundy's memory is faulty here or, as likely, the advertisers were attempting to create a more exact fit between Shaw and his surrogate. Either way, at the inception of his professional career, Kenneth Tynan's talent was located in a tradition.

But what were the dominant characteristics of this tradition? Irving Wardle sees the mid-point of the century as the cusp between two epochs. Before the 1950s, he writes, 'the independence of the British theatre – and the tradition of reviewing, such as it was – was grounded in two things: Shakespeare, and heroic acting' (Wardle 1997: 128). In the 'glorious revolution of the 1950s', however, everything changed. The New Wave militated against that previous actor-managerial, Shakespeare-dominated tradition, and profoundly altered the status of the actor, the playwright and the director. In the second part of this chapter, I argue that Tynan's Shakespearean reviews should be read in the light of this epochal shift from a tradition of production and reception based on Shakespeare and 'heroic acting' to one increasingly dominated by new playwrights, ensemble acting and the preeminence of the director. Before doing so, I want first to explore Shakespearean reviewing in the decades before 'the glorious revolution'.

In *1956 and All That*, Dan Rebellato makes a persuasive case for revising the orthodox perception of postwar British theatre history, in which Tynan and *Look Back in Anger* are synonymous. Both have come to symbolise a moment of abrupt upheaval, a decisive infusion of Leavisite 'life' (Rebellato 1999: 21) into the sclerotic body of British theatre. The 'obsessive date-stamping' of 8 May 1956 in theatre discourse has created a habit of thought through which one is taught to believe that 'everything changed' on a particular day. But, Rebellato argues, the privileging of *Anger* has depended on an underestimation of the vitality of British theatre before 1956, as well as an exaggeration of the resistance the play met when it was premiered. Indeed, an anecdote from Tynan's *Diaries* reinforces not only Rebellato's argument about the mythical position of *Anger* in theatrical discourse, but also Tynan's own awareness of the constructed nature of cultural memory.

In 1976, on the twentieth anniversary of the play's premiere, Tynan was interviewed by Robert Cushman in the *Observer* and asked to reminisce about its opening night. Tynan (2001: 337) found the 'subject so staled by repetition' that he determined 'to do a little myth-making'. In the interview he consequently 'remembered' seeing Kingsley Amis, Evelyn Waugh and Binkie Beaumont at the first night, all responding with parodic and predictable hostility to the play. All of these false memories subsequently appeared in print. 'Thus', Tynan reflected, 'are legends born' (338).

Bearing Rebellato and Tynan's caveats against the selectivity of cultural memory in mind, it is important to place Tynan in some historical context and avoid the temptation to represent him as an *ex nihilo* sensation, the parentless wunderkind who flared brightly for a few stellar years before burning up. That this was Tynan's own preferred self-representation ('I will either die or kill myself when I reach thirty because by then I will have said everything I have to say' (Dundy 2001: 104)) should further encourage one to seek precedents, influences and contexts for his Shakespearean reviewing. The publicity departments of the *Daily Express* and *Evening Standard* puffed Tynan as the successor to Shaw, and the paternal link has proved durable in many accounts of Tynan's significance. But comparisons between Shaw and Tynan generally recall only the Shavian aspects of Tynan's criticism: the iconoclasm, the chutzpah and the advocacy of a leftist social theatre. What the comparisons tend to forget, and what this chapter seeks to remember, is the contradictory ideological impulses in Tynan's work, and particularly how his construction of Shakespeare owed as much to his immediate predecessor, James Agate, as to Shaw.

The previous chapter argued that, with the advent of the signed article and other corresponding shifts in journalistic culture, the theatre reviewer was encouraged to foreground his or her individuality and critical personality. This in turn facilitated an attitude, even a pose, towards Shakespearean authority – whether of the actor-manager or the playwright – that was openly playful and often subversive. Here I concentrate on two distinctive strands of Agate's Shakespearean reviewing that both emerge from the reviewing culture of the 1890s and reflect the climate and concerns of the immediate postwar period. The first consists of an openly heretical attitude to the Shakespearean play-text and seems to be a direct hangover from the sceptical tradition of the New Journalism. The second is more distinctive to Agate and the tensions of his particular personality and period. Broadly, it concerns the imperative to accommodate shifts in the power structures of Shakespearean production. The decline of the actor-manager and the correspondent rise in the status of the producer-director fed into a wider critical anxiety about the decline of the lead actor as the centre of any given production's meaning. If Wardle is right in claiming that the tradition of British reviewing before the 1950s rested on the interaction between the critic, Shakespeare and heroic acting, how did critics of the interwar period negotiate the first challenges to this tradition? I argue that Agate's response was a series of recuperative gestures that sought to arrest historical change by self-consciously reinforcing the mainstream tradition of British theatre reviewing. Later I argue that a comparable tension between modernity and tradition is evident throughout the Shakespearean reviewing of Kenneth Tynan.

'That modern nuisance': Agate, the producer and the death of the actor

James Agate (1877–1947) was the liveliest, most productive and most widely read British theatre critic of the interwar period. A relative latecomer to journalism, he began his career in Manchester in the family business, the cotton industry, and only in his very late 20s started contributing reviews to Manchester newspapers. He served a formative apprenticeship of seven years on the *Manchester Guardian* (working as third string to the eminent duo of C.E. Montague and Allan Monkhouse), before descending on London, where he spent two years on the *Saturday Review* and twenty-three as chief critic of the *Sunday Times*. As a boy he had imbibed his father's memories of the great actors of the mid nineteenth century, and he had seen with his own eyes many of the finest of the 1880s and 1890s, including his own immortal beloveds, Sarah Bernhardt and Henry Irving. These performers set a standard against which he would judge the thousands of actors whose efforts he would appraise in the decades to come. At the end of his life, he reflected that he had for forty years 'felt about H[enry]. I[rving]. what Iago pretended to feel about Othello: "I am your own for ever." It has not been in the power of Time to weaken this' (Agate 1948: 323).

His appetites were eclectic and intense: French literature, show-ponies, golf, Ibsen, boozy lunches at the Ivy, Berlioz, cricket, Damon Runyon. His dislikes were no less various, but he was especially allergic to anything he considered highbrow, a condition that he defined as 'pseudo-intellectual. A mind thinking above its class. A mind in corduroy trousers' (Agate 1948: 281). Most contemporary music, modernist literature and experimental film fell into this category. Poetic drama, Orson Welles and cubism baffled and irked him. Bartok, especially, was a *bête noire*. In his twin positions as theatre critic of the *Sunday Times* and book reviewer for the *Daily Express* (the latter with a circulation of 3 million), Agate was well placed to campaign against the type of work a sympathetic correspondent, signing herself 'An Old Lady of Ninety-Three', was pleased to call *'masturbitic'* (1948: 68). He was 'a philistine with the conscience and equipment of an intellectual' (1948: 284) and refused to be 'gammoned' (a favourite verb, meaning to be humbugged) by 'silly-symphony', 'too-clever-by-half', 'namby-pamby' displays of 'brains'. He was most delighted to be described as 'ungullible'. Yet he was nothing if not paradoxical, and his was not the conservatism of Clement Scott. Agate's philistinism — cheerfully irritable — coexisted with a deep love of Ibsen and Chekhov and an incorrigible tendency to quote, often without translation, inches of French literature. His frames of reference were, then, by twenty-first-century standards, highly intellectual and demanding. But at a time when 'even three-ha'penny papers quote Kafka and Kierkegaard' (Webb 1952: 41), it was not his level of intellect that formed his reputation and earned a devoted readership. According to Alec Guinness:

> Agate was a great critic because, although there were sometimes lumps of Racine in his columns, he managed in a neat, clean phrase to show you the essential characteristic of an actor's work and often its profundity... if the performance or play was dull, his journalism remained superb and his love of the theatre constant. (Webb 1952: 7–8)

The chief characteristic of good acting, according to Agate, was that the performer 'takes hold of the dramatist's conception, absorbs it, and then gives it out again re-created in terms of her own personality and delighted imagination'. In the detailed analysis of this transmigration, the 'twofold joy of one fine talent superimposed upon another' (Agate 1943a: 71), he was superb.

Ostensibly and sometimes actually sybaritic, he also had a phenomenal work ethic. By the end of his career he had published over 7 million words: twice the amount, he proudly calculated, in Balzac's *La Comédie Humaine*. His corpus included novels, belles-lettres and, most impressively, twenty-five books on the theatre and nine volumes of his hugely popular autobiography *Ego* (1932–47). As a theorist of criticism, he subscribed wholeheartedly to the doctrine of personal criticism articulated and practised by the critics of the 1890s. He cited approvingly in his diary Anatole France's dictum that the critic always speaks of himself '*à propos* of Shakespeare' and Shaw's that good journalism can only emerge from a strong personality. It was not untypical for him to launch a paragraph with a formula such as 'Speaking for myself – and one's self is the only criterion...' (Agate 1943a: 223). By the end of his career, he was certain where his strength as a reviewer lay: 'I not only think, I *know*, that I am the best critic of acting during the last hundred years' (Agate 1948: 335).

Agate recognised at an early point in his career that his best shot at immortality lay in hardback publication, and, in doing so, he saw himself fulfilling the responsibility and the privilege of the theatre critic 'to see to it that the memory of the great player does not perish utterly' (quoted in Harding 1986: 207). Agate prefaced *Brief Chronicles: A Survey of the Plays of Shakespeare and the Elizabethans in Actual Performance* with a dedicatory letter to fellow critic and long-term amanuensis Alan Dent. In this he reflected on the history of British theatre reviewing and its relationship with the book. 'Nobody', he wrote, 'will deny that there is one respect in which the soil during the last fifty years has been less generous than in Hazlitt's day, and how poor in the way of criticism surviving in book form it has been from that day to this' (Agate 1943a: 14). Agate's account of reviewing history since Hazlitt was, with notable exceptions, lapsarian. If the capacity and will to republish reviews in the higher cultural format of the book is an indicator of the prestige of the critic, then the reviewing tradition, from Agate's perspective, had consistently been on the verge of extinction. Agate could only cite Lewes, Forster and the last of Leigh Hunt in the second quarter of the nineteenth century, and Morley and Knight in the third, as examples of critics who had reprinted their journalism. But the case was altered in the 1890s. In *Those Were the Nights* (1946), Agate offered the straightforward assertion that 'In 1895 criticism had become once more a serious art' (Agate 1946: 49); 'Henry Morley and Dutton Cook had gone, and Clement Scott was going. They were succeeded by G.B.S., William Archer, Max and J.T. Grein – the most brilliant critical galaxy that has ever coruscated at one and the same time' (54). Yet even this stellar period was, according to Agate, short-lived in terms of reprinted reviews; and even in reprinted collections, especially those of Grein and Beerbohm, omission of Shakespearean reviews was 'the order of the day' (Agate 1943a: 15). Agate had therefore decided 'to bring together my notices of the Shakespeare productions I have seen since I joined the *Sunday Times* in 1923' for 'any student wishing to know how Shakespeare fared in the London theatre between the two great wars' (Agate 1943a: 15).

One of Agate's most obvious inheritances from the New Critics, Shaw and Beerbohm in particular, was an unpredictable attitude to the value of Shakespeare's plays. He was 'a fanatic of Shakespeare on the stage as well as in the study' (Agate 1943a: 87) and wrote in the last year of his life that the plays had afforded him more delight than all the operas, art galleries and books, 'all the rounds of golf I've played, all the ponies I've shown, all the whisky, all the cigars' – and that was much (Agate 1948: 106). And yet he devoted a considerable measure of his critical gusto to slaughtering sacred cows. Consider the Shavian ethos and atmosphere of Agate's criticism of *Measure for Measure*: 'My own objections to the play are simple. The first is that the Duke in the long speech, "Be absolute for death," talks the most absolute bosh that ever fell from human lips... The rest of the Duke's speech, considered otherwise than as music, is beneath modern contempt!' (Agate 1943a: 31). The incongruous colloquialism, the belief that some of Shakespeare's verse works more on the level of sound than sense and the appeal to modern sensibility as an arbiter of value are all Shavian habits. Isabella's obsessive retention of chastity also seemed to Agate a hopeless anachronism:

> In plain English, if Isabella had yielded to Claudio's [sic] request she would not only have been more ensky'd and sainted than ever, but proved herself a decent sort as well. What Elizabethan [sic] audiences thought of this aspect of the play it is difficult for us to guess, since encrusted upon those notions must be the inherited layers of Restoration raillery, Victorian prudery, and neo-Georgian flippancy. (Agate 1943a: 30–1)

But the original act of reception was, for Agate, irrelevant. Seeing a revival of *The Duchess of Malfi*, Agate asked: 'What is there about this play which made it acceptable to the playgoer of 1614? Is there that about it which makes it acceptable to the playgoer of 1935?' The answer to the first question lay with scholars; 'for an answer to the second one need only consult oneself' (Agate 1943a: 148). Agate read and revered some Shakespearean scholarship, but he would not defer to it when evaluating performance. To do so might have been to expose his own vulnerability as one who, in the words of his self-penned obituary, 'felt keenly the lack of a university education... His shop-window was superb, and perfectly concealed the meagreness of the academic stock within' (Harding 1986: 115). What mattered was the litmus test of modernity: were Isabella airlifted out of Vienna and into a contemporary Hollywood film, she would say 'Sure! I'm no angel. Tell Angelo to come up and see me!' and this would chime with 'what every man and women who is honest with himself or herself knows to be the truth' (Agate 1943a: 31).

This was far from an isolated incident of anti-bardolatry. *The Merchant* is 'a pretty poor play about a Jew who has the minimum of Jewish characteristics, a hero who may or may not be a cad, and a great lady who at one moment is prepared to buy her lover and at another desires only to stand high in his account' (Agate 1943a: 57); *All's Well that Ends Well* 'was Shakespeare botching and bungling at his worst' (61); '*The Comedy of Errors* always strikes me as the most excruciatingly boring farce ever devised by a man of genius' (66); *Cymbeline* is a 'mud-hovel... prettified by a master-decorator' (47); 'any schoolboy will tell you that Brutus is an ass' (171); 'Cordelia is a "gumph" or, as we say in Lancashire "gormless"' (193). Of *King John*: 'What a bad play this is! All about a war in which it is not possible to take the slightest interest' (89). Furthermore, Agate took great delight throughout his career in running a competition for the 'Worst Bit' in Shakespeare, his candidates including such passages as Jaques's 'All the world's a stage' (59), Portia's 'The Quality of Mercy' (54) and Hal's 'Yet herein will I imitate the sun', of which he wrote 'if there is a more revolting passage in Shakespeare... I have still to read it' (100). He was no fan of Prospero – that 'endless chunnerer' – and concluded his review of this *Tempest* with characteristically amplified indifference to his readers' sensibilities: 'Postage stamps may be saved by readers desiring to tell me that the opinion set down above is uniquely crass. *Je m'en fiche*' (17).

If Agate inherited Shaw's propensity to test Shakespeare's thought against that of the contemporary world, he also shared Beerbohm's comparable taste for representational, modern (although not modern*ist*) staging. Of Tyrone Guthrie's 1934 *Macbeth* at the Old Vic, he complained that 'This going back to Elizabethan conditions because they were the only ones Shakespeare knew seems to me like saying that Rameau, Couperin and all that push would have refused to avail themselves of the pianoforte if they had known of it' (Agate 1943a: 230–1). Like Beerbohm (and some critics of the 1990s), Agate argued that the authenticity movement had unnecessarily restricted Shakespeare's intention to the technically limited age in which he lived:

> Shakespeare's choice of modern setting would, I am convinced, have been strictly representational, and the nearest possible approach to historical accuracy... He would have made Macbeth's soldiers carry actual firs and real larches from Birnam to Dunsinane. He would have insisted upon an authentic wood for his midsummer night's dream. He would have been of the school of Tree. (Agate 1943a: 35)

But to a greater extent than Max Beerbohm – or indeed his half-brother – Agate was fighting a rearguard action against new movements in Shakespearean production. His preference for 'the school of Tree' was, as he admitted, a predilection for 'the old-fashioned method of presentation'

(Agate 1943a: 39). Here, he felt, he was in tune with his readership: 'Nine-tenths of playgoers are, in my computation, still essentially Victorian as far as this play [*A Midsummer Night's Dream*] is concerned' (44). But unlike Victorian critics and audiences, Agate was confronted with the work of producers who were inspired by and had built on the scenographic revolutions of Craig and Granville Barker. Agate's preference for representational scenery was predicated on the belief that such an aesthetic – no matter how ostentatiously sumptuous – rendered both producer and designer invisible. When he took issue with the designs for Henry Cass's 1934 Old Vic production of *Much Ado* ('a cobwebby steeple from the top of which sombrely gibed a stringy, featherless fowl') it was because the design had intervened between actor and audience: 'I hold that getting itself immediately forgotten is the first function of all scenery in plays that speak to the mind' (34). But this credo would be challenged by new schools of production which were motivated in part by the ability of the visual to 'speak to the mind' through emblematic, metaphoric and thematic treatments of Shakespeare's texts.

The shift of interpretive locus from actor or actor-manager to producer and scenographer is perhaps most simply put at the opening of *The Times* review of Theodore Komisarjevsky's 1933 *Macbeth* at Stratford. Relishing the prospect of a season of productions by Komisarjevksy, William Bridges-Adams and Tyrone Guthrie, the reviewer concluded: 'In former days it was the actor who tried to keep the plays vivid and vital: now it is the producer who assumes the responsibility' (Anonymous 1933). W.A. Darlington's collection of reviews, *Six Thousand and One Nights* (1960), also offers an exemplary narrative account of this interwar transference of 'responsibility'. Darlington, who had been reviewing since 1919, wrote in his foreword:

> Though I hardly realized it at first, I was a witness of the theatrical revolution which changed the position of the actor completely. Before the revolution the actor was supreme in his own world; after it, he was no more than the equal, or even the subordinate, of the dramatist or the producer. Whether you see him as a giant diminished or as a king deposed is a matter of choice of metaphor. The effect is the same; he is now an ordinary human being, finding for himself a new way of life among his fellowmen. (Darlington 1960: 8)

Barely concealed beneath Darlington's language of 'revolution' and of deposed kings is the theatrical-political fantasy of continuity (noted in Chapter 1; see p. 37) in Downes's interregnum-effacing account of the unbroken chain of Hamlets stretching from Shakespeare to Betterton. Not only did the rise of the producer pose a threat to theatrical tradition, it also complicated the critic's job. In 1924 Darlington responded in the *Critics' Circular* to Arnold Bennett's claim that reviewers 'ought to look upon the entire [theatrical] spectacle as primarily the artistic creation of the producer' (Darlington 1924: 4). With some exasperation, Darlington enquired how the critic might 'set about the task of disentangling the work of the producer from that of the actor'. Citing one of his own attributive gaffes, in which he had mistakenly blamed the producer for 'an amazing piece of over-acting', Darlington reflected that: 'If it were a regular part of the critic's duty to apportion praise or blame between actor and producer he would be continually faced with the task of making such invidious and difficult distinctions' (4).

James Agate had little difficulty making such distinctions. The apportioning of praise and blame generally depended on how successfully the producer had rendered his work inconspicuous and thus ceded stage authority to the actor. Of Stephen Thomas's 1946 *Macbeth* he concluded simply and representatively that 'the production was unnoticeable and therefore in every way first-class. Not once did Mr Stephen Thomas obtrude himself between us and the play' (Agate 1961: 253). Of Wolfit's *Lear* in the same year Agate was again grateful for the lack of obtrusion: 'The scenery was bare yet simple, and blessedly there was no nonsense about "production"' (248). For Tyrone Guthrie and Michael Benthall's 1946 production of *Hamlet*, starring Robert Helpmann, Agate's view was figuratively blocked by 'fashionable' scenery and directorial ideas. Agate averred that, although this was 'one of the most exciting theatrical events for many a long day', it was nevertheless 'a disappointment for the favourite's [i.e. Hamlet–Helpmann's] supporters': 'How so? Because, in racing parlance, the Lord Hamlet after a good start fell away in the middle, came again and lost by a short head to Production, whose clever jockey rode the race throughout in the way he had obviously planned' (243). Had Helpmann been given free rein/reign it might have been different. Agate began the review with a sideswipe at modern ideas of production and ensemble playing. Quoting Ellen Terry's opinion that Irving 'was always quite independent of the people with whom he acted', Agate followed up with: 'Art thou there, Mr Team-actor, likewise Mr Producer?' (242). In the second review he devoted to the production, he reiterated the point. In another allusive throwback to theatre history, Agate quoted a passage from George Henry Lewes on the power of such actors as Garrick, Kean and Kemble 'in swaying the emotions of the audience'. 'What', Agate demanded, 'have our team advocates to say to my passage from Lewes? Will they never realise that a great actor's punch is more potent than a hogshead of team-spirit' (245). Whether this *Hamlet* was in any sense played as an ensemble piece is not clear from his review, but for Agate 'team-acting' and overtly interpretive direction and design were associatively linked in the assault on the great actor. The directors' power seemed to be growing by the week; by the time he wrote the second part of the review, Agate regretted that 'On reflection I must hold that Messrs Guthrie and Benthall's production beat Mr Helpmann's Hamlet not by a head but half a dozen lengths' (243).

Agate's resistance to shifts in the power structure of Shakespearean production was perhaps most clearly registered in his review of Komisarjevsky's 1936 *Antony and Cleopatra* at the New Theatre. Komisarjevsky 'was the first director of Shakespeare in the English mainstream theatre to insist that his ideas were as important as the words of the play, and to insist that acting style follow from the visual concept' (Kennedy 1993: 132). In this review, Agate (1943b: 9) reiterated his frustration with the subjugation of the actor and Shakespeare to 'that modern nuisance, the producer'. He opened by drawing attention to the division of theatrical labour as found in the 'tail-end' of theatre programmes of the time. There, he wrote:

> You will read 'Shoes by Thingummy' and 'Stockings by Thingumbob'. One turned to the New Theatre programme the other evening to see whether among the informative rag, tag, and bobtail, one would find: 'Words by Shakespeare'. One did not. The time-honoured phrase was in its usual place under the title of the play. But alas! the information turned out to be, in part and in the most important part, false... Beneath the words 'by William Shakespeare' one read in thicker and blacker type: 'The Production is devised and directed and the Scenery and Costumes designed by Komisarjevsky.' (Agate 1943a: 180)

With a journalist's alertness to the semiotics of typography, Agate took the bold type bestowed on the director as symbolic of appropriated power. 'Words by Shakespeare', instead of being placed beneath the play's title, should more accurately have been relegated to the below-stairs of the theatrical economy, somewhere between the anonymous purveyors of shoes and stockings. It is hard in this context not to recall Terence Hawkes's description of the traditional belief that the meaning of each of Shakespeare's plays 'is bequeathed to it *ab initio* and lies – artfully concealed perhaps – within its text... It is as if, to the information which used to be given in theatrical programmes, "Cigarettes by Abdullah, Costumes by Motley, Music by Mendelssohn", we should add "Meaning by Shakespeare"' (Hawkes 1992: 3). For Agate, Komisarjevsky had ignored

Shakespeare's bequest and instead introduced an array of illegitimate meanings through design, costume and direction.

If the tradition of English Shakespearean theatre reviewing depended on the symbiosis between lead actor and critic, if the critic's historical function was to memorialise the individual talent, where did the advent of the producer lead or leave this tradition? For Agate, the threat to the indigenous tradition could conveniently be cast in nationalist terms. Komisarjevsky had postponed the opening scene of *Antony and Cleopatra* and inserted in its place the interchange between the soothsayer and Cleopatra's attendants. Agate (1943a: 181) wrote, 'I do not think that foreign producers, however distinguished, should permit themselves to take such liberties.' Although he had fun at the expense of the Russian and heavily accented Cleopatra, Leontovich, Agate made it clear that this was not an objection to foreign accents per se. Komisarjevsky's 'formalized settings', eclectic costuming, and textual rearrangements and excisions were, however, critiqued in such a way as to foreground nationality: 'If Mr. Komisarjevsky does not know, he must be told that "Call to me all my sad captains" and "To-night I'll force the wine peep through their scars" are to the English ear and mind sacrosanct' (183). This tension between the English ear and the European eye is apparent in Agate's verdict that, had Shakespeare been alive in 1934:

> he would have thrown under foot and trampled on the choicest designs of Messrs. Craig, Komisarjevsky, Bakst, and Picasso. I utterly decline to believe that he would have approved a crazy night on a geometrical heath with Lear on a spiral staircase defying an algebraical night. Not for William any gyring and gimbling in that wabe! (Agate 1943a: 34–5)

Of the designers and producers mentioned, only Craig was British, and even he had only directed one Shakespeare play in London (*Much Ado*, 1903). As a boy, Agate had heard Richter conduct the first performance of Tchaikovsky's Sixth Symphony in Manchester; at the end of his life, he remembered chiefly the moment when Richter 'laid down his baton in the second movement and let the orchestra conduct itself' (Agate 1948: 140). In that moment, perhaps, lay a parable about directorial humility.

Unchanging Cockaigne: Agate and the recuperation of tradition

I argued above that Agate frequently critiqued Shakespeare's plays on the grounds of what Shaw called their 'philosophy'. Like Shaw, he could apply the litmus test of contemporary relevance and find Shakespeare wanting.

Such an attitude depends on a belief in historical differentiation and contingency, in the fundamental otherness of the past. 'Nor is there any earthly reason why the King's Evil speech should be retained. King James is dead' Agate (1943a: 216) wrote baldly in a review of a 1926 *Macbeth*. It is interesting, therefore, that this strand of Agate's Shakespearean criticism was accompanied by a stronger contradictory impulse to affirm national-historical similarity and continuity. This impulse expressed itself in two distinct, but mutually supportive strategies. First, in Shakespearean (and other early modern play) reviews, Agate frequently commended the play as appealing to an unchanging British consciousness. Second, in both his reviews and publishing projects, Agate sought to reinforce a national tradition of reviewing. In this tradition, the individual talent (whether of the lead actor or the prominent critic) lay, timelessly, at the heart of a production's meaning. The tradition was stable and, perhaps most crucially, quotable.

In 1923, in one of his first Shakespearean reviews, Agate (1943a: 22) wrote of *The Merry Wives of Windsor*: 'How modern this play is!... at the Welshman's "Your wife is as honest a woman as I will desire among five thousand, and five hundred too" we realize how little three hundred years means in terms of national character and expression.' In the same year, he wrote of an Old Vic *Henry V*:

> It is amusing to note how modern this play is. The pow-wow between the two kings is like our own peace conferences. The boy's 'Would I were in an alehouse in London!' is that Tommy, 'fed to the teeth', who would so willingly have exchanged Bagdad [sic] for Bolton. Even the appeals to glory are our recruiting-posters in better English. (Agate 1943a: 111)

In Agate's reviews, the expression of timeless British sentiments is not the sole preserve of Shakespeare. Of a 1926 revival of *The Shoemaker's Holiday*, he wrote 'the theme of this comedy is equally near the general heart to-day':

> It is not pretended that the audience at this theatre [the Old Vic] is composed of anything but simple, middle-class people. Well, here is the play for them. Watching it, and noting how the wage-earning spirit of the late sixteenth century called to the wage-earning spirit of the early twentieth, one realized that there is an unchanging England which does not know serfdom and ignores plutocracy. (Agate 1943a: 70–1)

Warfare, infidelity and middle-class acquisitiveness are timeless features of the English mental landscape: 'Recent years have re-taught the world, if indeed the world had ever forgotten, that Jack is as good as his master in such things as dying for his country, or hating to find his woman another's' (Agate 1943a: 70). Agate, noting how the Old Vic audience 'proved its kinship with the enduring wit of the London streets', concluded that 'Cockaigne is a country which never changes' (70). 'Cockaigne' here seems to denote not only the later humorous sense of 'the country of Cockneys' (OED 2), the sense in which Elgar's overture of that name is an ode to London, but it also evokes that 'imaginary country, the abode of luxury and idleness' (OED 1). Imaginary and perhaps idyllic for Agate, unchanging Cockaigne represented a stable, transhistorical idea of Englishness, and of an England 'which does not know serfdom and ignores plutocracy'. (As he neared death, he thought he had 'discovered or invented a new limbo' in which 'anything that you want to happen, happens and goes on happening, always. For ever Sir Toby has his "*Pourquoi*, my dear knight?" And longer than any figure on a Grecian urn Traddles looks forward to union with his dearest Sophy' (Agate 1948: 270).)

While the notion of an unchanging Cockaigne was central to Agate's high opinion of Dekker's play, he also invoked it to explain the failure in performance of a 1932 production of *The Knight of the Burning Pestle*:

> Perhaps that is the reason why the play when it was first produced was a complete failure, for if human nature does not change neither do theatre audiences, and we know that even to-day no burlesque succeeds which is at the expense of that to which the public is genuinely if sentimentally attached. (Agate 1943a: 76)

Agate's representation of an essential and unchanging Cockaigne sought to efface historical contingency. At these moments he seems to possess Eliot's 'historical sense', the 'sense of the timeless as well as of the temporal and of the timeless and the temporal together' that for Eliot made a writer 'traditional' (Eliot 1964: 14). If neither human nature nor theatre audiences changed, if history were the spatial poem of modernism, then the pressure of contemporary upheavals could be subsumed by a gesture towards the timeless. In the extracts above, this gesture is forthright and explicit, but Agate also had a more subtle critical method for overcoming historical difference.

Agate's reviewing was insistently, incorrigibly intertextual. Time and again he began a review by quoting the opinion of another critic, whether journalistic or literary. Very rarely was the cited critic a contemporary of Agate. This use of quotation could be restrained, almost epigrammatic, as in his verdicts on *The Taming of the Shrew*: 'Johnson said "The whole play is very popular and diverting." May I put it that it is much too popular and does not divert me?'; or on *Love's Labour's Lost*: 'Schlegel talks about the "lavish superfluity of labour in this play's execution", and I cannot help suggesting that for some there is lavish superfluity of labour in listening to it' (Agate 1943a: 65, 50). But more often the use of quotations was expansive, detailed and discursive, a springboard either for focused debate or wholesale divagation. Occasionally Agate presented himself as dependent on this springboard for the production of criticism. After he had decided that *All's Well* was 'Shakespeare botching and bungling at his worst', he appeared to have run out of steam. 'This, I said, will never do for Sunday, and began to look round for that wherewith to buttress this column. Wasn't there an old article by William Archer? There was' (61): the column had found its buttress. He was frequently rebuked for this habit by readers whom he suspected of wanting their money's worth or, more seriously, by fellow critic Beverley Baxter, who saw in it a symptom of fundamental intellectual poverty: 'when you want real thought you summon the thinkers of the past. In fact, you are something between a resurrectionist and a cloakroom attendant for other men's thoughts' (Agate 1948: 157).

Agate's reviews summoned in quotation authorities as diverse as Granville Barker, Coleridge, Allardyce Nicoll, C.E. Montague and Shaw (among many others). His pre-show preparation usually involved a quick trawl through the tools of his trade, the reviewing anthologies that lined his study. At the end of his career, he reflected:

> I should not dream of going to see an Ibsen play without having a look at what Shaw and Archer had had to say. In the case of the big Shakespeares I do much the same thing. Before to-night's Valk–Wolfit battle I looked up G.B.S. on Wilson Barrett's Othello. Magnificent, of course – I mean the criticism. (Agate 1948: 55)

While Beerbohm had 'quoted' Pepys and Aubrey to playful effect, and as a marker not only of his vaunted lack of qualification, but also his independence of thought, Agate's use of quotation and allusion served a more serious cause. Derrida's concept of iterability is based on the premise that any utterance 'can be *cited*, put between quotation marks; in so doing it can break with every given context, engendering an infinity of new contexts in a manner which is absolutely illimitable' (Derrida 1988: 12). If a phrase can be recycled, it has an afterlife divorced from its original context, referents and intentionality. David Roberts argues that, in the process of inducting their readers into a tradition of stage interpretation, reviewers habitually offer paradigms of interpretation, paradigms that often take the form of recycled quotation:

> To know that Olivier's Macbeth 'gave you the sense that he had committed the act of murder many times in his imagination' [as Michael Billington wrote in his review of Adrian Noble's 1993 production] is to be suitably equipped: even if you never saw the performance in question, this repeated observation of it retains its currency when you see another. (Roberts 2002: 352)

But, Roberts goes on to argue, the effect of such iterability in theatre criticism is not fragmentary or dislocating, as Derrida would have it – rather, the reverse: 'the endlessly iterable quotations of theater criticism do not so much engender "an infinity of new contexts" as yoke every new context to an all-too-obvious finitude of old ones' (Roberts 2002: 353). I want to pursue Roberts's insight in relation to Agate and his construction not only of an acting tradition (Roberts's chief focus), but also of a tradition of reviewing.

Agate could quote the opinions of past critics as counterpoints to his own verdicts. These disagreements were largely on matters of character, meaning and style, what could be called literary as opposed to strictly theatrical issues. Agate's favourite source was Hazlitt, and on several occasions Agate distanced himself from the canonical critic. In a review of *The Merchant of Venice*, for example, Agate (1943a: 53) detailed his dislike of Shakespeare's characterisation: 'Jessica is unworthy of her race. Hazlitt makes the silly remark that he should like Lorenzo better if he had not married a Jewess; it should have been the other way round.' Elsewhere, Agate disagreed with Hazlitt's description of Jonson's verse as 'dry', 'literal' and 'meagre', and argued that Hazlitt's real difficulty with Jonsonian comedy was based on character rather than poetry: 'The point is that the great essayist is a sentimentalist and will take no pleasure in a play unless he can find in it some nice person with whom to identify himself' (82).

If past critics' readings of play texts were open to argument and revision through contextualisation, their responses to live performance were not. When Agate quoted past reviews of individual performances, the evidential nature of these passages was unproblematic. If both human nature and theatre audiences are unchanging, it follows, in Agate's use of iterability, that the language used to describe performance (and by implication the performance itself) is comparably impervious to ostensible changes in context and history. Just as Agate buttressed his *All's Well* column with a backwards gesture to Archer and Shaw, so his 1935 review of Abraham Sofaer's Othello began with a textual invocation:

> Watching Mr. Abraham Sofaer the other night I could not get out of my mind a picture in words of an earlier player who produced upon a critic of

his day the exact effect that Mr. Sofaer produced on me. When I got home I rummaged about, and in Leigh Hunt found this... (Agate 1943a: 296)

Agate then quoted Leigh Hunt at great length, concluding that 'Almost every word of this describes my view of Mr. Sofaer's performance' (Agate 1943a: 296). The reiterability of theatre criticism performed a similar function throughout Agate's Shakespearean reviews. They consistently placed Shakespearean performances within a tradition in which interpretive or physical virtues and vices were shown to be timeless phenomena, in which the 'pictures in words' of earlier critics could ideally encapsulate contemporary as well as past performances. Here again, Eliot's essay 'Tradition and the Individual Talent' offers a useful context for understanding Agate's critical method: 'No poet, no artist of any art, has his complete meaning alone. His significance, his appreciation is the appreciation of his relation to the dead poets and artists. You cannot value him alone; you must set him, for contrast and comparison, among the dead' (Eliot 1964: 15).

This book has already shown how this tenet of contrast and comparison between the living and the dead, and between successive generations, structured the reception of Shakespearean acting throughout the eighteenth and nineteenth centuries. For Agate, placing the new individual talent within theatrical tradition necessitated the resurrection not only of dead artists, but also inevitably of dead critics. Of Olivier's Hamlet in 1937, Agate (1943a: 270) chose to consider the actor in 'the frank, brutal, and altogether sensible way in which the old dramatic critics considered the old actors. What is the first thing G. H. Lewes tells us about Frank Lemaître?' Lemaître's qualities and defects were subsequently matched to Olivier's; Agate later cited Lewes again: 'The same critic whom we have been quoting has a significant passage about Charles Kean, which I would apply almost word for word to Mr. Olivier' (271). In responding to Olivier's Iago, Agate again depended on a textual precedent, in this case Hazlitt's essay on the character and his review of Edmund Kean's performance. Hazlitt had complained that 'Kean "abstracted the wit of the character", and that it was "too full of trim levity and epigrammatic conciseness". And that in a nutshell must be our reproach against Mr. Olivier's otherwise clever and always admirably mimed performance' (302).

The recycling of criticism was itself a Hazlittian strategy. Hazlitt first reviewed Kean's Othello in *The Times* in October 1817; the critic then reproduced that review, with very minor alterations, on two further occasions: first, in 1820, for the *London Magazine* in the pseudo-anonymous format of 'the words of a contemporary journal, a short time back' (Hazlitt 1930–4:

XVIII 302), and then eight years later in *The Examiner*. The reproduction of the review in 1820 was prompted by Hazlitt's disappointment with the instability and contingency of Kean's performance. The reprinted review is prefaced: 'Mr. Kean's Othello the other night did not quite answer our over-wrought expectations. He played it *with variations*; and therefore, necessarily worse. There is but one perfect way of playing Othello, and that was the way in which he used to play it' (362). If there was only one perfect way of playing the role, there could only be one worthy textual response, recycled and reiterated in defiance of the heavy wear, tear and variation visited on Kean's performance.

It is appropriate, given Agate's recurrent engagement with Hazlitt's criticism, that the later critic should mimic the reiterational tendencies of the earlier. Such a strategy reinforced Agate's attempt to induct his readers into a tradition of British criticism, in which the primary relationship was between the individual actor and the critic. That the critic's evaluative 'pictures in words' were transferable across centuries tended to blur issues of theatrical history, performance practice and reception. The project to construct an informal canon of British theatre reviewing that (as argued in the previous chapter) can be traced in part to the publishing projects of Archer and Lowe, and the reprinting phenomenon of the 1890s, reached fruition in Agate. Take, for example, his review of Frederick Valk's 1942 Othello. Agate's opening thesis was that the part of Othello 'goes against the English grain': 'Over and over again this unique rôle has defeated the English actor' (Agate 1943a: 303). Agate then proceeded to conduct a whistle-stop tour of the part's performance history, summarising each actor's failure with an unattributed quotation: 'Macready "whined and wimpered" ... Young "left no recollection". Phelp's performance "was far from his best"' (303). As this role call of inadequacy reached the present, the regular reader of Agate would have felt an even stronger sense of *déjà lu*: 'Abraham Sofaer "lacked that on which the whole nature of Othello is built – temperament" ... That fine player Donald Wolfit "wanted a banjo"' (303). It is only at the end of the paragraph that one learns, in a Foucauldian sense, 'who is speaking' about these actors: 'Authorities: Hazlitt, Leigh Hunt, Dutton Cook, Knight, Shaw, Grein, Agate' (303). Shorn of a few limbs and branches, this is the genealogical tree of canonical British theatre criticism. (These names are prominent in Agate's 1932 anthology *The English Dramatic Critics*.) Among the many denotations of 'canon', perhaps the most useful here is that of the musical form, 'a species of musical composition in which the different parts take up the same subject one after another, either at the same or at a different pitch, in strict imitation' (OED 7a). All of these voices or 'parts', these textual memories of performance, were, as shown by Agate's preface to *Brief Chronicles*, easily accessible in book form. Indeed, in this respect, *Brief Chronicles* is a potentially ambiguous title for a collection of Shakespearean reviews. Who or what are the brief chronicles: the actors or the review texts? If actors are the brief chronicles of their time, the chroniclers can escape history and mortality: performance is short, criticism is long.

'Post-mortem on the egoist': style, paternity and the dynamics of succession

In his final years, Agate brooded on his legacy and achievements. He coveted recognition and had hoped to have his prodigious work as a critic rewarded with a knighthood. It would have been the first awarded primarily for services to theatrical criticism and would have crowned his career with a moment of legitimation: what Irving had done for actors, he would do for critics. The knighthood was not forthcoming, perhaps because rumours of Agate's homosexuality were rife in establishment circles and were, according to Harold Hobson, one of the reasons that Agate was retired from his column (Hobson 1978: 210–13). (Hobson would succeed Agate at the *Sunday Times* and, in 1977, would himself become the critics' first knight.) In upbeat moments, Agate (1948: 210) joked about expiring during the second act of a substandard comedy and being 'received into a Technicolor Hereafter by Hazlitt, G.H. Lewes, George Jean Nathan (who has unhappily predeceased me), and the M.-G.-M. choir of angels'. In a more melancholy letter to Alan Dent ('Jock'), he did to himself what he habitually did to actors, and staged an unequal competition between the quick and the dead:

> I am not in the running with Hazlitt. In the spectrum of dramacology I approximate to mauve, and you remember Whistler's 'Mauve is only pink trying to be purple.' Compared with Hazlitt my purplest passages are a sickly puce. And then I haven't Shaw's knowledge, Max's wit, Walkley's urbanity, Montague's style. Besides, I don't particularly want the stuff to live. I might have wanted if there had been an Irving to write about, but there hasn't. I tell you, Jock, that I would give the whole of Olivier, Richardson, Wolfit, and Gielgud for the smile the Old Man gave the little serving maid at his first entry in *The Bells*. (Agate 1948: 293)

Not wanting the stuff to live is either disingenuous or a remarkable volte-face. He had placed himself as the last great reviewer in his anthology of

The English Dramatic Critics, and it was in this terminal position that Dent remembered his old friend in 1953 when he claimed that 'none of us writes half as well – nowadays – as the great line which began with Leigh Hunt and concluded with the death of Agate' (Webb 1952: 41).

Agate spent many of his last years convinced that 'this country, as I knew it, is finished'. Cockaigne was changing, and he despaired at the reforming, egalitarian zeal of Attlee's government: '*I am just not interested in the working conditions of coal-mines*. What I am interested in is a first-class performance of *Rosenkavalier* with a bottle of champagne at the Savoy afterwards. To me inequality always has been, and always will be, the spice of life' (Agate 1948: 309). If nothing would shake his belief in the 'Non-educability of the Masses' (128), the educability of precocious undergraduates was a different matter. On the day after his diary despaired of the future, he received a letter from Kenneth Tynan, an Oxford student who had initiated the correspondence in July 1945 when he was still a sixth-former at King Edward's School, Birmingham. In their correspondence Agate signed himself 'Polonius' and offered advice to Tynan ('Hamlet') on the art of reviewing. In one letter, Agate included extracts from Shaw, Walkley, Beerbohm and Montague in order to illustrate the correct use of quotation. Agate advised that the young critic's writing was too densely allusive and his own voice lost in the melee: 'I do not want you to write like any of those four great critics . . . I want you to make for yourself a style – which can be done only out of your own bowels and nobody else's – that will make readers say, "That's Tynan," just as people say, "That's Hazlitt" or "That's Lewes"' (quoted in Kathleen Tynan 1987: 46).

The letter Agate received shortly before his death was encouraging to the man who felt that distinctions were being squashed and all was slipping away. Tynan had composed a long, virtuosic and defiantly old-fashioned review of Donald Wolfit and Frederick Valk in *Othello*. On the spectrum of dramacology, it was deep purple, or, as Tynan (1966: 98) would have it in another gaudy patch, 'tyrianthine'. Agate (1948: 311) was delighted. 'Anybody reading this in a hundred years' time should know what these two actors had been like in these two great roles. And that, and nothing else, in my view is dramatic criticism. In other words, here is a great dramatic critic in the making.' Furthermore, although Agate could hardly have guessed it, this was a great dramatic critic in the making who would be interested both in the working conditions of coal-mines and in a first-class performance of *Rosenkavalier*. Tynan (1961b: n.p.) would later describe Agate as 'politically an ignoramus (or unadmitted right-wing anarchist)', who could not, at the end of his life, 'understand why the arts were moving away from him in the direction of what seemed to him ugliness, coarseness and obscurity'.

Agate died in 1947, Shaw in 1950; Beerbohm died in 1956 after years of quiet isolation in Rapallo, Italy. Tynan (1961a: 152) found Shaw's childlessness symbolic, but the same could be said of all three men. There is perhaps more fruit for the symbolist in the fact that Tynan was born out of wedlock, barely knew his father and resented his mother. He was therefore self-orphaned, and 'when one hasn't had a good father, it is necessary to invent one' (Nietzsche quoted in Bloom 1997: 56). As outlined at the opening of this chapter, Tynan was hailed as Shaw's successor when he was appointed theatre critic of the *Evening Standard* in 1951. In fact, he combined key qualities of all three influential predecessors. He experienced this tension as a crisis on the level of style. In 1964, he reflected:

> My chief problem is to walk the hazardous tight-rope of my prose style, which is that of a provincial writer who fell out of love with the mandarin class too late to foreswear his early love of mandarin prose. The result is a bizarrely quilted amalgam in which patches of exhortation and colloquial simplicity are joined together by embroidery remembered from Max Beerbohm. (Kenneth Tynan 1964: 11)

The key images of high-wire performance and class-based seduction are strikingly anticipated in a 1961 review of *James Agate: An Anthology* entitled 'Post-mortem on the Egoist': 'James Agate was the first drama critic who ever fascinated me. Behind his style, which was the work of a butcher-boy hypnotised by Beerbohm, an elephant walking a slack-wire, there lurked a lawyer with a case to plead, always posing rhetorical questions and anticipating objections' (Kenneth Tynan 1961b: n.p.).

Prose style is politics in a more or less convincing disguise. Cyril Connolly – much admired by both Agate and Tynan – had, in the first part of *Enemies of Promise* (1938), anatomised the mandarin and colloquial styles and the political implications of each: 'left-wing writers have tended to write in the colloquial style while the Mandarins, the wizards and prose charmers remain as supporters of the existing dispensation' (Connolly 1961: 81–2). When Beerbohm replaced Shaw on the *Saturday Review*, the dandy style (which tends to mature into mandarin) replaced the direct, colloquial register of the reformist. Tynan would assimilate both influences and, like Connolly's autobiography, compose 'in a language which combines the rapidity of the colloquial with an elasticity permitting incursions into the Mandarin of prose poetry' (Connolly 1961: 10). When Tynan arrived on the critical scene in 1951, therefore, he sounded like no one else before him; or perhaps he sounded like everyone else before him at the same time.

Tynan saw style as his 'chief problem', but it was merely the most visible symptom of a more profound malaise. The hazardous tightrope he walked was strung between political extremes. One of his talents as a journalist was to offer his reader vivid and memorable antitheses. (Connolly (1961: 30) again: 'Literature is the art of writing something that will be read twice; journalism what will be grasped at once.') To read Tynan was to grasp and then be equipped with strong contrasts: Arthur Miller is a Scandinavian playwright, Tennessee Williams a Mediterranean: 'Miller's plays are hard, "patrist", athletic, concerned mostly with men. Williams' are soft, "matrist", sickly, concerned mostly with women' (Kenneth Tynan 1964: 141). His book-length analysis of bullfighting was largely structured around 'two contradictory views of bullfighting, the clash of two schools, a tauromachic civil war' (Kenneth Tynan 1966: 90). Equally typically, he wrote of himself: 'Can seldom banish from his mind the fact of approaching mortality. This may account for his instinctive sympathy with Socialist-maternal ideal of equality and mercy rather than with Conservative-paternal ideals of hierarchy and authority' (Kenneth Tynan 1967: ix). There are countless ways of recasting the central dialectic; here are a few that Tynan would have recognised: Right / Left; High Tory / Socialist; Pessimist / Humanist-Optimist; Patrists / Matrists; Cavalier-Royalist / Roundhead-Puritan; Mandarin / Colloquial; Dramatic Theatre Spectator / Epic Theatre Spectator; Art for Art's Sake / 'Art for Our Sake' (Kenneth Tynan 1961a: 116); Star-system / Ensemble; Hierarchy / Equality; Tragedy / Comedy; Fate / Free Will; Dionysian / Apollonian. Intellectually, he was aligned with the qualities of the latter half of each pair; somatically, sensually and more or less subconsciously he would frequently succumb to the former.

In an article of 1959 Tynan described the mediocre theatre critic:

> His task, or so he conceives it, is to keep out of his criticism the values and convictions that govern his attitude, if he has one, toward society. The great test comes when he brings out a book (imaginably entitled *Rogues and Vagabonds*) of his collected reviews. Considered singly, they may glitter; *en masse*, they resemble nothing so much as a bag of unstrung beads. (Kenneth Tynan 1961a: 295)

Tynan published three review anthologies: how well strung, to adopt his metaphor, were Tynan's reviews, and specifically those that concerned Shakespeare in performance? What did Shakespeare consistently stand for in the writings of the most influential critic of a generation? How did the values and convictions that governed Tynan's attitude to society as an 'opinion monger, observer of artistic phenomena, [and] amateur ideologue' (Kenneth Tynan 1967: vii) affect his recording of the theatrical experience of watching a Shakespeare production? I will argue that the heroic theatre of the individual and the anti-heroic, social theatre were not consecutive, but simultaneous desires for Tynan, and this tension clustered around a series of figures, the most important of whom were Brecht, Shakespeare and Laurence Olivier, the man 'on whom our whole tradition of heroic acting rests' (109). Tynan's relationship to one play, *Macbeth*, is analysed for its degree of continuity with or independence from the tradition of *Macbeth* reception described in the second chapter of this book. I also examine how the heroic atavistic idea of Shakespeare and Shakespearean acting in Tynan's writing changed under the influence of anti-heroic trends in modern theatre, focusing on the disjunctive moments in his work when he was torn between contradictory and mutually exclusive constructions of Shakespeare. But I begin with the Infant Phenomenon who so dazzled the dying James Agate.

He That Plays the King: enter Tynan, stage right

He That Plays the King, a collection of undergraduate reviews and essays, was published in 1950 when its author was 23: a precocious entry into theatrical criticism reminiscent of the 21-year-old William Archer's co-authorship with Lowe of *The Fashionable Tragedian*. The book is full of bold, aphoristic pronouncements and extensive, cosmopolitan reading worn less than lightly. It could be described as a *jeu d'esprit* if so much of the content did not morbidly dwell on the nobility of stoicism and the centrality of death to great literature. The book's main theme, however – the strand that endows it with 'a kind of gothic unity' according to Tynan (1950: 17) – is heroism and hero-worship. From beginning to end, it is predicated on the great individual.

Tynan's response to Agate, as his most illustrious forerunner, was suitably ambivalent – one might, recalling the pen names they used in their correspondence, remember that it is Hamlet's fate to kill Polonius. In 1950, three years after Agate's death, Tynan offered a tribute that began by describing the distance between their styles and attitudes to drama but also allowed for identification and sympathy, the overall tone balancing satire and homage. As part of a general survey of the state of dramatic criticism, Tynan executed a series of parodies of the incumbent national reviewers. Like Max Beerbohm in the 1890s, Tynan projected his talent through mimicry and impersonation. His pastiche captured Agate's frequent tone of lively and exclamatory bluster and his addiction to quotation:

> Let it be said at the outset that this little play is, as Mr. Gimpish said in that other novel Dickens ought to have written, 'a ruddy Brave Try, my bucko!' Which means (or ought to mean) that parts of it are possibly good, and other parts impossibly bad. Which makes nonsense! Now the older critics had a word for this sort of thing. The word is (or was) 'Patchiness'. Whereat I turn up my Walkley, and what do I find? (Kenneth Tynan 1950: 29)

'He was often rambling and often vulgar, and nearly always too emphatic' wrote Tynan (1950: 30), but on one key point Tynan aligned himself with his predecessor:

> He looked first for uniqueness, and always argued for the hierarchic principle of drama: for him plays were, or ought to be, pyramid-shaped, with one giant surmounting a horde of carefully grouped lesser men. It was not that he did not admire expert teamwork: it was just that he felt that the single virtuoso was rarer and therefore more to be prized. It is that feeling which we lack, and for want of which our criticism is languishing. (Kenneth Tynan 1950: 30)

Tynan (1950: 31) concluded his survey of dramatic criticism with an appeal to reinstate the 'single virtuoso' to the centre of reviewing: 'There is no critic alive who can suggest quite clearly the breadth of the chasm that parts great acting from good acting; the heroic actor is finding more and more that his treasures are swallowed up unnoticed and unrecorded. So: "What must the king do now? Must he submit?"' 'No critic alive' was brazen self-advertisement. Tynan's review shared the ethos and the organisational structure of a typical Agate Shakespearean review: pyramid-shaped and premised on the (highly traditional) image of the lead actors as rare giants, dwarfing anonymous supernumeraries. As he wrote in the Wolfit–Valk *Othello* review that had so impressed Agate:

> I think I perceive that other players flickered intermittently across that bare stage... Who they were, I have not the slightest notion. They lie *perdu*: an irrelevant flurry of colour and dim noise in the midst of which gigantic things were going forward. They it was, I think, who buzzed and rattled when the big gladiators fell fatigued. I should prefer to ignore them, thus dismissively. (Kenneth Tynan 1950: 84)

Throughout *He That Plays the King* the undergraduate presented himself as both saviour of and rightful heir to a tradition of theatre and theatre criticism that was widely perceived to be endangered by developments in performance practice. If the tradition of British reviewing over the previous two centuries had depended, as Wardle claims, on a symbiosis of Shakespeare, heroic acting and the gifted critic, Tynan could only reinvigorate that tradition by urging the centrality of the lead actor in the theatrical economy.

At this early stage, Tynan resembled Brecht's spectator of the dramatic theatre, that easily moved, febrile creature who responds to theatre with fatalistic identification: 'Yes, I have felt like that too – Just like me – It's only natural – It'll never change – The sufferings of this man appal me, because they are inescapable – That's great art; it all seems the most obvious thing in the world – I weep when they weep, I laugh when they laugh' (Brecht 1964: 71). ('Great art' in this account is predicated on transhistorical notions of human nature and artistic value, notions central to Agate's reviewing.) The 'human beings' who laughed, or more probably wept, in front of the young Tynan were almost invariably monarchs. As the title suggests, the actor who plays the Shakespearean king was welcomed as almost the sole object of Tynan's critical gaze at the opening of his career. On substantive issues, especially the yearning for heroic acting and a theatre of devastating bravura, Tynan's voice was hardly unique or distinctive at the time. W.A. Darlington, who was, as mentioned, a staunch defender of the actor's theatre, wrote in the late 1940s in a similar vein to the young Tynan:

> There are no giants to-day . . . the breed has died out. It died with the passing of the actor's theatre and the coming of the dramatist whose interest was in the ordinary doings of ordinary people as much as, or more than, with the passions of supermen. The giant's robe still lies where Irving let it fall. (Darlington 1960: 235)

This appeal to breeding sounds throughout early Tynan. Having stated that 'the history of theatre is a chronicle of kings not republics' (Kenneth Tynan 1950: 30), he devoted the second and longest chapter of his book to the description of the 'titanic performances' between 1944 and 1948, 'which made us a little ashamed of our glad acceptance of democratic values' (32). Already in his criticism there was an interplay between the politics of acting and the politics of society, here with the emphasis firmly on a high Tory view of each. The entire theatrical experience is predicated on the outstanding individual, the exception not the rule. This preference had a formative effect on Tynan's attitude to genre. Comedy as a genre in most ways antagonistic to heroism and productive of social reintegration could play little or no part in Tynan's aesthetic scheme, and a strong bias towards tragedy and history emerged in his reviewing and commemorative habits. Shakespeare's original audience, for example, was depicted in Tynan's own image as solely interested in the vicissitudes of monarchs: 'the only symbol to remain in Europe to-day of the old, tougher aristocratic heroism is the *matador*: under his power the same crowds are mesmerized who were first drawn to watch the exploits and deaths of Shakespeare's kings' (Kenneth Tynan 1950: 238). Elsewhere, writing of Anthony Quayle's qualities as a director, Tynan noted that 'comedy is his forte, and the very greatest directors are never quite at home in comedy' (146). While this claim is far from self-evident, it is certainly true of Tynan that he was more memorably 'at home' writing about tragedy than comedy. In this he would appear to have consciously aligned himself with the predominant trend of Shakespearean theatrical criticism.[1]

A final feature of *He That Plays the King* relevant to the genesis of Tynan's relationship to Shakespeare is the young critic's attitude to actors and the art of acting. Of the 'dozen best performances' (Kenneth Tynan 1950: 137) he saw between 1944 and 1948, all were by male actors, seven were Shakespearean, and six were given by Frederick Valk and Laurence Olivier. While Tynan was so impressed with Valk's anti-poetic, highly physical performance of Othello in 1946 that he claimed never to want to see another performance of the part, pride of place in the young critic's heroic pantheon was reserved for Olivier: 'The one unquestionably heroic thing in English drama to-day is the sound of Laurence Olivier's voice' (250). There was 'no dramatist alive who could write a line worthy of the noble ferocity, the almost muscular fury of this actor's best cadences' (250). Tynan's verdict that Olivier's voice in his film of *Henry V* made it 'momentarily impossible to be cynical about patriotism' was a first indication of an attitude that would recur throughout Tynan's criticism, in which Olivier's muscularity would overwhelm any political convictions Tynan might otherwise have cherished.[2]

'When comes there such another?' Tynan, Olivier and Macbeth

Tynan's critical relationship with *Macbeth* began in 1947, when the 20-year-old saw Michael Redgrave in the part at the Aldwych. A page of *He That Plays the King* is devoted to a review that criticised the production's use of six witches, passed swiftly over Ena Burrill's Lady Macbeth, commented that Redgrave 'did all that lungs of leather and power of movement could do for Macbeth, but it was not enough', then concluded by panning out to offer the first of a line of criticisms of Shakespeare's play:

> There is no death-scene, and as we have said, Mr. Redgrave is especially good at death-scenes. *Macbeth* has never been the most effective of Shakespeare's plays in our theatres; nobody is remembered for having played it; and it fails, in the last analysis, as a tragedy for this very reason – that tragic heroes do not die offstage in battle. (Kenneth Tynan 1950: 81)

Clearly this criticism is informed by Tynan's taste throughout the book for the theatre as the arena of the heroic and spine-tingling demise. His personal fascination with ritualised death, which would soon find some relief in the bullrings of Spain, is here frustrated by Macbeth's off-stage slaughter, a vanishing that cheats the critic of a virtuoso moment of display and the opportunity to compete with Hazlitt on the death of Kean's Richard III, or indeed Hazlitt on the *in extremis* vein-swelling and convulsive hand motions of Kean's Othello (see p. 1 above).

In 1952 Tynan reviewed two further *Macbeth*s, experiences that substantiated his aversion to the play. The disappointment generated by the first of these – Ralph Richardson directed by John Gielgud – was widespread. Gielgud had surrounded the play with settings of total black 'which is about as subtle as setting Saint Joan in total white' (Kenneth Tynan 1961a: 24). But equally at fault was Richardson, 'the glass eye in the forehead of English acting', whose Macbeth, rather than exhibiting manly courage, struck Tynan as nothing more than 'a sad facsimile of the Cowardly Lion in *The Wizard of Oz*' (25) – again the spectre of cowardice haunted the Macbeth actor. The second *Macbeth* Tynan saw in 1952 was that of Bernard Miles at the Mermaid, in which the text was spoken entirely in what the director believed to be seventeenth-century English pronunciation, and which for Tynan had the result that 'Shakespeare's weaknesses [were] paraded with new and quite unexpected clarity' (29). Exactly what these weaknesses were Tynan did not divulge in any detail, but he returned to a key motif first sounded in *He That Plays the King*:

> I realised for the first time why Shakespeare had not bothered to provide death scenes for either Macbeth or his lady. He gave one to each of his other heroes; but in the fate of the Macbeths, he must have decided, there was nothing to regret. I believe he had simply stopped liking them. And so, at the Mermaid, did I. (Kenneth Tynan 1961a: 29)

Macbeth fails in the theatre because Shakespeare has made his protagonist a substandard hero. The critic's disappointment is not due to the lead actor's failure to reach some near-inaccessible pinnacle of representation. Miles's Macbeth, whether intentionally simple and anti-romantic or not, actually impressed Tynan; strutting about like a prize rooster, rarely rising above the spiritual level of the thugs he employed, Miles was described as 'gaudy and ostentatious', 'all of which [is] absolutely faithful to the play' (Kenneth Tynan 1961a: 29). Tynan's disappointment was rather with a Shakespeare whom he imagined, in one of his own self-images, as an unprofessional dilettante, bored with his own creations.

Michael Benthall's production at the Old Vic in 1954 did nothing to cure Tynan of his dissatisfaction with *Macbeth*. Playing second fiddle in the review space to some opening paragraphs on a *Hedda Gabler*, the *Macbeth* review cursorily mentioned the few adequate performances of the evening. Then, sparing Paul Rogers the scorn he had lavished on previous Macbeths, Tynan (1961a: 78) merely damned with faint praise: 'The part needs lungs plus genius; Mr. Rogers does all that lungs can'; like many Macbeths before him, Rogers was seen to be 'at his best in the last act, [which] he plays all out for wild white hair and bellicose ecstasy'.

As if in answer to Tynan's prayer for 'lungs plus genius', Olivier played Macbeth a year later at Stratford, and this marked a decisive turning-point in Tynan's relationship to the play. The context of the production is important. In 1954 Anthony Quayle had initiated what he hoped would be a three-year plan to develop a young troupe of unknown actors into a strong, cohesive repertory company at the Memorial Theatre. The proto-democratic Stratford season of 1954 suffered poor attendance and a luke-warm critical response, prompting Quayle to complain, 'all the press are interested in are stars' (quoted in Holden 1988: 288). Responding to market forces, the management lured Olivier and Leigh to Stratford for the following season. The enormous public reaction – half a million applications for only 80,000 seats before the box office had even opened – seemed immediately to justify the move. Following an adequate *Twelfth Night*, the season was still artistically, if not financially, on trial when Glen Byam Shaw's *Macbeth* opened. Olivier's performance was unanimously praised, many pronouncing his the best Macbeth in living memory. Tynan for the first and last time in his career enjoyed a production of the Scottish play. This was a performance he had anticipated for some time. In his first article for the *Daily Sketch* in October 1953, Tynan (1953: 4) had found the week's theatre so tedious that he chose to review 'instead of the things I saw, the things I would *like* to have seen'. At the top of his list was the desire to see:

> Laurence Olivier summoning up all his powers and having a giant stab at 'Macbeth,' which he first played in 1937 and is now ripe to play again. Since the tremendous Old Vic seasons just after the war, when he seized English acting by the scruff of its neck and brandished it aloft in sight of all the

world, he has dawdled disturbingly, and given us only one stage performance in the rough, grand manner he inherited from Edmund Kean. (Kenneth Tynan 1953: 4)

When Olivier answered Tynan's call and had his second stab at Macbeth, Tynan was impressed not only by the originality per se of Olivier's reading, but also by the fact that the interpretation somehow ran against the grain of the play as Shakespeare wrote it. The review began: 'Nobody has ever succeeded as Macbeth, and the reason is not far to seek. Instead of growing as the play proceeds, the hero shrinks; complex and many-levelled to begin with, he ends up a cornered thug, lacking even a death scene with which to regain lost stature' (Kenneth Tynan 1961a: 98). (The complaint about the death scene manqué is now familiar.) Tynan further argued that most actors who play the part are aware of this diminution of complexity and power and therefore peak pretty quickly, 'and have usually shot their bolt by the time the dagger speech is out'. Olivier 'reverses this procedure, turns the play inside out, and makes it (for the first time I can remember) a thing of mounting, not waning, excitement' (98). That Olivier, in Tynan's sexually suggestive language, does not shoot his bolt prematurely and makes the play's trajectory one of rising excitement is a tribute to the actor's virility. A great Shakespearean performance is usually praised in terms of the actor having done rare justice to the scope and magnitude of Shakespeare's creation. Here it was a case of Shakespeare not doing justice to the magnitude of Olivier's creation; on the battlements towards the end of the play, Olivier's 'throttled fury switches into top gear ... his voice rising like hair on the crest of a trapped animal. "Exeunt, fighting" was a poor end for such a giant warrior. We wanted to see how he would die; and it was not he but Shakespeare who let us down' (99). If Olivier's performance was one of 'mounting' excitement, Tynan felt robbed of the climax, and one does not have to strain too hard to hear the Elizabethan double sense in Tynan's wish to see how Olivier's Macbeth would 'die'. Tynan's writing switches gears as he instinctively prepares to rise to the challenge of the Hazlittean death description. 'Exeunt, fighting' is a poor end for the critic as much as the actor.

It should come as no surprise that Tynan was thinking about sex when he watched Olivier and Leigh in *Macbeth*. His writing on Olivier frequently cast the critic as ravished spectator, wooed, exhilarated and exhausted by the actor's overwhelming assault. 'Most plays follow the pattern of the sexual act', Tynan wrote in 1960, in an attempt to explain what made the arm's-length detachment of Brecht's *Life of Galileo* so distinctive:

> [Most plays] begin evenly, work up to a climax of emotion, and then subside; and the actor's job is to make the audience feel exactly what the characters on stage are feeling. Acting thus becomes a form of love-making, and is accounted successful when the spectator proclaims himself (or herself) ravished, overwhelmed or taken by storm. In costume pieces, the wooing tends to be noisier and more importunate, and if the period is the Renaissance, it is likely to border vociferously on rape. (Kenneth Tynan 1967: 23)

When Tynan watched bull-fighting – 'a rite in which, on a good day, heroism and beauty, the great absentees of Western Europe, may be seen happily and inextricably embraced' (Kenneth Tynan 1966: 92) – he instinctively reached for Olivier to explain the somatic thrill of witnessing an electrifyingly close pass, a *dosantina*, executed by Emilio Ortuño 'Jumillano':

> *Valse melancolique et langoureux vertige*; the solemn rhythm of the pass sent Baudelaire's line surging into the mouth, and the body surging up from its seat. Jumillano was now keyed up for adventure, and the rest of his faena was the purest war-poetry, a bodying forth of the emotion contained in Olivier's delivery of 'Once more unto the breach . . . ' (Kenneth Tynan 1966: 82)

At the inevitable death of the bull 'we stood and sobbed' (Kenneth Tynan 1966: 82).

The interpersonal relationships between Olivier, Leigh and Tynan are doubtless relevant to Tynan's review of *Macbeth*, not least perhaps the surreal weekend that he and his first wife, Elaine Dundy, spent at the Oliviers' country mansion, Notley Abbey. Tynan, writing in a 1973 diary entry, dated the weekend 'in *c*.1955' – the year of *Macbeth* and *Titus* – but both Dundy and Kathleen Tynan place the visit some time in 1958. Tynan remembered being surprised by the invitation to stay, since 'I had written some pretty devastating things about Vivien, which Larry had deeply resented', which might refer to the *Macbeth* review, or to any one or all of the acidic notices he had previously given Leigh in performances such as her Blanche du Bois, or Lavinia, or Cleopatra. Tynan described the psychic pressure of the Oliviers' domestic life in terms of Olivier's stoic endurance of his wife's baiting: 'Vivien's manner with L[arry] is haughty and derisive: how can he bear it? But he does, bearlike staying the course' (Kenneth Tynan 2001: 133). The uncharacteristically clumsy repetition hints that Tynan saw the analogy with Macbeth – tied to the stake and who 'bear-like . . . must fight the course' (5.7.1–2) – as significant. Olivier was a latecomer to the party and had missed an eventful afternoon. Siestas followed a heavily alcoholic lunch, and no sooner had Tynan fallen asleep in a single bed than he became aware of his sheet being peeled back and a hand placed on his genitals: 'It was Vivien, naked under a *peignoir*. I began to respond and then suddenly thought how impossible it would be to cuckold a man I venerated under his own roof – a really cock-crinkling thought' (133).

There may be no other moment in the long and eventful history of Shakespearean reviewing in which the critic – the eunuch in the harem – faced the piquant dilemma of whether or not to cuckold Macbeth. Dundy makes no mention of Leigh's attempted seduction of Tynan, or of what Tynan described as the women's subsequent sleepy embrace, which is odd, given her pains elsewhere to stress her glamorous intimacy with Leigh. Perhaps this was a tale Tynan reserved for other men; Irving Wardle – Tynan's second string on the *Observer* in the early 1960s – remembers Tynan recycling the story as homosocial banter: 'when we met in the local pub he was very direct and friendly. At the same time sort of bubbling over with show business stories about Vivien Leigh in some terrible state, and her clasping her hands on his cock' (Shellard 2003: 176).

According to Olivier, Tynan always 'felt Vivien was an interloper between myself and my fucking genius' (Kathleen Tynan 1987: 119). To return to the 1955 *Macbeth*, it should therefore come as no surprise that Tynan devoted very little space to Vivien Leigh's Lady Macbeth, a performance he described, callously, as 'quite competent in its small way'. In the 1953 *Daily Sketch* article in which he had claimed Olivier 'owes us a Macbeth', he had added that Olivier also owed 'it to himself to hunt out a more challenging Lady Macbeth than his charming wife' (Kenneth Tynan 1953: 4). But it is questionable how much Tynan really wanted Olivier's on-stage authority to be challenged. Juliet Dusinberre (1996: 60) has argued that Tynan's negative response to the 1951 Olivier–Leigh repertory pairing of *Antony and Cleopatra* and Shaw's *Caesar and Cleopatra* was fuelled by an anxiety that 'a great male actor' was throwing his career away on a 'pert little miss'. Tynan, according to Dusinberre, wanted Antony–Olivier 'to be more of a hero; in the theatrical competition between the two stars he believed that Antony must win' (59). Tynan wrote that, throughout Shaw's play, Leigh kept 'a firm grip on the narrow ledge which is indisputably hers; the level on which she can be pert, sly, and spankable, and fill out a small personality' (Kenneth Tynan 1961a: 9). 'Spankable' was not a disinterested compliment from Tynan, and all might have been well had Olivier taken advantage of this submissiveness and dominated the stage. Tynan would no doubt have preferred the Olivier of the Old Vic pre-war *Coriolanus*, an actor who, in his own words, had 'quite a lot of spunk and guts in the way I marched on to the stage' (Burton 1967: 21). But Olivier failed to be 'more manlike / Than [his] Cleopatra' (1.4.5–6), and Tynan (1961a: 10) saw a potentially great actor neutered by infatuation: 'Sir Laurence, with that curious chivalry which some time or other blights the progress of every great actor, gives me the impression that he subdues his blow-lamp ebullience to match her. Blunting his iron precision, levelling away his towering authority, he meets her halfway.' In a reversal of the play's fourth-act hydraulics, 'Antony climbs down; and Cleopatra pats him on the head' (10).

Shakespeare thwarted Tynan's desire for Olivier to dominate *Antony and Cleopatra* by exclusively devoting his fifth act to the female protagonist. In *Macbeth*, of course, the situation is almost reversed: Lady Macbeth is last conscious in 3.4 and makes her final appearance in 5.1. However powerfully her somnambulism is performed, the rest of the fifth act belongs to the actor of Macbeth. Tom Stoppard said of Tynan at his funeral that 'his paragraphs – paragraphs were the units of his prose, not sentences – were written to outlast the witness' (Kathleen Tynan 1987: 405). Tynan's review of *Macbeth* ran for five paragraphs, four of which were dominated by Olivier's performance. Leigh was granted twenty-one words at the opening of the last paragraph. While suddenly appearing, Mercadé-like, in the fifth act of a play can be powerful, its *mise-en-page* equivalent is not generally an auspicious space in which to find oneself as an actor. Tynan also barely mentioned either the settings or Shaw's direction: this was a piece of high heroic acting by the rightful heir of Edmund Kean, and Tynan's witness-outliving paragraphs spoke only of one man's achievement.

Reviewing Donald McWhinnie's 1962 production with Eric Porter in the title role, Tynan offered his most detailed critique of Shakespeare's play, a play that he could not conceive of as artistically successful without Olivier. Tynan (1967: 115) began with the *ubi sunt*, 'Seven years have passed since Olivier annexed the part and left us marvelling: When comes there such another?'. The choice of the verb 'annex', like the notion of Olivier turning the play inside out, was Tynan's way of paying tribute to the virility of Olivier's personality, the quality of self-imposing he admired in so many of his idols. Tynan continued:

> Without him, the play's faults obtrude – its narrative monotony, once Banquo is dead; its summary abandonment, halfway through the evening, of the relationship between Macbeth and his wife, who never meet after the banquet, and the near-sameness of its major supporting characters. Here, if anywhere, in the upper reaches of dramatic literature, is a play in desperate need of a sub-plot. (Kenneth Tynan 1967: 115–16)

Tynan would try to remedy many of these problems when he acted as co-screenwriter with Roman Polanski on his 1970 film of *Macbeth*; thanks to the nature of the medium, Tynan at last had the pleasure of seeing Macbeth die 'on stage'. Ultimately, however, the heroic trajectory could only be provided by Olivier's annexation of the part. But over the next decade Tynan's attachment to Olivier's Shakespearean annexations would come to appear increasingly anachronistic when contrasted with other, self-consciously contemporary approaches to staging classic texts.

Re-enter Tynan, stage left: anti-heroic Shakespeare and the possibility of radicalism

From the outset of his professional career Tynan was in the vanguard of the movement against plays set in an area he baptised 'Loamshire', a mythical county in which living standards were high and conversation trivial, and in which most playwrights chose to set their West End plays. There was a world elsewhere. Across the Atlantic, Miller was writing Ibsenite tragedies of the little man, relatively unheard of in England (the Lord Chamberlain's ban on *A View from the Bridge* on the grounds of homosexual content aided and abetted this ignorance); and, in East Berlin, Brecht had since 1949 made social relevance the credo of his unofficial national theatre. At the same time that Tynan was lauding Olivier's Shakespearean heroism, other cross-currents were bringing him to an awareness of a social theatre distrustful of heroism and the cult of the individual.

The first clear sign of a shift in attitude towards Shakespeare can be found in two reviews written in 1955. In the same year that Olivier overwhelmed Tynan with his Macbeth and Titus, the critic elsewhere found evidence for the modernity and potential radicalism of Shakespeare. Tynan's review of Douglas Seale's productions of the *Henry IV* plays is one of the most remarkable – and contradictory – of his responses to Shakespeare. It begins:

> I suspected it at Stratford four years ago, and now I am sure: for me the two parts of *Henry IV* are the twin summits of Shakespeare's achievement. Lime-hungry actors have led us always to the tragedies, where a single soul is spotlit and its agony explored; but these private torments dwindle beside the Henries, great public plays in which a whole nation is under scrutiny and on trial. (Kenneth Tynan 1961a: 93–4)

Here is the first and most explicit rejection of what Shakespeare had meant to Tynan as a younger critic. Contrasts are made between private and public, the individual and the social, and, by implication, between an actor-manager's and a director's theatre, and, for the first time, the latter half of each dichotomy is privileged. In one evening Tynan appears to make the leap from being a dramatic to an epic spectator; what he admires is the finely balanced argument of the plays, the fact that there is no 'true villain... on whom complacent audiences can fix their righteous indignation. Hotspur is on the wrong side, yet he is a hero; Prince John is on the right one, yet his cynical perfidy at the disarmament conference would have astonished Hitler' (Kenneth Tynan 1961a: 94). Not only is the spectator forced into an active engagement with the debate, but the debate, through that anachronistic phrase 'disarmament conference' and the invocation of Hitler, is given the urgency of recent and current history. Shakespeare as the playwright of a society, rather than of the romantic individualist, develops, in Tynan's review, a heavy Brechtian inflection; he becomes a playwright interested in a dramatic consideration of the way people ought to live, rather than the way some men ought to die, more the activist than the fatalist: 'More than anything else in our drama they deserve the name of epic. A way of life is facing dissolution; we are in at the deathbed of the Middle Ages. How shall the crisis be faced?' (94). Furthermore, the style of presentation has complemented the democratic even-handedness of the play's exploration of this crisis: 'the Old Vic company, which lacks star quality, exactly fits a pair of plays which lack star parts'. In the same season that Olivier's success dealt the final blow to Quayle's plans for a starless company at Stratford, Tynan praised a Shakespearean production at the Old Vic precisely because it had no Oliviers. Tynan concluded by commending Seale for putting Shakespearean production 'on the right realistic track' (95).

In the same year, Tynan saw Joan Littlewood's production of *Mother Courage*, a piece that, like *Henry IV*, places one uncomfortably at the death bed of the Middle Ages. Having described Brecht's play as 'a chronicle play about warfare in which warfare scarcely appears' (Kenneth Tynan 1961a: 99), he reached for a Shakespearean point of reference that would throw Brecht's bracing anti-heroism into relief: 'It is *Henry V* without the dear friends and the breach and the nonsense about not wishing one man more' (99). Tynan had an ambivalent relationship to the most potentially heroic of the history plays and could only really swallow its appeal to nationalism if that invitation was issued by Olivier; without Olivier, Harry is merely a 'butcher and a sophist' (113). However, *Henry V* without the dear friends, etc., begins more closely to resemble *Henry IV, 1* and *2*, and indeed those now favourite plays were invoked in a further comparison between Brecht and Shakespeare, and one that again allowed for similarity more than difference. Tynan commended Brecht for presenting his audience not with a downtrodden peasant oppressed by fascists, but rather with a:

> bawdy cynic who can barely recall the names of the men who sired her children. Her code of honour is Falstaff's, and her moral code Doll Tearsheet's. She is in the war for what she can make out of it; and in return the war robs her of her children, the very reasons for her avarice. (Kenneth Tynan 1961a: 100)

Lurking behind this comparison is a line of descent from Falstaff's callously realistic view of recruitment, via Farquhar's *The Recruiting Officer*, to Brecht's adaptation of that play, *Trumpets and Drums*, a production of which the Berliner Ensemble brought on their first trip to London in 1956.

Tynan's writing throughout 1956 displayed a growing awareness of how Shakespeare and modern dramatic trends might cross-fertilise to produce a contemporary Shakespeare. In that year he saw the Berliner Ensemble perform *The Caucasian Chalk Circle* at the Paris Drama Festival:

> If I was unmoved by what Brecht had to say, I was overwhelmed by the way in which he said it... In the British theatre everything is sacrificed to obtain sympathy for the leading characters. *Chez* Brecht, sympathy is nowhere; everything is sacrificed for clarity of narrative. No time is wasted on emotional climaxes. (Kenneth Tynan 1961a: 390)

At the end of the review, Tynan (1961a: 390) offered the warning that unless the British theatre assimilated the work of the Berliner Ensemble in the near future, 'the ideal way of staging *Henry IV*, *Tamburlaine* and *Peer Gynt*, and a hundred plays yet unwritten will have been ignored'. On a trip to Moscow he was impressed by the apparently egalitarian and democratic nature of Russian theatre companies:

> I made the childish error of asking an actor to name the star of his company, and my interpreter gently signified to me that the concept of a 'star' was something his language was barely capable of rendering. Outside Russian theatres the names of the plays are billed, but never the names of the actors. (Kenneth Tynan 1964: 266)

A shift of emphasis from heroic to collective drama was also central to Tynan's essay 'Social Drama', in which he aligned himself with Arthur Miller in deploring the cult of the individual in drama, a stark volte-face, considering his early critical tenets. With his newly held conviction that public drama was more important than the tragedy of the individual, Tynan (1961a: 123) could now identify which parts of Shakespeare were intrinsically unradical: 'The first English play to set up personal fulfilment as a tragic ideal happened, unfortunately, to be a masterpiece: *Hamlet*.' Tragedy, far from being the stoic decline of the magnificent exception that it was in *He That Plays the King* and throughout Tynan's reviews of *Macbeth*, was now measured against the more recent template set down by Miller, the tragedy of the representative, sociologically identifiable type written by the socially committed dramatist: 'I shall continue to applaud all plays that are honestly frivolous, devoutly disengaged; but I shall reserve my cheers for the play in which man among men, not man against men, is the well-spring of tragedy' (124). That is, for *Death of a Salesman*, not *Coriolanus*.

Bearing in mind Tynan's call in the mid 1950s for a more Brechtian approach to the classics and a more egalitarian definition of tragedy, it is instructive to analyse his responses to productions that attempted to create a dialogue between classical texts and modern political engagement. For example, three years after describing the presentational style of the Berliner Ensemble as 'the ideal way of staging *Henry IV*', Tynan saw Roger Planchon's Brechtian-inspired conflation at the *Théâtre de la Cité de Villeurbanne*. Tynan (1961a: 418) described how the plays were 'boiled down to the bare social bones; each point was made, coolly and pungently, on a rostrum backed by a map of medieval England... Individual characterisation was subjected to the larger image of declining feudalism.' Despite this textbook application of 'the ideal way of staging' the play, Tynan was notably reserved in his judgement. Whereas his review of Seale's *Henry IV* in 1955 had argued that the depiction of 'declining feudalism' and momentous social change were part of Shakespeare's achievement, here the socialist emphasis of the production was evaluated in terms of reduction rather than fidelity: 'The result was not Shakespeare; it was abundance reduced to relevance, riches cut down to a living wage, a jungle turned into a cartographical survey' (418). The anti-heroic is most easily spatially imagined as reduction, a cutting down to size, yet his summary clearly showed that, for Tynan, that reduction and relevance were 'not Shakespeare'. It is also clear from the generally neutral, if approving, tone of Tynan's review that the production failed to excite him.

Tynan's response to a socialised Shakespeare was most indicative and revealing at the moment in his writing when Brecht and Shakespeare came directly into contact, in his review of the Berliner Ensemble's production of *Coriolanus* in 1964. Tynan (1967: 161) describes the historically accurate 'tribal, barbaric', setting, the detailed characterisation of the plebeians, the stylised Chinese operatic fighting, the finely nuanced political content, and concludes that until Coriolanus' banishment the production 'is a masterpiece: politics and theatre exquisitely wedded'. From then on, however, 'Shakespeare lets Brecht down by stressing personal relationships (e.g., Coriolanus and Volumnia) in a way that goes against the Brechtian grain' (161). Yet, in a revealing penultimate paragraph, Tynan wrote of Brecht's decision to underplay the importance of private emotions:

> Thus Brecht makes his point: that the play's theme is the downfall of 'the individual who blackmails society with his indispensability.' But Shakespeare's play, no matter how you revamp it . . . is the work of a man who genuinely believed that heroes *were* indispensable. Brecht's anti-hero is historically convincing; but after the banishment, stripped as he is of emotional complexities, he becomes theatrically uninteresting, if not redundant. (Kenneth Tynan 1967: 162)

Anti-heroism may be historically convincing, intellectually appealing in its leftishness, but Tynan failed to find it theatrically interesting. To compare his review of Brecht's *Coriolanus* with his description of Olivier in the part in 1959 is to be struck by the difference between a critic's intellect and his instinct. The review begins 'we will skim over the inessentials of the Stratford *Coriolanus* as quickly as possible' (Kenneth Tynan 1961a: 239–40). These inessentials included: the sets, Peter Hall's direction, and the performances of Edith Evans as Volumnia and Harry Andrews as Menenius. The remaining space (over 80 per cent of the review) was devoted 'to the heart of the production, which is Olivier's performance as Coriolanus'. In Tynan's account – to paraphrase Martius on his fluttering of the Volscian dovecote – alone Olivier did it. The extent of Tynan's description of Brecht's Coriolanus, Ekkehard Schall, was that he was 'a stubby, crew-cut figure'; the anti-heroic performance was intrinsically less eye-catching, less conducive to description. Olivier's performance, in contrast, demanded Tynan's memorialising pen. Olivier, 'the nonpareil of heroic tragedians', alternately chilled and scorched Tynan's sensibility, and provided him with the sense of an ending Brecht's would frustrate. Dangling, held by his ankles 12 feet above the stage, Olivier gifted Tynan with the beautiful, unsentimental heroic death he always demanded of Shakespeare's tragic protagonists.

Despite his intermittent advocacy of a Shakespeare who is our and Brecht's contemporary, Tynan consistently, not least in his review of Brecht's *Coriolanus*, remained sceptical of the theatrical effectiveness or the fidelity of radical Shakespeare. Unable still to believe wholeheartedly in a Shakespeare for whom heroism was a dispensable or even questionable commodity, Tynan reserved his most ecstatic, hyperbolic praise for a manifestation of Shakespeare that appeared to transcend history or social relevance:

> The dark imprint of Olivier's stage presence is something one forgets only with an effort, but the voice is a lifelong possession of those who have heard it at its best. It sounds, distinct and barbaric, across the valley of the many centuries, like a horn calling to the hunt, or the neigh of a battle-maddened charger. (Kenneth Tynan 1961a: 241)

As a young man, Tynan had written of Olivier's voice as the only unarguably heroic thing on the English stage. Many years later it was indeed proving to be 'a lifelong possession', a vocal reminder of the tougher aristocratic heroism of theatrical tradition.

Conclusion: Roundheads and Cavaliers

In June 1973, Tynan made the trip to Stratford-upon-Avon to see John Barton's production of *Richard II*. As his diary entry records, Tynan (2001: 139) was unenchanted: 'It is bloodless, with the curiously pedantic flamboyance for which this company is nowadays praised. The RSC (a director's theatre) has not discovered one star actor in the twelve years since it was founded. When you lack actors, you need "interpretation" – to supply the bloodstream that is missing.' In the same month, Tynan saw Patrick Garland's production of *Twelfth Night* in the gardens of Worcester College, Oxford. He found it 'the most joyful and moving Shakespearian occasion I've attended for years: real Cavalier stuff after the Roundhead aridities of Stratford, totally unafraid of such unmodish qualities as emotional impact and – worst of all – charm' (144). Tynan (199) elsewhere referred to himself as 'a Roundhead in politics but a Cavalier by temperament', and this nicely captures the champagne-socialist ambivalence in his career as newspaper reviewer. But, more generally, the Roundhead–Cavalier distinction offers a useful metaphor for the changes in Shakespearean theatre to which Agate and Tynan responded.

W.A. Darlington saw the four decades between 1920 and 1960, when nearly all of Agate's and Tynan's theatre criticism was written, as witnessing 'the decline and return to grace of the actor' (Darlington 1960: 9). This 'theatrical revolution', like the English Civil War, deposed the king and sought to replace his privilege with a greater concern with 'the ordinary doings of ordinary people' (235). But, as Tynan (1950: 30) wrote in the late 1940s, 'the history of theatre is a chronicle of kings not republics'. In Agate's reviews of Shakespeare and his early modern contemporaries, one sees a strong resistance to the Roundheads who threatened the sovereignty of the actor, whether that threat came from the 'modish' designer, the 'team-actor', the producer, or the very idea of 'production'. This he combined with a highly allusive, quotational strategy that read contemporary performers against reviews of their antecedents, thus insistently foregrounding, despite the emergence of 'production', the primacy of the actor–critic relationship to the classical theatre tradition. When Tynan began his career as a critic, he approvingly cited Agate's 'hierarchic principle of drama' and enthusiastically agreed that the 'pyramid-shaped' production, 'with one giant surmounting a horde of carefully grouped lesser men' (30), should be defended. In his subsequent career, the tensions between Roundhead and Cavalier Shakespeare resurfaced recurrently, usually resolving in an ecstatic submission to Olivier's masculine and individualistic heroism.

After Olivier's Macbeth Tynan asked, 'When comes there such another?' As the following chapter shows, that question would in turn be asked in the 1990s by reviewers who were acutely aware of the absence of any comparably influential critic in the late twentieth-century reviewing community. Tynan's career began with the question of succession ('another Shaw?'). His posthumous reputation has equally prompted widespread reflection on questions of inheritance, surrogation and the status of the reviewer.

CHAPTER FIVE

New contexts, new crises (1997–2012)
Reviewing from the opening of Shakespeare's Globe to the World Shakespeare Festival 2012

In the summer of 2008 London's Tate Gallery ran an advertising campaign on the Underground transport system. Headlined 'Instant Critic', the poster hailed the male traveller, encouraging him to take a date to the Tate and impress her with his knowledge of the museum's layout and contents. No matter if the reader had never been to the Tate: everything he needed to know, including an itinerary and strategically smart comments, was spoon-fed to him in the text of the advert. Take her to this room first; point out that painting; don't say 'between', say 'juxtaposed with'. Thus, in the three minutes before his train arrived, the commuter could make of himself an 'Instant Critic', acquiring the cultural capital that might buy him love in this capital of culture. The implication was clear: art criticism, no less than artworks themselves, could be faked, and the only thing separating the stuck-up professional critic and the man on the Tube was a little *savoir faire* and a smattering of swanky vocabulary.

Everywhere one looked, at the opening of the twenty-first century, the authority of the professional arts reviewer was in crisis. Instant critics of every conceivable level of expertise populated the Internet to such an extent and with such apparent influence that American regional newspapers haemorrhaged arts reviewers. In the UK, even a quality daily national such as the *Independent* consistently muddied the once clear blue water between professional and amateur critic: many 'official' reviews were accompanied by vox-pop audience verdicts, and a regular feature – 'You Write the Review' – invited readers to do just that, filling valuable copy space that might have been occupied by professional opinion. As Rónán McDonald (2007: ix) argued in *The Death of the Critic*: 'The public critic has been dismembered by two opposing forces: the tendency of academic criticism to become increasingly inward-looking and non-evaluative, and the momentum for journalistic and popular criticism to become a much more democratic, dispersive affair, no longer left in the hands of the experts.' What hope for the review in an amnesiac culture that pushes compulsively forward and lives in a state of feverish, insatiable and almost permanent *pre*view? What hope for the past (even the very recent past) unless it can be commoditised as nostalgia and repackaged into profit? And what hope for the professional critic in the age of the celebrity reviewer, the quick-fire blogger and the citizen journalist?

In 1997 a number of theatre practitioners were asked what they thought should be 'the role of the critic in the overall theatre process'. Jonathan Kent, then artistic director of London's Almeida Theatre, responded that criticism was vital as 'a way of disseminating the news of the play', but that it should also 'in a purer sense . . . be a record of a crucial artistic strand of the nation' (Stefanova 2000: 123). In Kent's opinion, contemporary criticism had veered too far in the direction of mere punditry, had succumbed to a hit-or-miss mechanism that shirked the ethical imperative to analyse and memorialise the theatre, 'the repository of our national soul'. Kent concluded: 'Theatre criticism is going through some sort of a crisis now. But just as a nation is supposed to get the government it deserves, perhaps a theatre gets the criticism it deserves' (123).

This chapter discusses the new journalistic and cultural contexts in which criticism took place over the last two decades and the multiple crises – of belatedness, status, authority and authenticity – that have confronted the contemporary Shakespearean reviewer. The sample is vast, so I proceed by way of five case studies, each of which re-examines themes raised and arguments made in previous chapters. In the first three sections, I discuss the influence of Kenneth Tynan on the practice and psychology of contemporary criticism, before placing that criticism within the context of the journalistic revolutions of the late twentieth century. In discussing broad changes in newspaper production, ownership, cultural coverage and size, I link these material and social dynamics with the revised forms and function of Shakespearean reviewing. I then return to *Macbeth* as a touchstone of Shakespearean reception, and particularly to a spate of revivals in 1995–6 that afford a focused insight into the interpretive habits critics brought to Shakespearean performance. The day job of the Shakespearean newspaper critic changed with the first full season of productions at Shakespeare's Globe in 1997, and this chapter's longest sections analyse the critical reception of the Globe in the first six years of its existence as a working playhouse (1997–2003), focusing particularly on revealing patterns in the rhetorical presentation of the Globe audience and space. Then I examine some of the changes required and inspired by the advent of the Internet, not least the ability of the audience – so reviled in early Globe reviews – to contest the authority of the critic in 'comments' sections and other online fora. In the chapter's final section, I analyse the ways in which reviewers responded to the multiple forms of Shakespearean production presented around the UK in 2012 as part of the World Shakespeare Festival.

My aim throughout this chapter is to draw attention both to the continuities and discontinuities, the constants and the variables between past and present Shakespearean reviewing. A key interest is the role reviewers play as cultural intermediaries. Pierre Bourdieu argues that artists and public intellectuals in general are:

> divided between their interest in cultural proselytism, that is, winning a market by widening their audience, which inclines them to favour popularization, and concern for cultural distinction, the only objective basis for their rarity; and their relationship to everything concerned with the 'democratization of culture' is marked by a deep ambivalence which may be manifested in a dual discourse on the relations between the institutions of cultural diffusion and the public. (Bourdieu [1979] 1986: 229)

This dual discourse offers a useful model for analysing the cultural work of the Shakespearean reviewer at the turn of the twenty-first century. In defining and disseminating legitimate high culture within the context of the mass media, reviewers are pulled in opposite directions. On the one hand, critics face the imperative to popularise. This requires that they answer the need to address the readership, distance themselves from the minority/elite discourses of academia, and respect the commercial basis of the newspaper enterprise by avoiding any form of writing that might alienate the reader-customer. On the other hand, this principle of inclusion is counterbalanced, if not frequently outweighed, by the concern for cultural distinction, a concern exacerbated by the peculiar pressures attendant on Shakespearean reviewing. Recent Shakespearean reception has been consistently marked by the principle of exclusion, by the need to defend high culture from the perceived threats posed by an array of low cultural and foreign sources. The recent reviewing histories of Shakespeare's Globe, of *Macbeth* and of the World Shakespeare Festival are reminders both of the fraught, contested nature of Shakespearean authority, and of the enduring centrality of the night-watch constable to the debate about what Shakespeare, as embodied in performance, should be permitted to mean.

'When comes there such another?' Tynan and belatedness

'We come *after*, and that is the nerve of our condition' (Steiner 1967: 22)

In March 2002 the Soho Theatre, London, staged *Smoking with Lulu* by the Canadian playwright Janet Munsil. Sibelius advised fellow composer Bengt von Törne: 'Never pay any attention to what critics say. Remember, a statue has never been set up in honor of a critic!' (although he did not live to see two of Broadway's theatres renamed after the great critics Walter Kerr and Brooks Atkinson). But *Smoking with Lulu* offered a different, aptly transient tribute to a theatre reviewer. The play portrayed a series of meetings between the silent-film actress Louise Brooks (Lulu in *Pandora's Box*) and Kenneth Tynan as both neared the end of their lives. Tynan, his fascination with great, iconic individual performers seemingly compounded by faltering health – the play was originally entitled *Emphysema (A Love Story)* – had interviewed Brooks for a piece that would later appear in the *New Yorker* as 'The Girl in the Black Helmet'. The play's arrival in London was well timed: following the recent publication of his first wife Elaine Dundy's gossipy autobiography (*Life Itself!*) and Tynan's diaries in John Lahr's edition, Tynan had been the subject of more publicity and posthumous celebrity than at any other time since his death in 1980.

Smoking with Lulu was warmly received. Some reviewers quipped that, on this evidence, there should be more plays written about theatre critics. Reviewers had featured as characters in other postwar plays, most notably perhaps in Stoppard's *The Real Inspector Hound* (1968). But, as Charles Spencer wrote in the *Daily Telegraph*, *Smoking with Lulu* was 'the first play to put a real-life theatre critic centre-stage' (*TR* 2002: 191), and it offered a very different image of the reviewer from that of the eunuch in the harem: urbane, unerringly eloquent and tragically doomed, 'Ken' even enjoyed the unconditional sexual availability of the young and nubile 'Lulu'. Here, surely, was another dose of 'pure theatrical Viagra' – as Spencer notoriously wrote of Nicole Kidman's performance in *The Blue Room* – for the predominantly male critical audience (Spencer, *TR* 1998: 1234). Spencer was not alone in finding in Peter Eyre's performance as Tynan 'the almost unbearable melancholy of a fading star who knows that his best days are long gone' (*TR* 2002: 191). Gone but far from forgotten, as *Smoking with Lulu* would prove to be only the first in a spontaneous trilogy of dramas that resurrected and celebrated Tynan two decades after his death. 'It takes a rare actor to bring a dead theatre critic back to life' (de Jongh, *TR* 2004: 1361), but Corin Redgrave's beautifully judged one-man performance did just that in Richard Nelson's *Tynan* (2004), an adaptation of Tynan's diaries.

(Richard Nelson had also brought Forrest and Macready back from the dead as rival Macbeths in *Two Shakespearean Actors*.) A few months later, in March 2005, BBC Four screened *Kenneth Tynan: In Praise of Hardcore*, a 60-minute film chronicling the strange and difficult years in the 1960s in which Tynan served as literary manager at the National Theatre while also devoting increasing amounts of his energy to private and public erotic projects.

Tynan's reviews had frequently outperformed the productions that prompted them, and here he was, three times in the space of three years, the louche father of modern criticism, at last in his rightful place, on screen and centre stage. All three works focused on the years of decline, the last decade and a half in which the memory of brilliance had become painful. Pain was also registered in the critical reception. Michael Billington wrote that it was 'difficult to write objectively about a man who was, for me both icon and influence: I earned my first fee in journalism by parodying him in the Observer, and have been dimly indebted to him ever since' (Billington 2004). Similar acts of emulative impersonation heralded the arrivals on the critical scene of Max Beerbohm and of Tynan himself.

Billington was one of very many critics who had wanted to be Tynan, or at least to attempt to fill the vast gap left by his retirement from weekly theatre reviewing in 1963. Tynan haunts *Who Keeps the Score on the London Stages?*, a collection of interviews with critics and practitioners on the state of theatre reviewing conducted by Kalina Stefanova in 1997. Stefanova (2000: 209) identified what she called 'the Kenneth Tynan's shadow problem, that is the subconsciously preconceived awareness by critics of the impossibility of ever surpassing his talent for fiery, brilliant prose. It is as if, from the start of their careers, they know that they enter a competition with a foregone conclusion.' 'Subconsciously' is questionable, and it is striking that, when talking of Tynan's influence on their careers, contemporary theatre critics echoed the rhetoric and values of Tynan's own criticism. Just as Tynan clung tenaciously to an ideal of the heroic theatre, so his successors habitually discuss his influence in terms of heroism and idolatry. When Stefanova asked 'Who do you consider your mentor in theatre criticism?' Tynan's name was rarely absent from reviewers' responses. Michael Coveney replied: 'I'm of the age when Kenneth Tynan was the great inspiration. He made theatre so sexy and important, and he was a genuine intellectual. So he was my idol really' (28). Sheridan Morley agreed: 'He made many of us want to be critics. He was the first one to make the critic a star' (29), while Benedict Nightingale reinforced the portrait of an epoch-defining presence: 'at the time I started we were all under the influence of Kenneth Tynan who seemed to speak up for our generation. At school I used to take *The Observer* religiously' (29). (When told by a fan that she read him religiously, Tynan (1967: viii) retorted that he would prefer to be read agnostically.)

Tynan bequeathed an image of the critic as erotic, exotic and influential. By contrast, contemporary critics are painfully aware of their low profile on the British cultural landscape. Stefanova asked critics to respond to a claim that Tynan made in a letter to Harold Hobson: 'The problem with our successors is that there is hardly anything at stake for them' (Stefanova 2000: 67). While several reviewers argued that there was still plenty at stake, many respondents registered a feeling of belatedness. Echoing Jimmy Porter, Coveney argued 'now it's very difficult to work out what the great causes are. Tynan and Hobson had all the great battles – about the subsidized theatre, new work, foreign influence...' (68); Ian Shuttleworth agreed that 'we know now that we can't change the world, we know that we can't even change the face of the art in that kind of revolutionary way that Tynan and Hobson helped come into effect in the '50s. And we are a lot more resigned about that' (72). The father figure emerges in Coveney's comment: 'I suppose we're spoiled thanks to Hobson and Tynan, and their legacy. We should thank them because they kept the debate about theatre going so vociferously and that we are their children' (68). While the fathers are to be revered and thanked for their aggression and bravery in fighting the battles of the past, they have also plundered the prerogative of their offspring, leaving them with nothing to kick against. 'Every talent must unfold itself in fighting' (Nietzsche quoted in Bloom 1997: 52); with no obvious outlet for their aggression, contemporary critics are no more like their fathers than Hamlet is to Hercules.

Theatre criticism, no less than the art it captures, is haunted by nostalgia. A diachronic awareness of past achievement and contemporary inadequacy pervades the genre. This *ubi sunt* theme is everywhere apparent in responses to Tynan. When asked what he thought were the main strengths and weaknesses of current British theatre criticism, Charles Spencer replied: 'I don't think we've got a great critic at the moment. There isn't someone of the stature of Kenneth Tynan and we need someone like that. It would possibly raise all our standards because we would all be in competition with him' (Bloom 1997: 51–2) – the presence of a latter-day Tynan might galvanise the critical community into a spirit of rivalry more typical historically of the relations between actors and theatres. Irving Wardle identified a contemporary weakness in the absence of 'really good descriptions of acting':

> This is one of the central lines of British criticism going back to Tynan. It was the actors who rescued the English theatre from the grip of Aristotle. And reviewers were part of that process. They've repaid the debt, paying an awful lot of attention to actors ever since. But we aren't doing that to the same extent now. (Stefanova 2000: 52)

Nicholas de Jongh commented, 'it's very sad to say so but theatre critics in England today have a negligible function' (Stefanova 2000: 110), while Kate Bassett argued that 'Theatre is less front-page news now, so you might say there's less at stake . . . In some ways they had it easier – Kenneth Tynan and Co. If theatre criticism is no longer hot news, the theatre critic is dangerously dispensable' (68). Bassett's reference to the *mise-en-page* of theatre criticism serves as a useful reminder of the context of performance criticism. What has happened to newspapers and journalistic culture in the recent past to make reviewing a 'dangerously dispensable' activity?

Matters of size and status: reviewing and post-Fleet Street journalism

Since Tynan retired from his job on the *Observer* to become literary manager of the National Theatre in 1963, the British newspaper industry has undergone what can only be described as a revolution in size, content, demography and print technology. Many of these changes can be directly linked to the fact that, as Bob Franklin (1997: 88) states, 'newspaper circulations have shown a relentless downward trend during the post-war years, and in virtually all newspaper sectors', even within the tabloid market. This circulation crisis has a number of causes: the near-universal ownership of televisions; the proliferation of specialist or general interest magazines; the rise of the free newspaper; and, most spectacularly, the advent of the World Wide Web.

But before the Web there was Wapping. The 'Wapping revolution' of 25 January 1986, a triumph for the new technology and for anti-trades-unionism alike, initiated a period of British journalism in which workforces were downsized, start-up costs reduced, a number of new titles were launched onto the market and, perhaps more than ever before, competition for revenue trumped commitment to quality. 'It is rare in history to be able to identify the precise date of a turning point. In the case of the fall of Fleet Street, however, we can' (N. Davies 2008: 61). Although some new titles – like the *Independent* – proved resilient, many quickly folded in a volatile atmosphere of price wars and market congestion. The main success story of post-1980 journalism has been the tabloid, both as a format and as a publishing philosophy. Franklin (1997: 4) observes: 'Since the late 1980s the pressures on news media to win viewers and readers in an increasingly competitive market have generated revised editorial ambitions. News media have increasingly become part of the entertainment industry instead of providing a forum for informed debate of key issues of public concern.' Furthermore, the success of tabloid journalism has had a contagious and corrosive effect, as the broadsheets' derision of the tabloid format has turned to 'mimicry': 'Tabloid-style banner headlines, alliterative and "punny" headlines, large print, less text, shorter words, bigger pictures, colour pictures and more of them, have become standard components of the broadsheet front page' (7). In such a context, any news item, be it foreign or parliamentary news, investigative journalism or, indeed, the 'news' of a theatre opening, without a clear tie-in to lucrative advertising became more or less expendable.

In his study of arts criticism in America, *The Critic, Power and the Performing Arts*, John E. Booth writes:

> Major factors governing critics and criticism are the character, the nature, and the complexity of the newspaper industry. Survival for the industry depends on advertising, and advertising depends on raising circulation. The arts are not considered important in increasing circulation and consequently do not command major attention on most newspapers. This combination of circumstances does not provide the most hospitable environment for encouraging the best criticism. (Booth 1991: 80)

When multinational (and multimedia) interests dictate the atmosphere and ethos of newspapers across the world, it is not surprising that the crisis Booth describes in American journalism has been equally evident in the UK. When seen in a long historical perspective, what is perhaps most distressing about the relegation of arts coverage is that this trend emerged during a period in which newspapers were generally *increasing*, sometimes exponentially, in size. While many papers have either shrunk to tabloid format or included tabloid supplements in the last four decades, all broadsheets have become thicker. An analysis of changing newspaper pagination in the decade 1984–94 underlines the importance of the mid to late 1980s in defining the contemporary newspaper (see Table 1).

This expansion did not lead to a corresponding increase in the space allocated to theatre reviewers. Generalising about review word-lengths is hard, but the broad trend over the course of the twentieth century was certainly towards diminution. While arts sections have grown, there is now greater

Table 1

	Pages in 1984	Pages in 1994
Guardian	28	72
The Times	32	72
Mail on Sunday	64	220
Sunday Times	178	362
Observer	96	196
Daily Mail	36	64
		(Franklin 1997: 90)

competition for space from cinema, popular music and books features and reviews, and 'lifestyle' coverage. In addition, two significant developments have constricted the size of theatre reviews since Tynan's day. First, length has been affected by the technological ability to reproduce a high-quality photograph of the production under review; newspapers have become more and more conscious of the appeal of a text that is accompanied and broken up by images. Here, a hundred years later, is the logical conclusion of New Journalism's concern with digestibility and visual variation. Second, theatre reviewing must now vie with a relatively recent phenomenon in arts coverage, the pre-publicity feature. In June 2000 Donald Sutherland complained about his disastrous, and as he saw it unfair, reception in Eric Emmanuel-Schmitt's play *Enigmatic Variations*. Michael Billington attributed some of Sutherland's hurt to the contrast between sympathetic pre-opening hype and the cold shower of post-opening criticism. Writing of the 'creative tension' between artist and critics, Billington argued:

> What I believe is distorting that relationship at present is the gradual shift towards a PR-led culture. Before any major film, play, musical or book is launched, there is now a barrage of pre-publicity in every available medium. Artists are wooed, cossetted, persuaded to bang the interview drum. Criticism, when it arrives, is consequently regarded as a form of belated impertinence, a spoiler at the publicity feast. (Billington 2000b)

This phenomenon has elsewhere been described as one of the by-products of 'churnalism', the work of 'journalists who are no longer out gathering news but who are reduced instead to passive processors of whatever material comes their way, churning out stories, whether real event or PR artifice, important or trivial, true or false' (N. Davies 2008: 59).

At the beginning of the twentieth century, Joseph Pulitzer invited Alfred Harmsworth (who founded the *Daily Mirror* in 1903 and was later made

Lord Northcliffe) to edit the New York paper *The World* for a day, 'remodeling it in the light of his ideas of newspaper development in the twentieth century' (quoted in Pound and Harmsworth 1959: 266). Harmsworth reduced the size of the paper and put a maximum limit of 200 words on each item. In his editorial in *The World* on 1 January 1901, Harmsworth wrote: '*The World* enters today upon the twentieth or Time-saving century. I claim that by my system of condensed or tabloid journalism hundreds of working hours can be saved each year' (267). At the end of the 'Time-saving century', Harmsworth's influence was, of course, apparent in the prevalence of tabloid journalism. Yet even in the ever-lengthening broadsheets (where, after all, most theatre reviews appear) the call for condensation led to such innovations as the widespread introduction of star ratings in arts criticism.

Since March 1999 Michael Billington and Lyn Gardner in the *Guardian* have awarded a production between one and five stars at the head of the review. Billington, who had been working for the paper for twenty-eight years at that point, admitted in interview that he was not consulted on the innovation:

> Without being disloyal to my employer, I don't like the star system. There are lots of reasons. For a start, it kind of preempts prose, because people glance at the top of the column and think 'Do I need to read this?', you know, 'it's only one star, why should I bother to read on?' But also I find it very difficult to apportion stars, because I see many things in the theatre that are partially successful and partially unsuccessful... very rarely are one's reactions clear-cut... star systems are arbitrary, whereas art is complex and multi-layered. (Billington 2000a)

In tandem with the rise of the star system, there have been many other signs of the simplification and commodification of criticism. The *Independent on Sunday* has frequently flirted with a vox-pop attitude to reviewing in its 'Exit Poll' section, asking members of the public what they thought of a production and publishing a soundbite version of their comments accompanied by a passport-size photograph of the interviewee. It is very hard for theatre critics to believe in their own unique cultural authority when criticism is, as in this case, presented as synonymous with opinion, as not requiring experience or qualification: in effect, as something anyone can do. The 'Exit Poll' democratises criticism, confronting the profession with its lack of a cognitive basis, the absence that caused so much angst for the members of the Critics' Circle in the first half of the twentieth century. As Larson (1977: 31) writes on the model profession's need for a principle of exclusion, 'where everyone can claim to be an expert, there is no expertise'.

One could argue that the adoption of iconic or shorthand evaluation is simply an honest acceptance of the economic function of arts criticism, and its utilitarian role in guiding a consumer to what is best (and best value for money) in an overcrowded market. Yet when the star system is accompanied by a diminution of space in which to justify or qualify those stars, and when there is a general demotion of criticism in the culture of newspapers, the reviewer's authority and ability are severely compromised. As John Gross put it:

> Tynan, Hazlitt, or Shaw, they could hardly be themselves, brilliant as they were, under these kinds of conditions. If the editor of the *Saturday Review* had said to Bernard Shaw, or the editor of *The Examiner* had said to Hazlitt, 'Right, next week you do five plays and you've got four hundred words and not a word more', yes, something of their genius would come across, but not much. (Gross 2000)

Like many critics, Gross deeply regrets the passing of the essayistic review. Before seeing Steven Pimlott's 2000 RSC production of *Richard II*, Michael Billington (like Agate before him) re-read C.E. Montague's review of Frank Benson in the part, 'a magnificent piece of writing' according to Billington.

> If you calculated the amount of words [in Montague's review], it was probably about a four- to five-thousand-word essay. And it was printed in the *Manchester Guardian*! It would take up a full page in today's issue. Even then it took up the bulk of a page. And that is what I find staggering, the way we were at one stage allowed to write these glorious essays... Now, none of us could be essayists, even if we had the talent or the skill. Because an essay requires space and room to digress... Criticism now is a functional process. It's there to tell the reader as concisely and clearly as possible what this event was about, whether it was possibly worth their investment. (Billington 2000a)

A community of the same? The cultural biography of contemporary reviewers

Stefanova's 2000 book offered a snapshot of the reviewing community of the mid to late 1990s, the community that greeted the opening of Shakespeare's Globe and that, sociologically speaking, is very similar to that at the time of writing (late 2012). As Robert Hewison noted in 1997: 'we are curiously homogeneous [sic] in our social background: all white, male, middle class, university educated. Some are heterosexual, some are not, but there are very few women critics, and there are very few critics who come from other than a narrow social and cultural formation' (Stefanova

2000: 49). No newspaper had a first- or second-string critic from an ethnic minority. In 1997 only the *Observer*, the *Independent on Sunday* and the *Guardian* employed female critics with any consistency: the majority of critics were still male. Class is, for obvious reasons, harder to gauge than ethnicity or gender and was rarely commented upon in reviews or interviews. But if educational background is taken as one of the indexes of class, the reviewing community was not only solidly middle class, but actually at the higher end of the social scale. Working from their responses to Stefanova's question about the evolution of their careers, one can deduce that only three of the twenty-seven practising critics working in 1996–8 had not attended university. Of the three, David Nathan and Jack Tinker entered local journalism at an early age. The vast majority of critics read English and/or drama at university. James Christopher studied at Edinburgh, Nicholas de Jongh at University College London and Matt Wolf at Yale. Almost half of the critics referred to an Oxbridge education: Herbert, Nightingale and Shuttleworth studied at Cambridge; Billington, Coveney, Hewison, Morley, Peter, Spencer, Taylor and Wardle at Oxford. In 1999 Ian Herbert (1999: 241) would describe himself as belonging to the species '*criticus rotundis Oxoniensis* – the portly middle-aged Oxford or Cambridge alumnus who today makes up the bulk (and I do mean bulk) of the English critical fraternity (and I do mean fraternity)'.

In one sense, the high degree of formal education evident in the theatre reviewing community is consistent with wider trends in journalism. While in the late 1960s only 30 per cent of specialist reporters, for example, had university degrees, the figure had climbed to 48 per cent by 1997, an increase no doubt partly motivated by the ever-expanding higher education sector (Franklin 1997: 50). With its absence of ethnic minorities, too, theatre criticism is entirely in keeping with British journalism's 'almost perfect system of apartheid' (56). Yet, in another sense, the social make-up of reviewers is anomalous when compared with the profession of journalism as a whole. In 1997 the number of women journalists was approaching 37 per cent of the profession (59). Thus the community of theatre critics, when compared with averages for journalism, is disproportionately male. There has been no research on the social and educational background of British arts critics in general, so it is hard to say whether theatre reviewers are representative of critics of classical music, opera, cinema or art. John E. Booth's comprehensive study of performing arts criticism in the United States (conducted in 1991), however, presents a familiar portrait, with a body of critics who are, if anything, even more formally qualified than their British counterparts: 'nearly two-thirds of the newspaper critics are male, the over-whelming majority are white, and their median age is around forty. Most critics have completed their B.A. and over half have taken some graduate courses; more than one-third have advanced degrees. Most theater critics majored in English and the liberal arts' (Booth 1991: 62).

The most obvious socio-educational factor among contemporary critics is the prevalence of Oxbridge educations. In 1997 (when many of Stefanova's interviews were conducted) Franklin reports that of the 48 per cent of journalists who had university degrees, roughly one-third had degrees from Oxford or Cambridge (Franklin 1997: 50). The figure was nearer 50 per cent with Oxbridge degrees for theatre reviewers. Indeed, the university background (as well as gender) of reviewers bore comparison with that of the editors of national newspapers, the most lucrative and influential jobs in journalism. In 1995 all nine broadsheet editors had been to university, six to Oxbridge. Franklin's comment that '[a] university education, ideally at Oxbridge, seems increasingly to be a precondition for editing in the national press' (63) might equally be applied to theatre reviewing in the late twentieth and early twenty-first centuries.

To summarise: over the last decades of the twentieth century – but especially after the newspaper revolution of the mid 1980s – theatre criticism had suffered a loss of prestige within newspaper culture. Despite growth in newspaper length, no corresponding extension had been made to the review text; this constriction had, if anything, been compounded by the partial introduction of an evaluative shorthand that, in theory at least, offered the reader a verdict without description. Reviews were written by a critical community more homogeneously educated than any group of reviewers before it. Furthermore, this community consisted of a high proportion of graduates from Oxford and Cambridge, and remained overwhelmingly white, male and middle-aged. Within this community (and perhaps beyond, in arts editing and popular opinion) there was a widespread perception that theatre criticism currently lacked wider cultural authority, and that, when compared with their immediate predecessors (most obviously Tynan), contemporary critics had neither a messianic mission nor a suitably virtuosic style through which to convey one.

Speak, memory: a misfortune of *Macbeth*s 1995–6

To examine comparative criticism as it was practised (or avoided) at the end of the twentieth century, I turn once again to the reception of *Macbeth*, here focusing on an intense period of revivals in the mid 1990s. Between September 1995 and May 1996, five productions (or 'a misfortune of

Macbeths' in Paul Taylor's collective noun) opened around England; with such a density of interpretation, comparisons were inevitable. The productions were diverse (and here I have to resort to a shorthand that will privilege director and designer): Bill Alexander's futuristic, urban wasteland at the Birmingham Repertory; Stephen Unwin's Jacobean-dress and bare-stage production for the English Touring Theatre; Mark Rylance's Waco-inspired Hare Krishna cult-setting at the Greenwich Theatre; Nicholas Kent's pyrotechnical but otherwise conventional Tricycle Theatre production; and, finally, Tim Albery's cerebral, anti-romantic expressionist *Macbeth* at the Royal Shakespeare Theatre. Reading across the receptions of all five productions casts light on how the critical community tended to read performance, how it constructed boundaries for legitimate interpretation and how the memories of past performance and criticism continued to ghost reception in the present. Again, issues of masculinity, cultural legitimacy, moral education and the role of the director were never far from the surface.

Alexander's and Unwin's *Macbeth*s, which opened in the same week, offered reviewers a neatly opposed set of aesthetic and interpretive values. Four national critics made the trips to Crewe and Birmingham and offered diverse evaluations. It says a lot about the relative unpredictability of UK Shakespearean reviewing that a generally conservative critic like Charles Spencer preferred Alexander's more audacious interpretation, while Michael Billington was more convinced by Unwin's 'old-fashioned Shakespeare': 'For all its plainness, I often felt closer to the world of the play than I did in the sophisticated, conceptual versions of Rylance and Alexander' (*TR* 1995: 1313). Spencer (2000), in common with many critics, admits to 'resent[ing] the very conceptual Shakespeare' and names Michael Attenborough as his favourite Shakespearean director, claiming that he 'invariably serves the text better than himself... there's a humility before the writer that a lot of other Shakespearean productions lack'. What might account for Billington's uncharacteristic preference for Unwin's conventional production?

Of the four critics who saw Unwin's *Macbeth* in Crewe, it is telling that Billington alone had already seen Mark Rylance's production at Greenwich, in advance of press night. Rylance's reception was interesting for a number of reasons, not least for the way it influenced the climate for subsequent *Macbeth*s. When Unwin's touring production reached London (and therefore most national critics) four months after Rylance's opening, it benefited from a residual backlash against the Greenwich production. In *The Times*, Benedict Nightingale wrote that it was 'a lot clearer and more solid than several other productions that have recently appeared under the same title. Anyone who has seen Mark Rylance moochng about a Hare Krishna Scotland in saffron robes will welcome the Tudor costumes and general sense and sanity' (*TR* 1996: 65). Jack Tinker in the *Daily Mail* put it more forcefully: 'Almost any Macbeth which follows so closely on the sandalled heels of Mark Rylance's bizarre and monkish thane... must begin with a plus' (*TR* 1996: 66). In both comments, Rylance's production was synechdocally represented by an item of costume, the strong implication being that to costume *Macbeth* in Shakespearean period dress represents a more sensibly neutral and faithful visual grammar. This appeal to Shakespearean authority was made explicit in Robert Butler's notice:

> He [Unwin] minimises the physical dimensions of his production to such an extent that you begin to wonder why he isn't doing it on the radio. Then you realise that he's determined to bring us a playwright worth listening to, with enough scenery, music and ideas embedded in the verse. Instead of Unwin's *Macbeth*, he's going to give us Shakespeare's. (*TR* 1996: 67)

As Worthen (1997: 160) writes of the function of 'Shakespeare' in Styan's *The Shakespeare Revolution*, comments such as Butler's 'finally represent modern performance almost exclusively as a mode of interpretation, committed to replaying meanings already inscribed in the text or, much the same thing, in the text's potential signification when performed in its original theatrical environment'. Butler's verdict was reminiscent of the phobia of 'production' in Agate's Shakespearean reviewing, predicated on the possibility of an unmediated communion with the author. Gary Taylor identifies this mode of thought as one of the characteristic defensive mechanisms of *Cultural Selection*:

> Traditionalists attack a new edition of a canonical text – a revision of a collective memory – by claiming that its latest editors have displaced the original author and substituted themselves. The revisionist editor is visible and, like all editors, can only be visible by being defective. The new transmitter is accused of trying to displace the dead makers and usurp their authority. (Taylor 1991: 227)

The experience of Rylance's *Macbeth* clearly affected the taste and tolerance of the reviewing community, making it more likely than ever to legitimise and value a production such as Unwin's in which the director had produced the illusion of his own invisibility and in which Shakespeare appeared to be unmediated. Whether or not Rylance's *Macbeth* was the perverse disaster most reviewers described is not the issue here; what is of interest is to note the interpretive and rhetorical strategies brought to bear in the review discourse. Before doing so, one should stress the context of this production in the politics of Shakespearean performance in the mid 1990s. In the course of their reviews, more critics mentioned Mark Rylance's appointment as the future artistic director of Shakespeare's Globe than the striking moment when Jane Horrocks's Lady Macbeth urinated on stage. Rylance's accession to a position of Shakespearean authority immediately raised the stakes of his critical reception. References ranged from anxiety for the future of the project in his hands ('The Globe is already in trouble... if Rylance offers a work like this, we can look forward to a fiasco of monumental proportions' (Spencer, *TR* 1995: 1333)) to relief that he might somehow have fully purged himself of eccentricity before taking the job.

Like Garrick and Irving when they produced their *Macbeth*s, Rylance was a potential, if not actual, figurehead of Shakespearean theatre, a surrogate-custodian of the national dramatist. Also, like Garrick and Irving, he was clearly aware of the transgressive nature of his production and sought to justify his interpretation in print. What the pamphlet was to Garrick and the critical essay to Irving, so the programme note to Rylance. But whereas his predecessors had both used writing as a defence of character interpretation, it was symbolic of profound changes in Shakespearean production that Rylance's notes were more concerned with substantiating the directorial concept and *mise-en-scène* in which he had placed the action. Many critics referred to these notes in review, if only to stress their inability to excuse what had happened on stage. Bill Hagerty wrote in *Today*: 'In a programme note, Mr Rylance declares Macbeth is "a tragedy of broken families who have lost the natural human ability to intuit their way from the signs that nature gives us". Perhaps he should intuit again' (*TR* 1995: 1331). Garrick, anticipating criticism, had prefixed his satirical self-criticism with the epigraph '*Macbeth hath murdered Garrick.*' The reality of Rylance's reception, no doubt fanned by an anxiety for the future of the home of Shakespearean authenticity, was not far from the one Garrick had feared two and a half centuries before: 'Just as Macbeth murdered sleep, so Rylance has systematically massacred Shakespeare' (Paton, *TR* 1995: 1330).

The stakes were high for the additional reason that all of this was happening in front of children. Not untypically, *Macbeth* was a GCSE set text in the academic year 1995–6, and many critics commented on the presence of school groups and 'the tyranny exercised by syllabus setters over the British theatre' (Billington, *TR* 1995: 1313). One way for the critic to express disapproval of the production in hand was to gauge its pedagogic usefulness for students sitting exams that had nothing to do with theatricality and everything to do with reading texts for themes and image patterns. Jack

Tinker wrote of Rylance's production that 'students hoping for enlightenment or instruction in their forthcoming GCSE exams, for which this is a set text, will seek in vain' (1329). Nick Curtis feared that Kent's version at The Tricycle 'would be of little help for an essay on Shakespeare's poetry or themes' (*TR* 1996: 66) – probably not top of Kent's priorities in staging the play. For those in search of basic instruction, though, David Nathan felt that the English Touring Theatre's 'Unwinised "Macbeth" will serve as a kind of Reader's Digest introduction to the full play' (67). Such moments make explicit the literary critical premises that underscore much newspaper (and academic) reviewing, tinged as they are by 'the notion that the end of performance is to illuminate and refine *readings* of Shakespeare's plays' (Armstrong 2008: 118).

In addition to the contextual influences on reception, and the echoes of the Shakespearean past these reviews threw up, perhaps the most noticeable feature of Rylance's reviews was the widespread invocation of Peter O'Toole's Macbeth (1980). Six of the thirteen national reviewers cited O'Toole's performance as the last time they had seen the play so badly produced: 'What a noble drama is here o'erthrown by Mark Rylance, director and star of the worst production of the Scottish play since Peter O'Toole's hilariously hammy Old Vic version' (Paton, *TR* 1995: 1330). This construction of an anti-pantheon of productions is common in postwar *Macbeth* reviewing. A series of negative benchmarks can be traced from Gielgud's 1952 production (starring Ralph Richardson), via Gaskill at the Royal Court (1966), O'Toole at the Old Vic (1980) and the series of 'failures' of the Eyre–Howard, Noble–Jacobi and Rylance–Rylance combinations of the mid 1990s. But what did it mean to label Rylance's *Macbeth* 'the worst' since O'Toole?

Revealingly, critics habitually refer to the 1980 Old Vic production as 'O'Toole's *Macbeth*', the possessive perhaps accurately reflecting the fact that, although the show was directed by Bryan Forbes, the resulting disaster was more the responsibility of the lead actor and his apparently executive control of interpretation. In the original reviews for this production, it is clear that the predominant critical complaint was that this *Macbeth* was an anachronism, a curious retreat to 'the kind of thing one used to get from Wolfit on a bad night' (Wardle 1980). Little more than a star vehicle, the Old Vic production lacked the kind of directorial conceptual vision that reviewers had come to expect in Shakespearean performance. Whatever else Rylance's 1995 production lacked, it made a clear attempt to impose a directorial vision on Shakespeare's play. In this sense, 'the worst since' formula rather cursorily homogenises two very different productions and their discordant aesthetics. But, as theorists of memory would argue, the important question is not how accurately the critics' recollection of O'Toole fitted with the reality of O'Toole's performance, but rather why that memory was (re)constructed in a particular way at a specific time. As David Middleton and Derek Edwards (1990: 11) write, accounts of the past are 'pragmatically variable versions that are constructed with regard to particular communicative circumstances. People's accounts of past events [should be] treated not as a window on to the cognitive workings of memory, but as descriptions that vary according to whatever pragmatic and rhetorical work they are designed for.'

The pragmatically variable nature of theatrical memory is evident in a series of *Macbeth* reviews by Michael Billington. Reversing the strategy of damning by comparison, Billington critiqued Rylance's production for *failing* to resemble other *Macbeth*s:

> In a lifetime of Macbeths – starting with Laurence Olivier at Stratford in 1955 – I have seen only three totally persuasive productions. One was Trevor Nunn's Other Place black ritual with Ian McKellen and Judy [sic] Dench. Another was Adrian Noble's Freudian study in childlessness with Jonathan Pryce and Sinead Cusack. And the third was Ninagawa's falling cherry-blossom Japanese version, which was about the transience of earthly power. Otherwise it remains one of those great plays that, as Agate said, in the theatre always slightly disappoints. (*TR* 1995: 1330)

(Whether a play that 'always slightly disappoints' in performance can still be considered 'great' is a moot point that Billington hasn't the space to explore.) By informally citing James Agate, Billington reinforces the authority of past performances with the authority of a critical predecessor, a very Agatesque gesture. But reading Billington's 1995 review against *Macbeth* reviews written in 1993 and 1999 reveals significant discrepancies. While the *process* of privileging and evoking memories of previous *Macbeth*s is constant in all three reviews, the *content* of those memories pragmatically varies. When reviewing Adrian Noble's 1993 production, he wrote, in extenuation of the director, that 'the play has defeated most of its interpreters throughout history ... In 40 years of theatregoing, I've only seen three unequivocally successful productions' (*TR* 1993: 1475). (Like the Porter, Billington has little respect for 'equivocators'.) What is surprising, however, is that this canon of three successful productions is different from the one he invoked two years later in the Rylance review. In 1993, Nunn, Ninagawa and Glen Byam Shaw's 1955 *Macbeth* with Laurence Olivier are the landmarks dwarfing the current production. Noble's 'Freudian'

Macbeth, for whatever reason, is not used as a yardstick with which to beat the same director's latest version of the play. This flexible canonicity appears once again in Billington's review of the John Crowley/Rufus Sewell *Macbeth* of 1999. Here he wrote that 'Macbeth itself is a role that has defeated most actors for 400 years, with the exceptions of Macready, Olivier and McKellen: it therefore seems peculiarly perverse to thrust it on Sewell at this stage of his career' (*TR* 1999: 282). Like buses and weird sisters, good *Macbeth*s / Macbeths seem only to come in threes. Indeed, the rhetorical penchant for triads and tricolons (most apparent in reviewers' use of adjectives) dictates the number of ghosts that are allowed to haunt the review.

Perhaps the most striking of all these *Macbeth* reviews strategically deployed a long-past performance to bolster the critic's own prejudices about gender and type-casting, with the whole capped by a subconscious (?) allusion to the pedagogic context of the touring production. Benedict Nightingale wrote of Paul Higgins:

> He makes a most unwilling regicide, one who has to kill half of what's best in himself in order to commit murder... It is a perfectly valid reading, sanctioned by no less an actor than David Garrick... But Garrick had Mrs Pritchard's awesome domineering Lady Macbeth to push him into murder, and Higgins has Hilary Lyon, a starchy-looking beanpole who is no worse than schoolmarmish. When she reproves Macbeth after the murder – 'a foolish thought to say a sorry sight' – it's as if she is giving him a D-grade in English. (*TR* 1996: 65)

One has to wonder what aspect of a slim physique disqualifies an actress from playing Lady Macbeth and whether comparing her to another actress 250 years her senior is in any sense meaningful, let alone helpful for the performer. One might also note that Nightingale began this review by quoting James Agate.

Tim Albery's production of *Macbeth* opened in the Royal Shakespeare Theatre in May 1996 and brought to a close this unofficial season of *Macbeth*s. With its expressionist set and apparently self-conscious denuding of the magniloquent and the 'tragic', the production provoked a largely negative critical response. Only a handful of critics (Billington, Coveney, Edwardes and Peter) sympathised with Albery's aims. In her review in *Time Out*, Jane Edwardes foregrounded the continental inflection of the production: 'The Euro expressionist train has arrived with a vengeance and theatre-goers are as likely to be as deeply divided as the Tories are over things European' (*TR* 1996: 626). A similarly political split was apparent within the reviewing community. Of the four critics who praised the production, three were writing in a newspaper or magazine with a centre-left political ethos. The fourth, John Peter, writing in the more conservative *Sunday Times*, based his approval not so much on the aesthetic of the event, but, more typically for this critic, on a more humanist concern with characterisation. Edwardes's analogy between critical reception of theatrical style and political attitudes to Europeanism should not perhaps be pushed too closely, but nearly all of the critics who panned the production were writing in newspapers that were broadly sympathetic to the then Conservative government and its prevalent Euro-scepticism. Just as submerged questions of whether the UK should succumb to an Americanisation of high culture would form a strand of Globe reviewing, so the issue of the UK's proximity to Europe underscored the reception of Albery's *Macbeth*.

Michael Billington thought that he detected in Albery's *Macbeth* the healthy influence 'both of German theatre and the ENO of the eighties', and found the 'stylised lighting, emblematic grouping and inventive use of space' vastly preferable to 'the old-fashioned Macbeth which Agate summarised as a mix of "tartan manners, berserk head-gear and uncouth whiskerage"' (*TR* 1996: 625). (Once again, Billington's allusive tic alights on Agate.) Billington concluded the review with a prophecy: 'the RSC is gradually moving away from the collective humanism of the Nunn years towards a more controversial neo-Expressionist aesthetic'. The evangelism of that closing statement met with a prompt response. As Billington told me:

> Trevor Nunn wrote me a very curious letter, as he often does, saying 'I really find this very worrying, you know. I thought that you, like me, were brought up on the sanctity and the holiness of the text as the centre of Shakespeare, and now you're telling us that these plays have to be expressionistically staged.' I wrote back to him, saying 'I'm not saying they have to be, I'm just saying there's a new generation that is not looking for the creation of a literal society.' (Billington 2000a)

That 'creation of a literal society' is how Billington characterises Nunn's approach to staging Shakespeare. This approach has, over the last two decades, combined the relocation of the play in a specific historical moment with a novelistic attention to stage properties and character. As Peter Holland (1997: 100) notes, Nunn's aesthetic since his production of *Othello* (The Other Place, 1989) has been 'materialist', consisting of 'emphatically naturalistic acting... and above all a belief in the play's explicability'. In his letter, Nunn's appeal to cultural socialisation, to being 'brought up' to view Shakespeare in a certain way, is another reminder of the homogeneity of intellectual background shared by critics and directors alike.

One of the reasons Billington's review of Albery's *Macbeth* caught Trevor Nunn's attention must have been the explicitness, rare in British reviewing, with which Billington expressed a theoretical preference for an emergent Shakespearean aesthetic. British reviewers are generally reluctant to theorise either Shakespeare or the cultural activity they perform. However, when critics are pressed to offer theoretical preferences for Shakespearean production, it is striking that these preferences are often contradicted in the practice of reviewing. John Gross (2000), for example, freely admits to being 'fairly small "c" conservative' and wary of deliberately politicised or heavily conceptual productions. Yet when confronted, in the summer of 2000, with two very different *Richard II*s (an embarrassment of Richards?) he found that, although the traditionalist Almeida–Ralph Fiennes version came 'in principle much closer to what I'm looking for', he actually preferred Steven Pimlott's modern-dress Brechtian production at The Other Place. The same was true of Charles Spencer (2000), who nevertheless claims that 'Brecht's influence [on British theatre] has been more or less entirely malign on every front'.

Many critics cite British criticism's perceived immunity to 'dogma' as one of its strengths: 'To me it's an entirely practical and instinctive job rather than something you should have any theories about. I see myself first and foremost as a working journalist rather than an academic, or as part of the theatre scene. I don't have a lot of dogmatic beliefs or theories' (Spencer in Stefanova 2000: 22). For both Billington and Peter, this resistance to theory distinguishes British critics from their European counterparts: 'Unlike a lot of criticism on the European continent, we are very aware of the needs of the reader. We tend to avoid elaborate technical terms, explanations and theorizing'; 'we have the ability to know how to address the reader and not get weighed down by theory. In France or Germany the critics are much more theoretically inclined than we are. We are much more pragmatic' (Peter and Billington in Stefanova 2000: 51, 45). Similarly, in interview, Billington (2000a) claimed that the difference lay not merely in critics' educational backgrounds, but in national mentality: 'I don't think in England or Britain we've ever had that conceptual Shakespeare that you find in Germany or France, because we're not that kind of society.'

This distinction between Continental, rule-bound, theorising and British pragmatic instinct has a long and complicated history in which Shakespeare has been cast as protagonist and example *par excellence* of the impertinence of theory. What Roland Barthes (1975: 22) has called 'the old reactionary myth of heart against head' is in play here. British critics may pride themselves on being part of a tradition that stretches back to Steele and Addison, on being, in Steele's words, the 'free critick, [the] free *Briton*' who 'is governed by the Laws which he himself votes for; whose Liberty is checked by the Restraints of Truth, and the Monarchy of right Reason' (quoted in Taylor 1991: 66). But this should not obscure the underlying theoretical strands in contemporary Shakespearean reviewing. When Billington complains that Adrian Noble's 1993 RSC *Macbeth* 'even lacks good design since Ian MacNeil has signally failed to find a coherent visual metaphor for the play' (*TR* 1993: 1475); or when Nicholas de Jongh wrote of the same production that 'it is... difficult to discern the production's guiding concept' (1474); when Ian Shuttleworth declared that he might have liked Tim Albery's *Macbeth* more 'if there were signs of an intelligent thematic vision' (*TR* 1996: 626); or when Nick Curtis averred that Stephen Unwin's *Macbeth* 'suffers above all from a lack of any real governing vision' (66) – at these moments (and they are very common) critics betray a theoretical disposition for the privileged taxonomies of New Criticism, for coherent metaphors, guiding concepts and thematic visions. Reviewers do not think of these standards of taste as 'conceptual' or 'theoretical' largely because, like Shakespeare himself, they are an invisible element in the national and educational bloodstream.

Inheriting the Globe: the reception of Shakespearean audience and authenticity in contemporary reviewing

Reviewing a 'misfortune of *Macbeth*s' or a cluster of Shakespearean revivals across different venues is bread-and-butter work for the UK newspaper critic. But in the mid 1990s the South Bank of London witnessed the most important innovation in British Shakespearean performance practice since the founding of the RSC in 1960–1, and one which profoundly changed the job of the night-watch constable. To distinguish it from the Globe Theatre on Shaftesbury Avenue, and presumably to sell more tickets, the new theatre was rebranded as 'Shakespeare's Globe'. The opening of this theatrical space within a few hundred yards of the original marked the climax of decades of campaigning and research. For the optimistic, the project offered an authorially intended, unmediated access to the plays, an education in their original performance conditions commingled with the chance to inhabit a quasi-spiritual location. For the cynic or agnostic, the enterprise too closely resembled the recently opened EuroDisney for comfort and threatened to descend into a commercial exercise in ersatz.

From its inception, the Globe has provoked controversy and has constituted perhaps the key theatrical site for the cultural contestation of Shakespeare. While it quickly proved its commercial value (regularly attracting audiences of 90 per cent capacity upwards), the Globe's cultural capital remains a subject of debate, a debate inevitably centring on the question of what constitutes Shakespearean authority and authenticity.

What follows is an analysis of that debate as it took place in the columns of national newspapers during the first seven years of the Globe's existence (1996–2003). The hundreds of reviews written in response to Globe productions in that time offer insights into both the characteristics of an interpretive community and the cultural status of Shakespeare at the start of the twenty-first century. Rather than offering a year-by-year survey of which productions and performances were favourably or unfavourably reviewed, and why, I instead focus on the representation of space and audience in the review discourse. The critical anxiety about Shakespearean authenticity was most complexly registered here, in the rhetorical depiction of the Globe audience and the evaluation of the Globe space. This anxiety is provoked, I argue, by unresolved tensions between national identity and global tourism, between high and low cultural forms, and between incommensurable constructions of Shakespeare.

Michael D. Bristol (1985: 5) argues for an awareness of the public playhouse as 'a politically significant *mise-en-scène*', a communicative space that is not 'an empty or uncluttered space in which a message is disseminated without interference'; on the contrary, the theatre is always and 'already full of sound and of other socially significant semiotic material. In such a state of affairs, a serious dislocation of authority is not only possible but likely' (111). In its emphasis on 'the immediate social purposes of theater ... over the specialized appreciation of durable literary values' (4), 'an escape from supervision and from surveillance of attitude, feeling and expression' (112). Such an escape enabled a subversive form of spectatorship, and with it the possibility of 'vernacular misinterpretations of high culture' (123). Similarly, Robert Weimann (1988: 403) claims that the early modern theatre was characterised by the presence of multiple, often discordant authorities: 'Contrary to the sanctioned modes of authorizing political, ecclesiastical, and juridical types of discourse, the theatre could not but acknowledge as authoritative the provision of pleasure.' What was so potentially radical about this acknowledgement was its situating of power in the act of audience reception: 'Authority in this theatre ... needed to be validated by the audience and was unlikely to result without the cooperative effort of the audience's "imaginary forces"' (405).

How can Bristol's and Weimann's insights into early modern playgoing speak to the last years of the twentieth century? Shakespeare's Globe has been since its opening one of the most popular performance venues in London. Does its distinctively festive atmosphere, buoyed up by the presence of so many tourists and holidaymakers (late modern equivalents of Bristol's carnival spectator, enjoying an interlude between periods of the authorised activity of labour) lead to the same dismantling of authority Bristol diagnosed in the early modern popular theatre? Might that dismantling of authority be all the more violent and noteworthy given the now high cultural status of Shakespeare? Finally, if Bristol's theatregoers were imagined to be free from the 'surveillance of attitude, feeling and expression', can the same be said of contemporary Globe visitors, given the presence of theatre reviewers, the 'uniformed members of the public' (Shuttleworth in Stefanova 2000: 83) who mediate and evaluate the cultural worth of the theatrical event?

Damn Yankees: reviewing the Shakespearean audience

Many reviewers praised the aura and authenticity of the Globe in its first seasons. In the first full season, Charles Spencer wrote that the staging of *Henry V* was 'as close as we are likely to get to what watching a play in Shakespeare's day was like' (*TR* 1997: 729); in the following season he reiterated that 'there are moments at the Globe when one feels closer to the spirit and the sense of Shakespeare than anywhere else' (*TR* 1998: 690). John Gross, in describing the 'magical' atmosphere of the space, concurred that 'every so often it makes you feel in touch with Shakespeare as no other theatre can – with the Elizabethan Shakespeare, that is, the one whom his first audiences actually knew' (691). Shakespearean presence also underlay Robert Butler's verdict on *Julius Caesar*: 'It's as if, inside this particular building and presented in a certain way, the cast luck into a forgotten radio frequency. When they hit on this waveband – as they do here – Shakespeare seems closer than ever' (*TR* 1999: 671). The unmediated strains of Shakespeare FM were also audible to Roger Foss, for whom the cast of *Cymbeline*'s 'communication with the audience resounds across the ages with digital clarity' (*TR* 2001: 909). The Globe represented 'Shakespeare as Shakespeare intended' (Holden, *TR* 1999: 673), offered a glimpse into 'Shakespeare's enigmatic heart' (Spencer, *TR* 1999: 702), promised 'a spine-tingling experience, listening 400 years later to the words of the poet in his own home, as it were' (Gore-Langton, *TR* 2001: 670). This strand of commentary confirms W.B. Worthen's analysis of how the presence or proximity of 'Shakespeare', in much performance criticism, still legitimates certain theatrical practice. What is surprising, however, is how infrequent this 'closer to Shakespeare' motif surfaced in most Globe reception. With the exceptions of Charles Spencer (*Daily Telegraph*), Michael Coveney (*Daily Mail*) and John Peter (*Sunday Times*), no critic returned with any consistency to the idea that the Globe afforded unmediated access to its proprietor playwright. Most reviewers found something irritatingly obstructing, both figuratively and literally, their access to the Shakespearean stage: the Globe audience.

A number of reviews mention the visible positioning of the standing audience between the critic and the stage, and the perspectival disruption this was felt to cause. In the 1999 season Michael Billington complained that 'seated in the lower gallery you become unduly aware of the chatting, chaffing and canoodling going on in the yard in front of you' (*TR* 1999: 1004); in 2003 Billington was again distracted by 'the endless gropings of the groundlings' (*TR* 2003: 817). Georgina Brown agreed in 2000 that 'if you sit in the stalls, there's a lot of drama to take in before you come to the stage itself with the groundlings lolling in the pit, eating, drinking, chatting, snogging' (*TR* 2000: 691). In these accounts, the piling up of verbs of consumption and concupiscence curiously recalls Phillip Stubbes's description of an early modern audience in *The Anatomie of Abuses*: 'such laughing and fleering, such kissing and bussing, such clipping and culling, such wincking and glauncing of wanton eies, and the like, is vsed, as is wonderfull to beholde' (Stubbes [1583] 2002: 203–4). The cumulative depiction of the Globe audience, and specifically the groundlings, that emerges from reading reviews may not be predicated on Stubbes's overheated anti-theatricalism, but it nevertheless shared his cultural critique of spectatorship and distrust of a carnivalesque crowd.

Notably, theatre reviews rarely allude to the audience. The number of comments devoted to the audience in Globe reception is partly a direct and inevitable consequence of its visibility in often day-lit outdoor performances. The critical awareness of the Globe audience was also predictable given the theatre management's policy of both encouraging an informal relationship between actor and audience as a marker of authenticity, and highlighting the contrast between conventional theatrical architecture and etiquette and those at the Globe. However, the frequency of critical comment on audience reaction or interaction in early Globe reviews was striking. It might be objected that critics are more likely to comment on and evaluate audience behaviour in any open air Shakespeare event. The Globe, after all, is not unique in offering a season of outdoor performances. To help tease out the unique rhetoric of Globe reviewing, let me briefly summarise the critical attitude to Shakespeare performances at the Open Air Theatre, Regent's Park.

Overall, the notable characteristic of Regent's Park reviews in comparison with those of Globe productions during this period was the absence of the open-air audience. It was rarely mentioned or characterised in reviews, and it was never represented synecdochally by an individual audience member. Of all the critics, only Madelaine North and Fiona Mountford in *Time Out* conveyed the anti-populist strain that, I argue, was so common in Globe receptions. Reviewing the 2000 production of *Dream*, North wrote that the lack of directorial innovation in the production would not 'worry the Open Air's average audience member', and concluded that 'it's serviceable Shakespeare for the deck chair crowd' (*TR* 2000: 762). Of the following year's revival of *Love's Labour's Lost*, Mountford wrote of the temptation for directors to 'stage an unimaginative Shakespeare-lite production, safe in the knowledge that the masses will flock to drink their alfresco Pimms anyway' (*TR* 2001: 759). Although Pimms is hardly the opiate of choice of the masses, these comments are consonant with the strain of Globe criticism that accuses productions of pandering to a lowest-common-denominator, culturally impoverished audience.

North and Mountford, however, were exceptional among reviewers of mid to late 1990s Regent's Park productions in foregrounding the audience. Most reviews ignored audience response. Michael Billington commented on the open-air audience, but only to contrast it favourably with that of the Globe. In his review of the 1998 *Troilus and Cressida*, he noted approvingly of how 'no one hisses Achilles or boos Diomedes as they might down at the Globe; the audience simply engages with the argument', adding that 'there is none of that hideous faux-naiveté which in Southwark turns Shakespeare's plays into The Perils of Pauline' (*TR* 1998: 784). In his review of the 2001 *Love's Labour's Lost*, Billington also praised Regent's Park Shakespeare for having 'none of that fatal audience self-consciousness you find at other open-air venues' (*TR* 2001: 758). The Globe was also, unwittingly, invoked in Robert Hewison's response to the 2000 *Dream*: 'led by Paul Bradley's am-dram aficionado Bottom, the groundlings stay solidly and entertainingly in the real world' (*TR* 2000: 761). Hewison could only have meant 'mechanicals' when he wrote 'groundlings', but the subconscious association is intriguing. Did the pantomimic, misguided efforts of the amateur theatricals, not to mention their low social status, remind Hewison of the Globe audience?

Unlike Regent's Park, the Globe theatre has a division of space (galleries, yard, stage) that unavoidably includes a defined body of spectators, the groundlings, in the rest of the audience's gaze. Although the Globe's publicity literature and booking brochure habitually claim that the best views of the stage come from standing in the pit, theatre critics are nevertheless given, as is customary, the most expensive seats in the house. Unless the critic then chooses to leave his or her seat and rove among the groundlings (as Billington reports doing on several occasions), the result is that a mass of highly visible spectators is interposed between the critic and the performance.

Many reviewers critiqued the Globe's early audiences in an off-hand, but loaded way; they talked of 'groundling-pleasing excess' or criticised an actor for 'playing to the gallery' – a metaphor, as the critic actually meant playing to the yard. On other occasions, the reviewer composed a group portrait. Since the staging of authenticity is a social event, many critics offered quasi-anthropological accounts of the neo-Elizabethans in the yard. Reviews of the 2000 season offer perhaps the least flattering portraits. On the press night of *The Tempest*, the heavens opened and many of the groundlings donned plastic Pacamacs, leading no fewer than three critics to compare them to condoms or 'a convocation of contraceptives' (Nightingale, *TR* 2000: 693). The condom, which affords short-term pleasure without long-term responsibility, is an apt symbol for an audience that critics depicted as more interested in cheap thrills than profundity. Responding to the controversial *Merchant of Venice* in 1998, David Nathan worried that 'when an audience is on its feet, it loses any sensitivity it might individually possess' (*TR* 1998: 691), a phenomenon known to group psychologists as 'risky shift'. A number of reviews registered a critical anxiety about the Globe audience's lack of sensitivity. Alastair Macaulay claimed that 'the audience is never so happy as when it can boo, hiss, cheer, or roar with laughter' (689), while Stephen Fay corroborated the image of subnormal intelligence: 'They respond well to music, especially if encouraged to clap' (*TR* 2000: 692). In these two accounts, actual noise, whether of hissing or clapping, becomes symbolic noise, signifying cultural incompetence.

These constructions of a vulgar, lowest-common-denominator section of the audience set the tone for much of the critical coverage of the groundlings in subsequent Globe seasons. In the third season, Roger Foss worried that '[m]aybe a Globe audience can't be expected to pay attention to a serious thought or a poetic allusion for much longer than a soundbite' (*TR* 1999: 998). Attention deficit disorder was also diagnosed by other critics. In the second season, both Billington and Rhoda Koenig rhetorically set the theatre management a stark choice: 'when it must choose between customers who care about poetry and those who want souvenirs, it's clear which kind it wants to cultivate' (Koenig, *TR* 1999: 1003); 'is it an artistically ambitious organisation? Or is it content to go on churning out inexpressibly dreary productions, such as this *Julius Caesar*, to restless, inattentive, largely tourist audiences?' (Billington, *TR* 1999: 673).

The presence of the audience in early Globe reviews was most striking when the critic shifted focus from the general to the particular. Many reviews featured a vignette of an individual audience member (almost invariably a groundling) whose stupidity and restlessness were offered as a synecdoche of the problematic audience. These would-be representative anecdotes often involved direct quotation and tended to specify the culprit's nationality. Thus, Macaulay was distracted by two men having a conversation in Spanish (*TR* 1999: 1000), while Paul Taylor's concentration on *Henry V* was broken by 'a young Japanese woman' sitting next to him, 'who kept a camera trained on the production throughout as though it were some extended alternative to the Changing of the Guard' (*TR* 1997: 726). Hannah Betts, in the process of despairing at some 'idiot gag-milking' in *Cymbeline*, dropped her head into her hands, only to witness 'a mulleted German youth, hitherto insufficiently impressed to raise his eyes from his Gameboy, [jump] up and down with glee' at the offending idiocy (*TR* 2001: 912). For Robert Gore-Langton, *Lear* 'even survives the backchatting of Americans ("Hey honey, he just got mad at Cordelia!") and confused Swedes' (670). This is the multilingual, even heteroglossic condition of both carnival and global theatregoing, and London's critical community was clearly uncomfortable with it.

As in Gore-Langton's anecdote, the foreign body foregrounded in reviews usually belonged to an American. On leaving his seat and descending among the groundlings at *Julius Caesar*, Billington found himself 'surrounded by snickering American jocks who were so caught up in the play that they supplemented the wails that greeted Caesar's ghost with their own derisive groans' (*TR* 1999: 673). The same critic's appreciation of 'To be or not to be' likewise had a transatlantic nemesis: 'some Yankee tourist... wrestling with his crinkly Pacamac' (*TR* 2000: 755). Charles Spencer claimed that the same tourist should have been 'tossed into the Thames' by the ushers, and, appropriating the authority of Hamlet/Shakespeare, found comfort in the fact that 'the Globe's audience got on Shakespeare's nerves too' (756).

In these anecdotes, American characters often functioned as culturally incompetent counterpoints to the critic. Carole Woddis began her *Herald* review of *Macbeth* with direct quotation: '"My heart sank," said the American beside me; "here I am at Shakespeare's Globe and they're all in tuxedos." There you have it in a nutshell,' Woddis asseverated. 'Is the Globe part of the English Heritage tourist trail or a living, breathing, risk-taking, theatrical organism?' (*TR* 2001: 750). As with Koenig's comment on the incompatibility of 'souvenirs' with 'poetry', Woddis presented tourism as inimical to theatrical health. The vocabulary of her Heritage-bashing betrays the intellectual genealogy of her position: 'living, breathing... organism' bears the unmistakable marks of New Left and New Wave rhetoric, and behind that, the socio-literary criticism of F.R. Leavis and T.S. Eliot. Fiona Mountford began her *Time Out* review of *Cymbeline* with a similar exposé of American cultural illiteracy: '"Is Cymbeline a tragedy or a comedy?" an American tourist asked me as I loitered outside the Globe' (909). On his way into the Globe in the opening season, Robert Butler walked past 'a dapper American TV presenter... talking to camera: "For an audience," he enthused, "this is as close as you can get to an Elizabethan theatre-going experience." It was a dismal endorsement', sighed Butler (*TR* 1997: 724). All three examples contrast the naivety of the American with the artistic, generic and cultural sophistication of the (British) critic.

Audience impropriety was similarly registered in a number of reviews of *King Lear*. Apparently, when Edmund asked the audience which of the sisters he should take, 'Both, one, or neither?' a woman in the crowd had responded 'Both!' Benedict Nightingale described the woman 'as a cheery bimbo in row C... sounding as if she were at a Chippendale's strip-tease' (*TR* 2001: 668), but Charles Spencer went further, describing her as 'the American lady' who behaved not only 'as if watching a baseball game', but also, to compound her low cultural profile, 'screamed like a member of the *Blind Date* audience'. Spencer, who had already flexed his emotional muscles in wishing for a Yankee to be drowned in the Thames, now felt 'like ramming her programme down her throat' (668). Maddy Costa in the *Guardian* at least had the honesty to admit that 'there's nothing quite like it for making one reel with snobbery' (669).

These anecdotes illustrate a general complaint about audience etiquette at the Globe, but that complaint could easily be made without reference to nationality. After all, the man wrestling with his Pacamac need not be identified and labelled as 'some Yankee'. These critics, perhaps unconsciously, chose to consider the nationality of audience members significant enough to flag in the reviews. More particularly, the presence of a generic American tourist in these reviews could be understood in a number of ways. First, it reads as a submerged anxiety in the critic about the financial provenance of the Globe, its American-born founder and the importance of the dollar in establishing and maintaining the Globe (and global) economy. A second and contiguous explanation relates to a general resistance to the phenomenon of Shakespeare's international popularity: anyone expecting the kind of one-nation microcosmic Merrie England Globe offered by the opening of Olivier's film of *Henry V* would have been jolted by the contemporary reality of the multinational and heterogeneous Globe audience. Either way, there is an overlap between responses to the postmodern and the early modern spectator. Like their early modern counterparts in Puritan accounts, tourists at the present Globe are skipping work, having a good afternoon or night out between periods of authorised activity. The carnivalesque elements of popular theatre that caused Puritan writers so much angst – the holiday cocktail of food, drink and sex – were also present in contemporary Globe reception.

The referential tactic of singling out incompetent audience members can be seen as part of a wider strategy of validating the critic's authority. As Barbara Herrnstein Smith points out in *Contingencies of Value*, normative evaluation and validation rely on standardising a community's preferences while simultaneously 'discounting or pathologizing' other people's tastes. 'Thus,' she continues:

> it is assumed or maintained... that the particular *subjects* who constitute the established and authorized members of the group are of sound mind and body, duly trained and informed, and generally competent, all other subjects being defective, deficient, or deprived: suffering from crudenesses of sensibility, diseases and distortions of perception, weaknesses of character, impoverishment of background-and-education, cultural or historical biases, ideological or personal prejudices and/or undeveloped, corrupted, or jaded tastes. (B.H. Smith 1988: 41)

The caricaturing of the Globe audience in newspaper reviews of the first seven seasons could be seen as part of a wider anti-heritage strain in contemporary journalism and cultural commentary, seeking to pathologise the tastes of the tourist.[1] 'The charge of vulgarity', as Raphael Samuel (1994: 265) writes, 'is a leitmotif of heritage criticism, and may account for the frequency with which heritage is bracketed with theme parks, toytowns and Disneyland'. Samuel continues:

> For the aesthete, anyway for the alienated and the disaffected, heritage is a mechanism of cultural debasement. It leaves no space for the contemplative or solitary. It forbids discrimination and the exercise of good taste. Its pleasures are cheap and nasty, confounding high and low, originals and copies, the authentic and the pastiche. It brings 'crowd pollution', in the form of mass tourism, to sacred spots. (Samuel 1994: 268)

All this is entirely consonant with the fears of most reviewers when confronted with the Globe experience. Whether it was the crudeness of the mulleted German, the underdeveloped tastes of the simple-minded groundlings, the perceived cultural impoverishment of the American who doesn't know what type of play *Cymbeline* is, or the weakness of character and lack of *savoir faire* that allows the 'cheery bimbo' to answer Edmund, the Globe audience members functioned not only as implicit contrasts to the trained competence of the reviewer, but as a damning commentary on a project that confounds high and low cultures and brought crowd pollution to the potentially most sacred spot in Shakespearean theatre.

'Arsenal/Tottenham': reviewing the Shakespearean space

The critique of the Globe audience, whether generalised or specific, was compounded by a series of analogies that ran throughout the theatre's early reception history. Comparing the heckler at *King Lear* to an audience member at *Blind Date* or a Chippendales show discursively transformed the Globe into a low cultural arena, no different from those that house tabloid television or soft porn. Similar critical manoeuvres many times compared the Globe, on numerous occasions, to the music hall or pantomime – traditionally working-class forms of theatre. Indeed, the word 'pantomime' had a very high frequency in Globe reviews (see in *TR*: Curtis, 1997: 1087; Macaulay, 1997: 729; Marmion, 1997: 729; Sierz, 1997: 730; Kingston, 1998: 689; Macaulay, 1998: 689; Curtis, 1999: 701; Kingston, 1999: 701; Gross, 1999: 1005; Hewison, 1999: 1005; Macaulay, 1999: 672). In 1997 Macaulay complained of *Henry V* that 'though Rylance & Co. could have invited audiences to behave with the high-spirited seriousness of Albert Hall promenaders, they have instead encouraged them to behave as if these plays were Christmas pantomimes' (*TR* 1997: 730). The Proms were also on John Gross's mind: '[o]ne wouldn't want to see the last-night-of-the-Proms treatment applied to *Hamlet* or *Lear*, but it doesn't seem unreasonable when it comes, say, to heckling the Dauphin' (731).

Popular sporting events were also invoked in the effort to describe the social atmosphere of the Globe. Jane Edwardes wrote in the 1997 season that 'the atmosphere is one of a football match and it demands its stars and their followers... If Rylance is a Ryan Giggs, the present company still needs a Shearer and a Seaman' (*TR* 1997: 724). The exact theatrical equivalent of David Seaman is now hard to imagine – when Edwardes wrote that, Seaman connoted 'a safe pair of hands', an association that afterwards lost some of its currency – but her analogy was misleading in the first place. Behaviour at football matches is governed, or sometimes fails to be governed, by very different codes from those pertaining at most theatres, no matter how much audience participation they encourage. Yet the comparison resurfaced in Patrick Marmion's verdict that 'the Globe's volatile dynamics... encourage actors to play to the gallery [read 'groundlings'], so reducing the intellectual atmosphere to the level of an Arsenal/Tottenham football derby' (*TR* 1998: 691), a sentence designed to strike fear into the heart of any sophisticated urbanite. (Incidentally, both Hagerty and Spencer, watching the murder of Cinna the poet in the 1999 *Julius Caesar*, were reminded of 'today's football thugs' (Spencer, *TR* 1999: 672), a memory-prompt that Hagerty at least found 'most distasteful' (*TR* 1999: 667).) Aleks Sierz was much closer to the mark when he wrote of the booing of the French in *Henry V* that 'with no lager-louts in the audience, this kind of patriotism is about as dangerous as a pantomime – and less serious than sport' (*TR* 1997: 731).

Globe conferences and publications that appeared under the auspices of the theatre circulated the analogy between a football crowd and the Globe audience more positively. At the International Shakespeare Globe Centre conference in April 1995, Franklin Hildy gave a paper on audience dynamics in which he 'related the Elizabethan playgoers to latter-day "fans" at sporting events or rock concerts and suggested that, given the right chemistry, future Globe audiences would react in a more fan-like manner at Globe performances than they would in a conventional theatre setting' (Nelsen 1995: 28). Six years previously, Andrew Gurr (1989: 53) wrote in *Rebuilding Shakespeare's Globe* that in Shakespeare's theatre 'The conditions and the time of day were closer to those for a modern football match than a play.' And in *Shakespeare's Globe Rebuilt*, the post-opening sequel to Gurr's study, Mark Rylance illustrated the theatre's 'Artistic Policy and Practice' with a footballing anecdote:

> At a football match some time ago a perfect stranger turned to me during play and gave me his full opinion of the quality of the game and what should be done about it. I experienced the same easy communication between strangers while watching [Northern Broadside's 1995] *A Midsummer Night's Dream* at the Globe. (Mulryne 1997: 171)

Curiously absent from these reflections on theatre, sport and social engineering is any mention of Bertolt Brecht. Indeed, Rylance's 'stranger', in his ability to step outside the excitement of the event and offer a reasoned analysis, closely resembles the ideal spectator of Brecht's smokers' theatre. In a fragmentary note, Brecht (1964: 8) wrote that 'I even think that in a Shakespearean production one man in the stalls with a cigar could bring about the downfall of Western art.' In the elision of sport and theatre lay a liberatory potential:

> There seems to be nothing to stop the theatre having its own form of 'sport'. If only someone could take those buildings designed for theatrical purposes which are now standing eating their heads off in interest, and treat them as more or less empty spaces for the successful pursuit of 'sport', then they would be used in such a way that might mean something to a contemporary public that earns real contemporary money and eats real contemporary beef. (Brecht 1964: 6–7)

Shakespeare's Globe clearly meant something to the contemporary public that patronised it in the first few years of its existence, but for critics accustomed to treating Shakespearean performances as interpretation rather than mere 'play' or 'sport', Globe productions tended to offer few interpretive, Shakespearean 'discoveries'. Michael Billington (2000a) argues that reviewing Shakespeare involves the optimistic quest for insights: 'one is always looking for new discovery, some new awareness, some moment in the text that you've never really discovered before. Discovery is what you are after.' Worthen (1997: 164) describes a similar terminology (and its interpretive implications) in academic performance criticism: 'Hapgood and others assign the Shakespearean text a more overtly theological function: the text determines a range of potential meanings which the performance works to discover.' In 2000 Billington (2000a) felt that he had not 'yet found any Shakespeare play coming alive in that space in the way that it does in a controlled environment', and that none of the productions had 'enhanced my understanding of Shakespeare in any way'. Could this be because an uncontrolled, playful environment such as the Globe is inimical to the presentation of 'discovery', if discovery is conceived as insight into character or theme? As Rylance forecast before the theatre's official opening: 'It will be very difficult to "present" a play there, to present a "solution" to a play. An audience responds to the playing' (Mulryne 1997: 171). In this sporting environment, the critic, denied a modern 'reading' of the play, in turn responds to the audience response.

Adapting the perspective of reader-response theory to the act of theatrical spectatorship illuminates a key dynamic of Globe reviewing. Hans Robert Jauss (1982: 23) argues that reception involves 'the carrying out of specific instructions in a process of directed perception, which can be comprehended according to its constitutive motivations and triggering signals'. Before encountering a work of art, the reader-spectator will have internalised a framework of ideas and values which form a horizon of expectations against which the new artwork will be judged. As Susan Bennett (1997: 49) writes, 'at its first publication/performance, a work is measured against the dominant horizon of expectations. The closer it correlates with this horizon, the more likely it is to be low, pulp, or "culinary" art.' When the Globe's actors and audience were associated with indigenous forms of popular theatrical entertainment, such as the pantomime or the music hall, or with *Blind Date* and the Chippendales, or with football – one of the chief expressions of British popular culture – critics found the theatre guilty by association of correlating too closely with low cultural forms. Indeed, some Globe reviews literalised the idea of culinary art by commenting on the food and drink available for purchase in the theatre. Alastair Macaulay's steady course of disenchantment with the theatre can be traced in his attitude to the culinary dimension of the Globe experience. Reviewing *The Winter's Tale* in 1997, he wrote: 'the atmosphere is relaxed, with drinks and food being quietly sold from time to time in the central promenade area. In the intervals, you can buy bagels and champagne and consume them by the Thames, looking over to St Pauls [sic]' (*TR* 1997: 723). Four years later, however, in a review that began with the bald verdict 'the worst Shakespeare in London is usually whatever's on at Shakespeare's Globe', the presence of the culinary was no longer so civilised. When Macbeth said 'Come, seeling night', the 'come' was apparently taken as a cue 'for uniformed flunkies in the middle-tier audience boxes to start serving chipolata sausages and other buffet food to the toffs seated there' (*TR* 2001: 748). In Macaulay's complaint we can see the results of optical chaos: the critic's gaze is torn between high and low cultures – even if they are 'toffs', the act of eating at a heightened moment in the drama marks them as philistines – and the meaning of Shakespearean performance must somehow reconcile Macbeth's soliloquy with an all-too conspicuous act of consumption.

Many critics spelled out the coordinates of their lowest expectations of the Globe in reviews of seasons 1997–9. In 1997 Benedict Nightingale wrote approvingly that 'the thatched-and-timbered cylinder opposite St Paul's is not going to be a theme-park for trippers or a playpen for academics' (*TR* 1997: 723; the phrase was recycled almost verbatim in his review of *Hamlet*, *TR* 2000: 756). These worst-case scenarios also surfaced in Paul Taylor's review of the same production: 'A tourist-trap-cum-playpen-for-cranky-academics? The Globe can be infinitely more' (*TR* 1997: 726). (Both Nightingale's and Taylor's images infantilise academic spectators.) Within two years many critics had decided that the Globe had failed to steer a consistent course past the Scylla of tourism and the Charybdis of academia. For Billington in 1999, the theatre was 'caught halfway between academic exercise and tourist totem', and needed to 'urgently rethink its future' (*TR* 1999: 673). In the theatre's defence, Sheridan Morley wrote that 'the Globe may well be at its best when filled not by theatregoers but by schoolchildren and scholars desperate to see Sam Wanamaker's impossible dream made timber' (1000). Despite differing attitudes to the value of the theatre, both Billington and Morley shared the assumption that tourists, schoolchildren and scholars are in a mutually exclusive category to that of 'theatregoers'. And this despite, or perhaps because of, the fact that the Shakespearean theatrical economy – whether in London, Stratford, North American festivals or elsewhere – depends heavily on tourist and school group bookings.

In their anxiety about the low cultural atmosphere of the Globe, these reviews revealed a more general concern about what conditions of production and reception are most appropriate, even authentic, for Shakespeare's plays. The critique of the perceived pantomimic, sporting, Disneyfied and multinational Globe audience was motivated by the assumption that none of these conditions is appropriate to the perpetuation of what is valuable in Shakespeare. Subtlety, subtext, psychology, thematic and linguistic complexity are the characteristically valorised concepts of twentieth-century Shakespearean criticism and reception. Since most reviewers studied English as undergraduates at a time when New Critical approaches dominated the discipline, the values of New Criticism inform their collective construction of Shakespeare. The Globe, seemingly led by its audience, was frequently found incapable of reproducing these values. In a bizarre trope, critics repeatedly called the would-be authentic space for Shakespeare, the facsimile of the theatre in which many of his plays were premiered, unworthy of his plays.

Writing about the Globe's second season, Macaulay opened his review of *The Merchant of Venice* with this injunction: 'Go to Shakespeare's Globe and discover why, in Shakespeare's day, his plays seemed no greater than those of several other playwrights' (*TR* 1998: 689). Macaulay's argument, in essence, was that the Globe space dumbs down all it contains, levelling Shakespeare to the reduced stature of his contemporaries. Implicitly, he suggested that Shakespeare's peerlessness, his supremacy over all other playwrights, only became apparent with the advent of naturalism and inhibited audiences. Indeed, surveying the reception of non-Shakespearean Globe productions in this period throws a revealing sidelight on reviewers' Shakespeare. Take, for example, Kate Kellaway's verdict on Middleton's city comedy: '*A Chaste Maid in Cheapside*, directed by Malcolm McKay, is a play for groundlings and last Wednesday a responsive audience had a great time of it – spitting, hissing and cursing [really?] – just as Middleton would have liked' (*TR* 1997: 1084). In addition to implying that there must also be plays that are *not* for the groundlings, that are so much caviar wasted on the general, Kellaway further invoked authorial sanction for the 'spitting, hissing and cursing'. I could not find one example of a reviewer using Shakespeare in the way that Middleton was used here: as authorising audience participation. On the contrary, in the Globe's first full season, Jane Edwardes commented that the open-air audience was so distracting that 'for all we know Shakespeare let out a sigh of relief when his plays were moved indoors' (1082). Robert Gore-Langton in a similar manoeuvre offered the hypothesis 'that when the original Globe burnt down, Shakespeare himself torched it out of frustration at the awkward working conditions that have now been so lovingly recreated' (*TR* 1999: 673). Hannah Betts, also speaking on behalf of Shakespeare's real feelings about the Globe, claimed that while the theatre may have captured Shakespeare's imagination when it first opened, 'it wouldn't do much for him today' (*TR* 2001: 912). The Lazarus Shakespeare had also appeared a hundred years earlier in Max Beerbohm's verdict on William Poel's Elizabethan Stage Society: 'if Shakespeare could come to life again he would give Mr Poel a wide berth, and would hurry to the nearest commercial theatre in which a play of his happened to be running' (Beerbohm 1969: 222).

In 1998 the Globe produced two more plays, *The Honest Whore* and *A Mad World, My Masters*, in which Middleton either had a hand or was sole author. Charles Spencer wrote that although both were in 'the dramatic Second XI' when compared with Shakespeare, he was 'not sure that such plays don't work better at the Globe than major Shakespeare. Their simpler language, he continued, 'strong plots and unashamed populism make them exactly right for this space, whereas Shakespeare's richness often struggles to communicate itself to those thronging the yard' (*TR* 1998: 1073–4). He then went on to describe *A Mad World* as 'the Jacobean equivalent of a Ray Cooney farce or even *The Benny Hill Show*'; the comedy of the latter is so independent of language that it enjoys greater popularity in some non-Anglophone countries than it ever did in Britain. The notion that the Globe is a more appropriate space for Shakespeare's less complicated, more rompish near-contemporaries can also be found in Edwardes's view that Brome's *Antipodes* 'suits Shakespeare's Globe better than the playwright after whom the theatre is named' (*TR* 2000: 1006). For most reviewers, the Globe was inadequate to the demands of Shakespeare. There was an underlying assumption, conditioned by naturalistic theatrical conventions, that the ideal atmosphere for Shakespearean reception is one of stillness, silence and reverence. Paul Taylor, reviewing the 2000 *Hamlet*, described the ushering of 'noisy late-comers' to their seats as an intolerable but characteristic obstacle 'to the requisite atmosphere of hushed concentration' (*TR* 2000: 754).

* * *

The staging of authenticity is a social event. In all theatre, as Anthony B. Dawson (1999: 62) writes, a 'habit is put into play, an institutional one specific to theatre in which we might say that social ritual is "remembered" and a temporary community nostalgically configured'. That nostalgic configuration is the subject of intense scrutiny in the staging of Shakespearean authenticity. In the 1890s and early 1900s, as we have seen, Max Beerbohm (1953: 258) objected that Poel's attempts at historical reconstruction were doomed, because 'we, in the twentieth century, cannot project – or rather retroject – ourselves' into the original audience's 'state of receptivity'. Beerbohm then devoted much of his review not to the production, *Twelfth Night*, but to an analysis of the contemporary audience and the motivation of its desire for this nostalgic configuration. Beerbohm's epithet for the members of the Elizabethan Stage Society was 'owlish', 'implying a certain rather morbid and inhuman solemnity and a detachment from the light of day' (258). Almost a hundred years later, the reception of Shakespearean authenticity was once again permeated by audience analysis. But that audience was no longer the archaeological, dusty and nocturnal Edwardians Beerbohm mocked; rather, the contemporary Globe audience was defined by its multinational, hedonistic and day-lit characteristics.

In reading theatre reviews for evaluative patterns and ideological subtexts, I do not mean to conduct a witch-hunt, outing some critics as xenophobic, others as conservative or elitist. Every theatregoer at some point has been irritated or distracted by fellow audience members. It could also be argued that much of the criticism levelled at these early Globe productions was justifiable. Freud, warning against over-interpretation, allegedly advised, 'Sometimes a cigar is just a cigar.' Similarly, sometimes a bad review is just a bad review, a bad show just a bad show. As W.B. Worthen (1997: 86) had to admit when discussing the antagonistic reception of a Peter Sellars production: 'It is possible, of course, that the kind of acting that Sellars developed for *The Merchant of Venice* was just plain bad.' Arguably, many of the productions discussed above were 'just plain bad', under-cast and/or unimaginatively directed. Yet much of what appears in early Globe reviews seemed to be energised by a response to something other than on-stage blocking, diction and characterisation, or any other component of what is traditionally defined as the performance. Rather, much of the hostility stemmed from a number of deep-seated cultural presuppositions: 1) that audiences at Shakespeare, if they must be seen, should not be heard; 2) that the requisite atmosphere for Shakespearean reception is one of silence and reverence, like that of the naturalistic theatre, or indeed, the act of reading; 3) that Shakespeare – but *not* his contemporaries – had a low opinion of the groundlings and preferred the higher culture of indoor theatre; 4) that foreign audience members are liable to be disruptive and incompetent readers of drama, and are prone to come between the Englishman and his Shakespeare; and 5) that Shakespeare should exist in a discrete cultural sphere, uncontaminated by contact with popular cultural forms such as television, pantomime or football. It would be quite possible to criticise Globe productions without holding any of these assumptions. Hannah Betts's verdict that 'the Globe serves up a lowest common denominator *non speaka da lingo* farce that you wouldn't wish upon your least favourite au pair' (*TR* 2001: 912) says more about the social situation and privileged child-care arrangements of the reviewer (and her presumed readership) than it does about the theatrical merits, or otherwise, of Mike Alfred's *Cymbeline*.

In a 1988 interview, Graham Holderness asked Sam Wanamaker whether he thought that the Globe, when constructed and opened to the public, would 'represent a genuine ground of international solidarity and friendship'. Wanamaker responded: 'If we are looking for forces to bring people together whatever their language, social status, culture, educational level; and if we seek within English culture a fitting representative figure manifesting the language and people, where else would we look but to Shakespeare and a few other great writers?' (Holderness 1988: 19). This is an attractive, idealistic image of the globally cohesive power of performance and of communal space. Much of the Globe's early reception, however, shows the results of the implicit tensions of Wanamaker's utopian project. If Shakespeare manifests English culture, language and people, *which* aspects of this culture does he embody? How is it possible to represent a distinct idea of Englishness – this is clearly what was at stake for Wanamaker – and simultaneously to include the foreign or the culturally incompetent without threatening the ideal self-conception of the privileged national culture? Bourdieu ([1979] 1986: 7) writes that 'the sacred sphere of culture' is defined by its denial of 'lower, coarse, vulgar, venal, servile – in a word, natural – enjoyment' and, in that denial, 'implies an affirmation of the superiority of those who can be satisfied with the sublimated, refined ... distinguished pleasures forever closed to the profane. That is why art and cultural consumption are predisposed, consciously and deliberately or not, to fulfil a social function of legitimating social differences.'

In July 1993 Wanamaker was made a CBE in recognition of his work on the Globe and for the 'remarkable contribution [he] has made to relations between Britain and the United States'.[2] Although it could not have been predicted at the time, the next decade proved that part of that remarkable contribution was to create a space in which the special relationships (or social differences) between the indigenous and the foreign, and between high and low national cultures would be provoked and brought to light through the apparently cohesive force of Shakespeare.

'Dear Mr Billington': the audience writes back

In May 2011 Michael Billington concluded his review of the Globe's new production of *Much Ado About Nothing* in a fashion not unfamiliar to his regular readers: 'But a carnivalesque evening would be better for a touch of self-restraint. In some theatres, actors play to the gallery. Here, they are in thrall to the groundlings' (Billington 2011a). For the reader of the paper edition of the *Guardian,* that was the last word on the matter. But for the reader of the *Guardian Online* there was more. The review was posted on Friday evening, and by the following morning John Morrison – according to his profile, a former Reuters journalist from Kent – had accepted the invitation the *Guardian* now extended to all its readers, whoever and wherever they may be, and posted a comment underneath the review: 'Michael Billington's reviews of Globe productions always damn with faint praise and fall short of his normal high standards. "In thrall to the groundlings" – this verges on intellectual snobbery' – and more in the same vein in defence of the Globe and contradiction of the critic. Thirty-eight minutes later, Billington wrote back: 'Needless to say, I totally disagree with John Morrison...It is also nonsense to suggest that I am opposed to democratic theatrical spaces. What I am against is letting the groundlings dictate the tone and termpo [sic] of the performance.' By Sunday lunchtime, 'mollfrith' – no profile information – entered the fray:

Dear Mr Billington

I'm writing out of concern that you may be lost in the wrong century. It appears you think the Groundlings are some sort of underclass of illiterate morons, pissing in corners and drunkenly groping each other while grunting with proto-laughter at the funny people on the stage. I always stand at the Globe. Partly because, as a theatre professional, I am too poor to afford a seat... Here is a space that acknowledges its audience and enjoys them being there, regardless of how much they have paid. Ticket price should never be a signifier for how worthy, intelligent or discerning the audience are.

Go read some Barthes, and I highly recommend that on your next visit to Shakespeare's Globe, you part with the necessary fiver, stand amidst the happy throng, and see if you can't remember how to be excited by live performance.

All the best, Moll (Billington 2011a)

Under the pseudonym (one assumes) of the historical personage, this Roaring Girl rode to the defence of the groundlings from the moral high ground ('I am too poor'), equipped with insider knowledge ('as a theatre professional') and armed with a copy of Barthes. Twenty-four hours later Billington wrote back ('Dear Moll'). He felt misunderstood: he was not 'really attacking the groundlings', rather the 'increasing tendency of actors to "milk" laughs and rely heavily on the ground-level spectators to respond'. Later that evening, Moll rebutted: 'There still seems to be a lingering assumption that ground-level spectators are more likely to laugh, which carries with it an implication that they are less discerning than those seated', and so on. A full week later, 'Hollar' – no profile information – weighed in: 'As regular groundlings, my wife and I are surprised that the *Guardian* keeps sending Michael Billington to the Globe when his reviews show clearly that he misses the point. We always read his reviews through a prism.' The comments section closed, as is typical in this newspaper, a fortnight after the review was first posted. A review of 321 words had spawned a commentary of roughly 1400, 234 of these by the critic attempting to justify his position to a more or less politely disgruntled readership (Billington 2011a).

To move from the decade and a half from the opening of the Globe in 1997 to the early 2010s is to fast-forward from a situation in which the audience was routinely rhetorically present in reviews to one in which that audience was capable of publishing reviews itself – or at the very least having its views aired beneath those of the salaried critic. The *Guardian*, for example, first introduced the comments function underneath its theatre reviews in late 2010 (Dickson 2012a), and such exchanges and threads will be entirely familiar to anyone who reads reviews online in the second decade of the twenty-first century. It is impossible to know what percentage of review-readers consume – and sometimes respond to – online criticism in comparison with those that read reviews only in hard copy. To know a newspaper's circulation is not to know how readers use the paper when it is in circulation. Tracking the way that readers have received reviews in the present or on an historical basis might be an impossible enterprise; as David Paul Nord (2006: 269) writes: 'the reading of journalism, however, is even more difficult [than that of books] to trace in the past because journalism is so ephemeral and the reading of it so commonplace and unremarkable and therefore so commonly unremarked upon in the historical record'.

It is nevertheless safe to say that the introduction of interactive online reviewing has changed the relationship between reviewer and reader, a shift even greater than that effected by the widespread introduction of the signed article at the close of the nineteenth century. Interactive online reviewing poses some profound questions about the function and status of reviews, and about the qualification and relative expertise of salaried and amateur critics. For theatre historians it also raises questions about the object of study: if the critic writes back to his readers, as Billington did above, one might wonder where the 'review' ends and whether all accounts of production reception must now pay attention (but how much?) to the crowd-sourced supplements that now cascade beneath many reviews. 'When a text is consumed, this is done by readers who have perspectives, agendas and background knowledge that may differ radically from that encoded in the text. Hence, the reader of a newspaper may resist, subtly counter or directly misunderstand the encoded meaning of the report' (John E. Richardson 2007: 41) – the comments section stages and makes visible those acts of resistance, subtle countering and misprision between critic and reader, and in so doing it not only creates a fertile space for the analysis of reception, it also makes anything the critic writes provisional and vulnerable to further review.

It is routinely argued that the advent of the Internet has ushered us into a post-authoritarian era of arts criticism. It will surely not be long before more reviews are read online via a range of electronic devices than are read in hard copy. It is the 'hunch' of Andrew Dickson, *Guardian Online* arts editor, that this is already the case with the consumption of reviews in his paper (Dickson 2012a). These 'official' reviews will typically be complemented, post-scripted and potentially undermined – more or less explosively – by readers' comments sections. (In some papers, the willingness of readers to enter these fora has been relatively weak, but papers like the *Guardian* and the *Daily Telegraph* have successfully nurtured a culture of participation.) The long-term effects of these shifts are very hard to gauge or predict. 'Boxes, annotations, sidebars, blogs, web-links, user generated content, responses to journalists' pieces in virtual debate, all contribute to changes not only in newspapers but in their relationship with readers' (Conboy 2010: 145): but what those changes might be is hard to say with any degree of confidence. The easy consensus is that the inexorable rise of interactivity and user-generated feedback is part of a wider democratisation of arts criticism in a postmodern culture that distrusts deference and tends to subjectify matters of opinion and taste. Hierarchical criticism, in which the critic speaks *de haut en bas* to his readers, is seen as effete, elitist and suspiciously Reithian. The arts pages of the quality press have for much of the twenty-first century regularly carried features pitting this established/establishment critic against the blogger or citizen journalist, invariably with the strong implication that the demise of one and the triumph of the other was close at hand. An *Observer* feature of 13 July 2008 traded in exactly these stereotypes in presenting the battle between different generations and their respective versions of criticism. 'Is it curtains for critics?' it asked beneath a photo of a pair recruited directly from central casting for such showdowns. Image right: Clement Crisp, the distinguished, white and septuagenarian dance critic of the *Financial Times* (*FT*) – eminently grey-suited, haughtily regarding the camera down the impressive length of his aquiline nose. Image left: Joseph 'JP' Patterson, a young black blog-critic of grime music, huge gold chain over a t-shirt bearing the words 'WASTE MAN' above a large arrow pointing to the ballet critic to his left. It is a common refrain among artists that many mainstream critics are similarly past their sell-by date. Nicholas Hytner, artistic director of the National Theatre, disgruntled with the reception of Emma Rice's production of *A Matter of Life and Death* at his theatre in May 2007, memorably described the critical fraternity as 'dead white men': 'They don't know it's happened to them but it has... I think it's a very good thing that at least on Sunday there's a female voice or two amongst the theatre critics'; but on the whole he bitterly regretted the prevalence of what he took to be an homogeneous and often prejudiced critical community (quoted in Jury 2007).

It is, then, the case that questions of expertise and qualification – the same questions that haunted the formation of the Critics' Circle in the first half of the twentieth century (see pp. 12–15 above) – are today more vexed than ever and that this has much to do with the rise of blogs and of spaces in the online editions of newspapers dedicated to commentary and manufactured controversy. When he first published an online piece on which comments were invited, Michael Billington reflected: 'I was suddenly aware that there was an army of people with opinions as strong as mine. Journalists of my generation have to adapt. And we have to accept that the printed word no longer has aristocratic supremacy' (Rayner 2008). Asked in 1997 about the crisis in criticism, reviewers tended to lament the lack of space, audience and influence; by 2012 those anxieties were compounded by the remorseless march of the new model army of citizen critics engaged in an apparently asymmetrical civil war with the erstwhile aristocrats of print. The battle described in the previous chapter between incommensurable models of theatre – the ensemble versus the heroic individual – is now replayed in the arena of the production and consumption of arts criticism.

Responses to Billington's review of *Much Ado About Nothing* at the Globe revealed a potentially vocal readership keen to challenge the critic's alleged prejudice against a specific theatrical space. Six months later, in November 2011, Billington's review of Ian Rickson's production of *Hamlet* (starring Michael Sheen) at the Young Vic provided an even more fertile demonstration of a polyphonic critique of the reviewer's interpretive competence (Billington 2011b). This review sparked a longer than usual thread of seventy-one comments, some in agreement with Billington, some which thought him too generous, but most of which took issue with the critic's interpretation of the production's governing concept and the fact of his awarding it 'only' three stars out of five. The thread is worth pausing over for the various examples it affords of reader feedback. The review was posted at 11.14 pm on 9 November. Two and a quarter hours later rebeccaphoenix wrote:

> This production is *not* Freudian – IT IS NOT A FREUDIAN DREAM!!!!! Anything but?!!!!, – I AM AN USHER AT THE YOUNG VIC, I have had the privilege to see the show many times and I can tell you, there is not much that is Freudian about it! that is a grave mistake to make. It is more than anything, Laing-ian.

Billington's review was 635 words long; rebeccaphoenix's first response was 527 words long and was conceivably composed and posted (at 1.30 am) after the usher had attended the first night party for the show. It sparked a number of running battles and thread spats about the relative merits of Laingian and Freudian psychology, most from people who had not yet (or never would) see the production and many of whom had apparently read neither Laing nor Freud. Billington's response to rebeccaphoenix's contention that he would have written a more informed review had he been privy to the production's rehearsal process was robust: 'rebeccaphoenix must be living in a dream-world, as intense as that of Sheen's Hamlet, if she thinks critics can follow the trajectory of a production from start to finish: we do have other shows to see apart from the Young Vic Hamlet'.

The embedded expertise of the usher contrasted to the mixture of theatrical innocence and pertinent professional experience displayed by another commentator, the medically punning KidKneestone:

> I'm back from seeing the production tonight. It's the first time I've seen the play. I saw a schizophrenic Hamlet hearing voices, confused, afraid, sensitive and intelligent put under lock and key and patronised but still uncowed. As someone who works with mental health service users I recognised him and Ophelia and their predicament and found it powerful and moving.

Elsewhere one could observe the emergence of improvised networks of correspondence between posters. JJ139 responded to offtheedge: 'When are you going? My ticket is for 23 November. if the same night, maybe we can compare notes?' In such an instance, the review text has acted as an inadvertent Pandarus bringing two readers together. But the notion of these two strangers seeing the show for themselves burns off the catalyst, as it were, and Billington's Uncle Pandarus is left behind as the new couple elope to 'compare notes' and perhaps make up their own minds.

Other comments revealed different user functions of the review. For at least one reader, the review offered a pretext for an airing of more general thoughts about Shakespeare. Byrani had 'not seen the production and have no intention (and no opportunity) so to do'. He or she had, however, read the review and the thirty-six comments that had been posted at that point 'with enormous interest', all of which served as a preamble for an anti-theatrical set-piece on the preferability of reading the plays in 'the theatre of one's own mind'. Most comments sections for reviews of high-concept productions of Shakespeare will feature at least one expression of despair at the liberties taken by directors and designers. 'Sussexperson', for example, appeared to be channelling the director-phobia of James Agate, right down to a version of the equine analogy Agate had employed to describe Helpmann's defeat by some lengths to 'Production' in the 1946 *Hamlet* (see pp. 103–4 above):

> Why do they *do* this? – get an actor whose Hamlet the world has been waiting for, then sabotage him with some god-awful directorial 'concept'? By all means try out experimental readings of the play, but NOT at the cost of a fine actor who could have illuminated the play Shakespeare actually wrote. (As opposed to the one the director thinks he should have written.) It's like giving a great horse his one chance at the Derby, then making him run it hitched up to a milk-float. Just *wrong*.

The ability to redirect through hyperlinks also poses a challenge to the authority of the critic by reminding the reader that there are worlds elsewhere. After forty-four comments had been posted in thirteen hours, Tonyhoward advised that 'John Morrison has written the best analysis of this superb production so far on his blog', to which he linked before signing off: 'if the Guardian would like to find a successor to Mr. Billington – look no further!' (Billington 2011b). The spectres of retirement, redundancy and succession are never far from the surface of Shakespearean reviewing.

The World Shakespeare Festival 2012: coverage, comment and the framer framed

The World Shakespeare Festival spanned seven months (April – November 2012) and was produced by the RSC in collaboration with a range of UK and international arts organisations. These included Shakespeare's Globe, whose 'Globe to Globe' seven-week season of thirty-seven plays performed in thirty-seven different languages was an obvious highlight of the Festival and accounted for just over half its productions. (See Edmondson et al. 2013; Carson and Bennett 2013.) Billed in publicity as 'the biggest celebration of Shakespeare ever staged', the Festival formed the centrepiece of the Cultural Olympiad that accompanied the London 2012 Olympic Games and brought thousands of artists from around the world to perform in almost seventy shows. While some effort was made to spread the Festival across the UK (including Birmingham, Wales, Scotland and Newcastle), the vast majority of these productions played in London or Stratford-upon-Avon. This section therefore bounces back and forth between these hubs in order to track the course of the Festival as it unfolded online and in the arts pages of national newspapers.

The World Shakespeare Festival officially opened with two RSC productions in the Swan Theatre, Stratford-upon-Avon. These versions of *Richard III* and *King John* simultaneously launched a strand of the Festival entitled 'Nations at War'. (Like the so-called 'Shipwreck Trilogy' – *Twelfth Night*, *The Comedy of Errors* and *The Tempest* – that opened in the Stratford main house in the following week, *Richard III* and *King John* were cross-cast but with different directors.) The cross-casting and thematic packaging sought to justify the choice of plays while also serving to steer critical and audience response. The reception of these two opening productions was instructive by virtue of its utter banality. Those critics who liked *Richard III* tended to value it as a relatively straightforward rendition of the text: in the *Daily Express*, Neil Norman approved of a *Richard III* devoid of 'tiresome directorial "concepts", just thrilling, brilliantly acted theatre' (*TR* 2012: 408). Those who found the production underpowered tended to articulate that lack in relation to previous interpretations. Michael Coveney argued that 'the greatest RSC Richards – Ian Holm and Antony Sher – had a vein of cold steel in their make-up. [Jonjo] O'Neill has only a sliver' (*TR* 2012: 408). For Charles Spencer, the choice of play was unfortunate, 'because memories of Kevin Spacey's thrilling performance' at the Old Vic in 2011 were 'still so vivid'. The critic then went on to mix memory with comparative masculinity: 'Fine actor though he is, Jonjo O'Neill sometimes seems like a boy sent to do man's work in comparison with Spacey in the title role' (408). Here again was an instance of ghost writing, of the repeating loop: Spencer had used the same analogy seventeen years before in comparing two of the Macbeths – Paul Higgins for the English Touring Theatre and Jeffery Kissoon at the Birmingham Rep – discussed earlier in this chapter. Then, Spencer had concluded of Higgins that 'after Kissoon he seems like a boy sent to do man's work' (*TR* 1995: 1312). Slightly later in the Stratford season, another adaptation of the play – *Two Roses for Richard III* by Brazilian company Companhia Bufomecânica – opened in the Courtyard Theatre, and here again memory was deployed rhetorically: as Neil Norman wrote in the *Express*, 'with the possible exception of Peter O'Toole's *Macbeth* this is the first time I have seen Shakespeare marred beyond measure' (570). Of the same show, Spencer wrote, 'we have quite enough gimmicky Shakespeare of our own. Do we really need to import it from Brazil, which, on this evidence alone, really is the place where the nuts come from?' (571).

Richard III reviews thus tended to issue forth from the 'heavy casket of reminiscence' (Beerbohm) and work comparatively, while those for Swedish director Maria Aberg's *King John* provided a critical echo chamber for normative British attitudes to director's theatre (and its potentially deleterious effects on the young). Libby Purves in *The Times* disliked the production's generally irreverent atmosphere, its recasting of the Bastard and Pandulph as female characters and its playful anti-heroism; she concluded her review: 'To school parties, let it be sternly said that while grown-up RSC directors get away with pointless, empty-headed larking, audiences don't. It would be very wrong to draw rude faces on the balloons [that flooded the stage after the interval] and bat them back. I resisted, so can you' (*TR* 2012: 410). It was odd but strangely typical of British Shakespearean reviewing that reception did not split predictably down party-political lines. Critics on the UK's two left-leaning daily papers did not like the production. Michael Billington felt that 'Aberg's hunger for innovation dwindles into idiocy'

(409), while Paul Taylor in the *Independent* deplored a 'stupefyingly dire modern-dress production' (410). Meanwhile in more typically conservative newspapers Dominic Cavendish (*Telegraph*) and Maxie Szalwinska, (*Sunday Times*) recognised the boldness of 'a Shakespeare most directors don't want to touch' (Szalwinska, *TR* 2012: 410); Cavendish acutely noted the ways the production caught 'the strained party ambience of our jubilee year' (*TR* 2012: 410), the jubilee in question being the sixtieth anniversary of the accession of Queen Elizabeth II. But perhaps most surprisingly, only six national critics reviewed *King John* (the norm for new Stratford productions was roughly twice that number). It is not impossible that advance news of the production's cross-gendered casting together with the starless nature of the company had combined to deter reviewers from making the trip.

Five out of six of these *King John* reviews appeared in the first week of Globe to Globe, and one could be forgiven for thinking that the diaries of British reviewers were so replete with Shakespearean engagements in the capital that they could not squeeze in a night in Stratford. Reviews of early Globe to Globe productions were full of eager anticipation of a busy late spring: 'It looks set to be a monumental seven weeks' (Mountford, *TR* 2012: 406); 'Roll on the next show, and the next' (Cavendish, *TR* 2012: 471); 'If Week One is anything to go by, Globe to Globe will be a culturally fascinating feast of languages, ethnic costumes and music, variously combining ancient traditions with modern and global sensibilities' (Bassett, *TR* 2012: 471). But despite this early enthusiasm, most critics were conspicuous by their absence at the festival. For the vast majority of readers of the UK press it was all too easy to miss these 'monumental seven weeks'.

Only one newspaper – the *Guardian* – reviewed every show (with the exception of *Venus and Adonis*) in the festival. The *FT* was the only paper whose coverage approached that of the *Guardian*, perhaps because the *FT*'s offices lie on Southwark Bridge, three minutes' walk away from the Globe, and are thus easily the most proximate of any newspaper to the theatre. After a slow start, the *FT* managed to review eighteen productions. In many cases, though, these reviews were confined to two paragraphs of roughly eighty words in total, thus severely limiting any scope for detailed analysis and in some places leading to positively telegrammatic results.

There were clear disincentives for newspapers to review Globe to Globe shows. The schedule was intensive, and most Globe to Globe productions ran for only two performances, so any notices that were written were often published and read after the show had closed. With the exception of the Q Brother's Hip-Hop *Othello: The Re-mix*, Deafinitely Theatre's British Sign

Language production of *Love's Labour's Lost* and the Globe's own *Henry V*, all productions were non-Anglophone and thus, arts editors might have felt, of less immediate interest to their readers.

Newspapers that would usually cover major theatre openings largely stayed away. The right-wing press – that is, nearly every UK paper – dispatched reviewers to a bare handful of productions. These were shows that had the most obvious appeal as a species of news: a controversial Israeli production of *The Merchant of Venice* or a *Cymbeline* from South Sudan, at that point the world's youngest country. The National Theatre of China's *Richard III* received some coverage, perhaps reflecting the media's increasing interest in the superpower; by contrast, some attention was paid to the Maori production of *Troilus and Cressida* as an ethnographical curiosity that could touch on a common reference point for readers (the *haka*, known widely as the prelude to New Zealand international rugby games) and that might metonymically stand for the 'exoticism' of the festival as a whole.

If one removes the efforts of the *Guardian* and the *FT* and discounts reviews of the Globe's own English-language *Henry V*, the national press published only fifteen reviews *in total* of the remaining thirty-seven Globe to Globe productions. By way of comparison, the opening night (22 May 2012) at the Hampstead Theatre of *Chariots of Fire* – a straightforward if imaginatively staged attempt to cash in on the Olympics and the popularity of the film on which it was based – was attended by no fewer than seventeen national critics. New productions at the RSC or the Globe can generally depend on notices to be published in at least a dozen national titles within a week of press night. Many who attended all or part of the Globe to Globe festival would argue that it offered an education in theatre aesthetics and an opportunity to see the work of some challenging – even revolutionary – theatre-makers. The benefits to British artists and audiences of exposure to such work might be vast. But as far as most newspapers were concerned, these foreign Shakespeares could be safely ignored. The revolution, as Gil Scott Heron warned, will not be televised.

Given this context of wholesale apathy and indifference, the *Guardian*'s coverage of the Globe to Globe festival was a great feat. Its first-string critics – Michael Billington and Lyn Gardner – could not have covered the whole festival even if they had wanted to, as there was the usual roster of other opening nights to attend over the seven weeks. Andrew Dickson (six reviews), Maddy Costa (one) and Kate Kellaway (one) ably supported Billington and Gardner, with the net result that the paper's experienced theatre critics covered sixteen productions in total. A scratch cohort of thirteen writers, drafted in from the paper's wider arts coverage, reviewed the remaining twenty-one productions. Most of these writers were expert in an art form other than that of theatre or, if they did write primarily about the stage, did so in a subgenre of theatre writing different from reviewing (interviews, profiles, previews, etc.). Care was apparently taken wherever possible to match the writer's expertise with some aspect of the production: music writer Kieran Yates reviewed the Q Brother's Hip-Hop *Othello*; Nosheen Iqbal – whose expressed interests included Pakistani politics and arts – reviewed the Pakistani/Urdu *Shrew*; comedy critic Brian Logan was given the highly physical South Korean *Dream*; Chris Michael, who 'writes about culture, Japan and William Shatner' (Michael 2012a), covered the Japanese *Coriolanus* (not, alas, starring William Shatner). But the fact remained that for most of these writers, their Globe review marked their first published theatre review in the paper – and perhaps anywhere – and that these were therefore purveyors of what one of them elsewhere described as 'humble, non-reviewer opinion[s]' (Needham 2012).

The most interesting features of the *Guardian*'s coverage of the Globe to Globe festival, then, were not the evaluations expressed in the reviews. These were largely sympathetic and averaged fractionally under 3.5 stars, with sixteen of the 37 productions awarded 4 stars. It would have been most unexpected if the quality of productions had been questioned on a regular basis. To do so would have been to query the purpose of the festival as a whole. These were often inexperienced critics writing about often unfamiliar plays, languages and performance traditions for a newspaper that had made a commitment to the festival, partly one assumes because of the festival's admirable (if far from uncomplicated) spirit of pluralism and multiculturalism, a spirit consonant with that of the newspaper and its presumed readership.

In the *Guardian*'s coverage of the Globe to Globe the competence of the critic was as likely to be questioned as the skills of the performers. The context was especially combustible given the national, racial, cultural and linguistic sensitivities that surround the production and reception of multi- and intercultural theatre. In only the third production, the Maori interpretation of *Troilus and Cressida*, Andrew Dickson described how the performance began with 'a bulging-eyed, tongue-waggling, foot-stamping haka-style war dance and rarely loses its energy thereafter', a sentence which sparked a heated dissection of the valence and connotations of each of the descriptors. In self-defence, Dickson responded that it was 'simply a description of what I saw, and an attempt (perhaps limited, but that's what happens when you have 55 minutes to write a review) to conjure it up for readers who weren't there'. CakeTin retorted that:

> References to 'bulging eyes' and 'tongue waggling' (I can live with the foot stamping) could have been better covered with something simple, like 'a ferocious haka' (people have the internet now – if they're that curious they can look it up. But when you've only got 55 minutes to knock out a review I guess it's hard to self-censor your inner Little Englander.)

With the advent of interactive Internet reviewing, Globe reception is now truly global: New Zealanders – whether expat or not was impossible to tell – weighed in, most gently to correct Dickson on the technical definition of a haka, while also defending him from the thinly veiled accusation of racism levelled by some commentators. Ehereni addressed the critic: 'Anyway, welcome to the great debate of NZ, you have successfully picked the top off the festering boil of resentment and barely disguised racism we get to listen to on talkback radio at home all the time... consider yourself blooded!' (Dickson 2012b).

Many of the *Guardian*'s critics might indeed have considered themselves blooded by the experience of reviewing the Globe to Globe festival. Andrew Gilchrist's observation that the Swahili in which *The Merry Wives of Windsor* was performed 'had an earthy gusto, an air of languor and sunshine, that made Shakespeare's prose seem prissy and verbose' perhaps deservedly got a kicking from the commentariat: 'Swahili has a long history of love poetry extending back to Shakespeare's day and beyond. It can be just as prissy and verbose as John Bloody Donne... still, The Guardian can be relied upon to be both patronising *and* ignorant while awarding five stars' (Gilchrist 2012). Kieran Yates's observation that hearing Shakespeare's lines rapped in *Othello* made one realise 'that Shakespeare himself is a master of rhythm and rhyme' provoked a flurry of scorn: 'The reviewer's comment is one of the most inane and ignorant observations I've ever read in a so-called quality journal. I take it the Guardian is now employing 14-year-olds with no prior knowledge of literature or drama to write its theatre reviews' (Yates 2012). CardinalPirelli deconstructed Chris Michael's review of *Coriolanus* in great and telling detail:

> 'There is no psychological realism here, and little trust in the essential drama:'
>
> Oh dear, it's all downhill from here, knowing Japan you should know your Japanese theatre which should give an indication as to what to expect and the 'essential drama' is not going to come from some western concept of psychological realism. (Michael 2012b)

In addition to this trend of trenchant crowd-sourced metacriticism, Globe to Globe reviews also evidenced a shift in the representation of the audience within the bounds of the review proper. It was generally the case that by the early 2010s reviewers of Globe productions devoted less attention to the audience and the nature of the space than they had in the late 1990s. By the 2010s, most critics had moved beyond grappling with the distinctive characteristics of Globe performativity to a more normative position of reading the production's major interpretive choices and individual performances. Critics could also assume that their readers did not need to be informed or reminded of the peculiar dynamics of a theatre that was by now well established. A significant minority of the Globe to Globe productions derived from earlier productions devised for indoor, often naturalistic environments. These productions – if not specifically re-engineered for the Globe space – therefore featured less audience interaction than shows expressly designed for an outdoor thrust space. It was also predictably the case that productions of the comedies tended to feature more audience interaction, and this interaction was harder for the critic to ignore when evaluating the salient features of the event. Of the eleven reviews that did not mention the Globe audience *at all*, seven were of tragedies (*Julius Caesar*, *Titus*, *Richard II*, *Othello*, *Macbeth*, *Timon*, *Hamlet*; the others being *Tempest*, *Shrew*, *Much Ado* and *Troilus*). Half the reviews (eighteen) mentioned the audience in a very brief or generic fashion (e.g. references to warm applause or a small attendance). Only three (*Merry*, *John*, *Merchant*) offered the kind of extended or personalised anecdote so common to the reviewing of the opening seasons.

The audience had broken out of the passive position of being framed by the review into a new and active role in which its comments – often the last word on the matter – became the frame. After many years of having its wildness and indecorum censured, the Globe audience was beginning to write its own sequel to the taming narrative, a sequel plausibly entitled The Framer Framed.

'Back to British business as usual': race, nation and regime change in *Henry V* at the Globe and *Julius Caesar* in Stratford

On Sunday 3 June 2012 the Lithuanian theatre company Meno Fortas brought to an end its three-performance run of *Hamlet*. Theirs was the last 'foreign' contribution to the Globe to Globe festival. In the following days, two new World Shakespeare Festival productions opened – one at the Globe, one at the Royal Shakespeare Theatre, Stratford-upon-Avon – the receptions of which would say much about the condition of

Shakespearean reviewing and indeed the state of the nation in the summer of 2012.

With the departure of the Lithuanians, the Globe was dark for three nights to allow for technical rehearsals for the final offering of the season, the theatre's own production of *Henry V*. This show was scheduled as both the culmination of the Globe to Globe festival and the curtain raiser to the theatre's annual summer season. Unlike all other productions in the festival, the show would bed in for a long run and would observe none of the restrictions of (e.g.) length required of the visiting productions. The choice to present *Henry V* as the home team's offering was – according to taste – mischievous, crass or knowingly celebratory. Consciously or not, it appeared to be based on the logic of the Proms, another annual festival in which weeks of very varied concerts by international performers and orchestras climaxes in – or perhaps descends into – the licensed merriment and soft-core patriotism of the Last Night of the Proms. The programming of Shakespeare's most triumphalist history play jarred with the dominant ethos the festival wanted to project but was nevertheless of a piece with one strand of the festival's self-image. Beside the assiduous and unimpeachable multiculturalism sat a quiet, stubbornly unreconstructed nationalism. The slogan 'Shakespeare's coming home' featured in advertisements for the Globe to Globe festival – a reference, probably lost on many tourists, to the chorus of the song 'Three Lions', the official anthem of the host nation's football team in the 1996 European Championships held in England: 'It's coming home, / It's coming home, / It's coming... / Football's coming home.' ('Shakespeare's coming home' was also stamped on the 'passport' of those who had bought groundling season tickets for the festival.) Appropriating and proudly 'owning' the type of football analogy previously used to smear it, the Globe's choice of slogan positioned Shakespeare as an English invention whose popularity had since spread across the world but whose ultimate expression could only be realised on home soil. The Globe to Globe festival – like the 1996 European Championship – would mark a moment of homecoming, but also of competition in which the pluck and pride of the host nation might win through. England did not win the 1996 European Championship. Whoever it was at the Globe that chose the slogan, one wonders to what extent they were aware of the fact that football, like Shakespeare, may have started 'here' but that is no guarantee of 'our' quality, let alone supremacy.

Despite multiple absences during the Globe to Globe festival, with the opening of *Henry V* the reviewers of the national press returned *en masse* and on message. 'After the enticing international extravaganza of Globe to Globe', Fiona Mountford wrote in the *Evening Standard*, 'it's back to British business as usual at Bankside. Indeed, it would be hard, in this summer of national celebration, to get much more triumphantly British than Henry sticking it to the French at Agincourt' (*TR* 2012: 657). The frame of reference that critics brought to bear was not the eclectic inter- and multiculturalism of the Globe to Globe season, but rather of an extended 'summer of national celebration' stretching from the Queen's Diamond Jubilee in early June to the Olympics and Paralympics of July and August. According to Tim Walker in the *Sunday Telegraph*, Dominic Dromgoole had:

> timed to perfection his production of Shakespeare's celebration of our country, our way of life and our willingness to defend it. It picks up the renewed sense of nationhood that the Diamond Jubilee celebrations engendered, and it will serve, I fancy, as a useful staging-post between them and the similarly upbeat and patriotic opening ceremony that Danny Boyle has created for next month's Olympic Games. (*TR* 2012: 658)

Dominic Cavendish in the *Daily Telegraph* concluded his review: 'In the end, though, the evening acts as a chastening reminder of what a country needs when it's up against it. Those rash souls at the Ministry of Defence, pruning the army to within an inch of its life, would do well to take note' (*TR* 2012: 657). In both reviews, the nation is besieged, under attack, up against it. The 'French' have become aggressors and an invasive threat to 'our way of life'. This has very little at all to do with Shakespeare's play, in which, of course, it is the English who attack (tenuously contestable?) French territory, and 'ways of life' are scarcely articulated. But in Walker's and Cavendish's accounts, Shakespeare's 'celebration of our country' becomes another version of the transhistorical Englishness and unchanging Cockaigne that so appealed to Agate, the Englishness that stands up to the Hun, that alone defies the Nazis, that defends civil liberties in the face of foreign onslaught. In 2012 the idea of defending the English way of life not only harked back nostalgically to the Second World War, Churchill's 'finest hour' and the stoicism of a people who, since the financial crisis of 2008–?, had bought in their thousands retro merchandise bearing the words 'Keep Calm and Carry On': 'Defending the English way of life' in 2012 was also code for resistance to a range of perceived contemporary threats, including immigration, Islamic radicalism and the legislative intrusions of the European Union. The dissemination and amplification of these threats were (and will always be) the stock in trade of many newspapers. Such sleights of hand – in which the action of Shakespeare's play is misrepresented as an inspiring, last-gasp defence against foreign invasion – are entirely consonant with the beleaguered xenophobia that characterises most of the English press (much of it, of course, foreign-owned). It is particularly poignant and dispiriting that such a fear of the foreign was articulated in the immediate aftermath of the Globe to Globe festival.

The Conservative-led coalition that had governed Britain since 2010 was predicated on severe fiscal austerity under the Orwellian slogan 'We're all in this together' first offered by Chancellor of the Exchequer George Osborne. The fact that (in May 2012) the cabinet of twenty-nine contained eighteen millionaires did not escape comment. This context of *noblesse oblige* and elite leadership also informed the reception of Dromgoole's *Henry V*. Jamie Parker's Henry, full of 'public-school heart-throb dash' (Taylor, *TR* 2012: 659), offered an idealised embodiment of Cameron and his cabinet – the apotheosis of the personable public school boy leading his country through tough times with slogans like 'We're all in this together' or 'We few, we happy few'. Although costumed in generic medieval finery, 'there's a touch of school captain about him, a touch of the corporate troubleshooter. Profoundly reasonable, but don't push him', noted Dominic Maxwell, approvingly (658). The Battle of Waterloo, Wellington is commonly thought to have said, was won on the playing fields of Eton – Maxwell's account offers a *bildungsroman* in miniature of the frictionless ascent of our hero from private education to private finance. If the protagonist of the piece was reassuringly familiar, it was disappointing to Tim Walker at least that the villains were not as recognisable as they might have been: unlike Olivia Ross's Katherine with her 'seductive Gallic accent', the actors playing the Dauphin and King of France did not 'make even the limpest stamp at being at all French' (659). Nevertheless, the net effect of the production was for many critics a comforting alignment of past and present. Walker continued: 'Doubtless, Henry would have doffed his crown to the present incumbent for what she managed to achieve [in the Jubilee celebrations] for her own somewhat demoralized "band of brothers" earlier this month' (659)

Here, more perhaps than at any point in recent memory, the critical fraternity lacked a 'G.B.S.' or a Tynan or anyone with a sharp pen and a nose for cant. William Charles Macready – who existed in a state of perpetual disgust with the press – would have warmed to the theme. Macready it was who in June 1838 complained of having to read in newspapers 'the perpetual *stuff* of [Queen Victoria's] Coronation', including a lickspittle article on the Duke of Nemours' 'stormy' passage across the Channel:

Mighty Heaven! – would it not be better that such trash as the Duke of Nemours, and all the fools and sycophants that make up their mob of idolators were buried fathoms below the surface, rather than that the reason *which God has given man* should be prostituted and abased to such vile purpose as communicating or reading such disgusting absurdity? *Can England ever be intellectually and morally free?* I think – never. (Macready 1912: I 465–6)

The reception of *Henry V* would not have calmed Macready's nerves. Even though Lyn Gardner in the *Guardian* argued that *Henry V* promoted something more cozily progressive than militarism and monarchy ('Few plays so obviously celebrate the collaborative nature of theatre as *Henry V*'), nevertheless Gardner – like many of the critics, left and right, who saw this production – was ready to submit to Parker's Henry: 'I swear if this Henry had strode off the stage and out of the theatre at the end [of the St Crispin's Day speech], everyone would have followed him' (*TR* 2012: 657). Those who followed Parker's dashing Henry out of the theatre might even have endured the 100-mile trek north to Stratford-upon-Avon, the other 'home' to which Shakespeare came in that week in mid June 2012.

Gregory Doran's RSC production of *Julius Caesar* ostensibly offered a very different experience from that of Dromgoole's *Henry*. Doran relocated the action of the play to a contemporary African state and created a one-off company consisting exclusively of black British actors. These bold decisions notwithstanding, the pressure was on here for a number of reasons. In the context of Globe to Globe and of the several non-Anglophone productions that visited Stratford during the World Shakespeare Festival, Patrick Carnegy had written in his review of the 'Shipwreck Trilogy': 'It is left to the RSC to fly the flag for Shakespeare in his native tongue with a dozen new productions... The challenge for the RSC remains to justify its special claim to the Bard with performances at least as good as those coming in from all over the world' (*TR* 2012: 479). But Doran was not only compelled to compete with those foreign tongues, he also had a more local fight on his hands. *Julius Caesar* offers a late Elizabethan analysis of a Roman succession crisis, but this production represented another trial of substitution: it was Doran's first since the announcement that he was to succeed Michael Boyd as artistic director of the RSC. As discussed earlier, such a charged context informed and amplified the negative critical reception of Mark Rylance's *Macbeth* in 1995. Whereas then critics had been frankly appalled by Rylance's eccentric conceptual vision, the reception of Doran's 2012 *Caesar* was characterised by a unanimous sense that the RSC was now in hands that were both 'adventurous and safe' (Spencer) and that 'this revival [was] the RSC at its best, celebrating Shakespeare our contemporary' (Brown, *TR* 2012: 675). How had Doran jumped through the hoop of Shakespearean legitimacy?

This was not the first of the World Shakespeare Festival's 'African' Shakespeares: five of the Globe to Globe festival's productions had originated in Africa. In common with most of the season's offerings, these had been largely unreviewed. A rare exception was Robert McCrum's disappointed *Observer* review of the collaborative production by Bitter Pill (London) and The Theatre Company (Nairobi, Kenya) of *The Merry Wives of Windsor*:

> take away the matrix of Shakespeare's language and 16th-century culture, toss in occasional references to baboons, Mombasa and Tanzania, and you're left with a one-dimensional comic strip about the ludicrous antics of some cartoon characters. Perhaps if the show had been more truly African, less faithful to the Folio, and had also made better use of the theatrical opportunities presented by the Globe, this could have been a night to remember. (*TR* 2012: 471)

Here, being 'truly African' was at tension with being fully 'faithful to the Folio'. The production was performed in Swahili in an adapted and heavily cut version of Shakespeare's play, so it is not entirely clear how McCrum wished it to be less 'faithful'. If an African company struggled to be 'truly African', how would reviewers feel about British actors impersonating 'Africans' at the RSC?

Doran need not have feared. Of the dozen national newspaper critics that reviewed the show, only one found the 'African' setting problematic (for thoughtful academic reviews of this production, see Peter J. Smith 2012 and Smialkowska 2013). For the rest, it held a revelatory force. Libby Purves began her review by making sense of Doran's concept to her reader: 'Tidy northern Italians, with a delicate shudder, say "Africa begins at Rome": flinching at the idea of heat, excitability, dark vivid faces, superstition, political volatility, corruption, dramatic emotional gestures and a general dearth of prudent bland modernity. So there is a Rome/Africa match, even before you consider [Doran's concept]' (*TR* 2012: 673). From a racist northern Italian perspective – and one from which Purves makes no effort to distance herself – Rome and Africa have many primitive, pre-modern features in common, and that was enough to justify Doran's concept. It did not trouble critics that the production was not explicit about *where* in Africa the action was set. Having identified the setting as 'sub-Saharan Africa', reviewers were happy to invoke a range of figures and places from across the continent – Winnie Mandela, Rwanda, Jacob Zuma, Charles Taylor,

Robert Mugabe, Idi Amin, with one quick detour to Saddam Hussein's Baghdad – without feeling the need to settle on any one. Although a generically 'unstable' African republic was portrayed, reviewers felt that the concept offered a 'startlingly close fit' (Bassett, *TR* 2012: 674) and a 'neat and thoroughly believable' analogy (Letts, *TR* 2012: 674). In the *Sunday Times*, Christopher Hart approvingly quoted a programme note expressing 'an African view' that 'Britain today would frankly "not interest Shakespeare". Africa is "more intense, more immediate", and "the western world feels grey and muffled in comparison".' Hart continued: 'This isn't self-abasement, it's the plain truth. Elderly, wealthy and safe, we have regulated real life out of our lives because it's too dangerous and hurts too much' (674). The 'African' setting therefore had the effect of 'resensitis[ing] you to the terrible dangers and risks' (Taylor, *TR* 2012: 675) in the play. Hart's 'elderly, wealthy and safe' implied readership was asked to forget the double-dip recession in which the UK currently languished, the austerity cuts, the widespread pensioner poverty, the inner-city riots of the summer of 2011 that had caused so much prospective apprehension about security and tourism ahead of the Olympic summer of 2012 – and instead to enjoy the spectacle of 'real' volatility, poverty and unregulated danger.

The fact that many reviewers described this 'Africa' as 'postcolonial' managed to imply that the range of ungovernable and volatile characteristics they thought so apt in this interpretation were functions and results of *post*colonialism, not of colonialism itself. Charles Spencer wrote: 'the dramatic concept works powerfully as we remember the continent's violent postcolonial history with its succession of dictatorships and bloody coups' (*TR* 2012: 673); to remember that is to forget the violent colonial history of, for example, the British Empire in Africa. If that was the case, it was part of a growing trend either to airbrush the horrors of empire or to rehabilitate its reputation by either stressing the 'achievements' of colonialism, or else trivialise the history in popular books such as Stuart Laycock's *All the Countries We've Ever Invaded: And the Few We Never Got Round To* (2012).

For such a potentially controversial production it was striking how similar most reviews were. Not one mentioned the dynamics of a majority white audience watching an all-black cast; not one found it significant that a white director had orchestrated this 'postcolonial' production. Alone of all reviewers, Ian Shuttleworth of the *FT* was alive to the complexity of the event. 'Especially at a time of heritage-centred celebration like this, it may evoke complacent (not to say racist) self-congratulation that we ourselves are not prone to such African-style instability and conflict'

(*TR* 2012: 674). For everyone else, though, Doran had passed through the succession crisis unscathed. Quentin Letts was delighted: 'Thank goodness Mr Doran, the Royal Shakespeare Company's incoming supremo, felt able to ignore the politically correct fad for colour-blind casting' (673); instead, according to Neil Norman in a typically bardolatrous formula, 'he allows the play to speak for itself' (673). Colour-blind casting is often an affront to conservative critics, but all-black productions, especially those that put British black actors in an 'African' setting, is another thing entirely. The fact of seeing black actors in Shakespearean roles is rendered palatable: the production is safely about Africa and not about contemporary multicultural Britain. For Susannah Clapp, 'Gregory Doran has gone to the heart of Shakespeare's play and set up a glow around his own future as artistic director – dictator? first among equals? sovereign head? – of the RSC' (674). Doran's intrepid Conradian journey to the heart of the play and that of the 'dark continent' had been strangely reassuring for critics. Opening in the same week as Dromgoole's *Henry V* and winning the same level of uncomplicated critical approval, it was indeed 'back to British business as usual'.

Epilogue: guarding the guardians, changing the guard

In 2012 the British Parliament was debating the recommendations of Lord Justice Leveson's inquiry of that year into the 'culture, practices and ethics of the press'. The key question is whether the press can be trusted to self-regulate – as has been the case since 1694 – or whether statutory legislation should be introduced to safeguard the public from the criminal and unethical excesses (the phone-hacking, police collusion, etc.) of the recent past that had prompted the Leveson Inquiry. Proponents of legislation argue that the Press Complaints Commission (PCC) – the body charged with self-regulation since 1990 – has been largely ineffectual. Here is section 12 on 'Discrimination' in the PCC's Code of Practice for newspaper editors:

i) The press must avoid prejudicial or pejorative reference to an individual's race, colour, religion, gender, sexual orientation or to any physical or mental illness or disability.
ii) Details of an individual's race, colour, religion, sexual orientation, physical or mental illness or disability must be avoided unless genuinely relevant to the story. (PCC Code of Practice)

Now consider these guidelines in relation to two reviews of *Measure for Measure* – a play about justice and the operations of the law – drawn from the last decade. On 25 November 2011 Quentin Letts reviewed the RSC's new production of *Measure* in the *Daily Mail*. Under the headline (not necessarily his own) 'Sensual? This Isabella is as sexy as a bar of soap', Letts wrote the following of Jodie McNee's performance:

> Shakespeare made her tender but brave, aristocratic, pretty enough to yank the lusts of two powerful men... This Isabella is not so much chaste as plain. She looks just like a dutiful, serious nun, no sexier than carbolic soap. Isabella needs to be much more than that for the play's balancing of sensuality and self-control to be humanized. (Letts 2011)

No doubt Letts would claim that this 'pejorative reference' to the actress's gender was 'genuinely relevant to the story'. But he was not only disappointed with McNee's looks: 'Miss McNee speaks with a northern accent. There is nothing wrong with that per se, but Isabella's brother Claudio (pretty Mark Quarterly) speaks RP, as do the rest of the Duke's court' (Letts 2011). As we have seen, Letts was relieved that the casting of Doran's *Julius Caesar* was not colour-blind; here he took firm exception to what he saw as the distraction of accent-deaf casting.

One might reasonably expect to find such self-conscious and showy political incorrectness in the *Daily Mail* – Letts is one of the highest-paid journalists in Britain, and he is rewarded for being both lightning rod and court jester to the prejudices of Middle England. But consider Rhoda Koenig's review of *Measure for Measure* that appeared in the *Independent* on 13 April 2002. Here was a rare example of a non-Globe review that dwelt at length on the audience. On the night she attended this touring 'educational' production of the play, Koenig wrote, 'the teenagers (whom I could see from the gallery) were all silent and caught up in the action, even the gum-chewers in FCUK [French Connection United Kingdom] jackets'. Koenig was not, however, impressed with what she took to be the production's bias 'toward issues rather than poetry':

> To put it another way, this frequently banal and sycophantic approach subjugated the play to the students' presumed interests and capacities, rather than attempting to make the students submit to something greater than themselves. Myself, I would have confiscated those jackets and sent them off to be burnt as a lesson in respecting the social contract and the language of Shakespeare. (*TR* 2002: 415)

In Koenig's review the audience was mentioned because it was *outré*, the typical audience being normative, predictable, unworthy of comment or critique. The 'elderly, wealthy and safe' audience of Christopher Hart's

Caesar review is effectively invisible in contemporary reviewing. But what does it mean to say that *Measure for Measure* is 'greater' than a GCSE student? And how can 'Shakespeare's language' be deployed as a stick with which to beat anti-social teenagers, given the fact that the playwright was hardly averse to the kind of bawdy that Koenig bemoans in modern clothes branding? As Aguecheek might have said: 'Her F's, her C's, her U's, and her K's? Why that?'

Despite the very different newspapers in which these criticisms appeared, the assumptions underwriting both reviews were discriminatory and elitist. Performer and audience members were stigmatised on the grounds of gender, region, accent and age. What Barbara Ehrenreich (1989: 3) wrote over twenty years ago remains generally true: journalistic reporting constructs white male middle class as 'a social norm... from which every other group or class is ultimately a kind of deviation'. Even when the writer is not male – as in Koenig's case – she will often assume that authoritative subject position.

In 2006 the Sutton Trust reported on the 'educational background of leading journalists' and found that the trend was towards decreasing plurality and social mobility within the profession. Of the top 100 journalists in 2006, 54 per cent were independently educated, an increase from 49 in 1986. In the context of an industry in which vital early work experience is frequently unpaid, in which expensive undergraduate and postgraduate qualifications are becoming requisite, and in which job appointments are often informal and based on word of mouth, reputation and contacts, the Trust concluded 'the signs are that the national media will become even more dominated by those from privileged backgrounds in the future' (Sutton Trust 2006: 2) – and this was before the introduction in October 2011 of £9,000 per annum undergraduate university fees following the application of the radical recommendations made in the 2010 Browne Report into Higher Education.

It seems unlikely, then, that the class and racial background of the mainstream theatre reviewing community will change any time soon. Indeed, if the Trust's predictions are correct, access to the best jobs in journalism will become more restrictive in the years to come. The more privileged that body of critics becomes, the more it is likely to value an establishment version of Shakespeare, one in which audiences are 'elderly, wealthy and safe', in which performers are monochrome and, unless they are in comic parts, speak RP, and in which directors – ideally men with similar backgrounds to the critics' – allow the plays 'to speak for themselves'. Under the revealing headline 'Classy Act', the *Spectator*'s theatre critic Lloyd Evans wrote:

> Michael Grandage, boss of the Donmar, is a most unusual director. He has no ideas. His rivals go in for party-theme, concept-album, pop-video Shakespeare (provincial folksiness in metropolitan disguise), but Grandage just goes in for Shakespeare. He arrives with no prejudices or pieties, only solutions. He's the bard's delivery boy. (L. Evans 2011)

Grandage is to be congratulated on finding solutions but avoiding ideas. This type of faithful 'delivery boy' will always win approval and work in a conservative theatre culture, especially one in which the critical guardians are unguarded.

Struggling to find a positive note on which to end his early stand-up routines, Woody Allen was in the habit of asking his audience if they would settle for two negatives. But there are some reasons to be optimistic about the future of the night-watch constable. It might offer some consolation to remember, as John Whiting claimed in 1956, that 'every present time is always a bad time for the theatre' (quoted in Rebellato 1999: 6), and that theatre criticism has throughout its history been dogged by nostalgia and a nagging sense that 'the odds is gone, / And there is nothing left remarkable / Beneath the visiting moon' (*Antony* 4.16.68–70). The 'acute longing for familiar surroundings' (*OED* 1) is a particular affliction in a profession such as theatre reviewing that straddles such mutable cultural spheres as journalism and the stage. In 1939 S.R. Littlewood lamented:

> Gone are the days – well within any middle-aged memory – when long and careful criticisms of plays, act by act and character by character, were written at leisure and welcomed and read in the London daily newspapers. The rival claims, too, of the cinema and the radio limit relations still more between the national Press and the flesh-and-blood theatre. (Littlewood 1939: 4)

Writing in 1941, A.E. Wilson claimed that:

> Dramatic criticism as an institution has, in fact, been in a sad decline for many years. Our allotted space had been gradually shrinking long before the war . . . The shrinkage of space has encouraged the cheap 'wise-cracking' notice and the notice which tells you how much the box office takings amounted to, and the clothes Lady Divorcay wore in the stalls. (A.E. Wilson 1941: 1)

These are constants of the tradition of complaint: the fear of cultural marginality, of impotence and of emasculation, anxieties that go with the territory and litter the beat of the night-watch constable.

But the emergence of the Internet as the dominant platform for theatre criticism offers the possibility of new dimensions of time and space. The constriction about which critics have complained at least since George Henry Lewes in the 1850s (see p. 18 above) is now a thing of the past, and there is nothing to stop critics writing to whatever length their subject demands. And while it is the case that 'technological developments in the pursuit of timeliness continue to impel news coverage towards "presentation" – that is, closing the gap between the event and its telling, with the goal of displaying events in "real time"' (Bell, 1996: 4), that present can be stretched in many directions. In the *Guardian*'s coverage of the Globe to Globe festival, for example, many reviewers used hyperlinks to expand the range of reference and indeed the remit of their criticism. In his review of *Macbeth*, Michael Billington wrote of the production's decision to cast the Witches as drag queens: 'These three sisters are undoubtedly weird, but you lose any sense of their connection with the concept of "wyrd" (Anglo-Saxon for "fate")' (Billington 2012b). The hyperlink took the curious reader from 'fate' to an online etymology of 'weird/wyrd' – it is hard to imagine such an erudite point being made without space-consuming elaboration in hard copy. Elsewhere Andrew Dickson began his review of an Afghan production of *The Comedy of Errors*: 'Though there's been plenty of error in Afghan politics in the past few decades, we've seen precious little comedy – as the most recent news, a triple suicide bombing in Kandahar and rumours of civilian deaths in a Nato drone strike in Logar province, mournfully confirms' (Dickson 2012d). Those underlined phrases represent links in the online review to detailed newspaper accounts of recent developments in Afghanistan. These hyperlinks served to connect Shakespearean performance with contemporary history, but the tool is equally useful in helping to induct readers into traditions of performance. Reviewing a production of *All's Well that Ends Well* presented by the Arpana Theatre, Mumbai, Dickson wrote: 'And unlike a long line in colourful "Indian" Shakespeare (from the RSC's 1976 Much Ado About Nothing, set during the Raj, to Tim Supple's acrobatic A Midsummer Night's Dream), this is undeniably the real deal' (Dickson 2012c). Here Dickson simultaneously introduced his readers – if they were not aware already – to two landmark RSC productions while at the same time calling into question those productions' authenticity in comparison with the show under review.

I have argued throughout this book that allusion and quotation are central to Shakespearean reviewing. Hyperlinks bring new intertextual opportunities for reviewers – they can be used to create or reinforce the reader's memories of performance traditions through the kind of diachronic references so common to Shakespearean reviewing of all ages. But they can

Epilogue

also liberate the reader from this relatively closed system of meanings to connect performance to political and intellectual worlds elsewhere.

* * *

Macready was inordinately fond of the word 'vile' but could not decide to which profession it was more aptly applied, that of the actor or of the critic. The opening of his diary entry of 18 July 1835 is often cited in this connection: 'I wish I were anything rather than an actor – except a critic; let me be unhappy rather than vile!' What is less often quoted is how he continued:

> If I meant by this that men who *usually criticize* are vile I should convict myself of equal folly and injustice. It is the assumption of the high duties of criticism (demanding genius and enthusiasm tempered by the most exact judgment and refined taste) by mere dealers in words, with no pretensions to integrity of purpose or the advancement of literature, that disgusts and depresses me . . . Generally speaking it takes its tone from faction. (Macready 1912: I 241; italics his)

British newspaper readers have been blessed with some superb journalist critics over the last three centuries, many of whom have tried to assume, in Macready's words, the 'high duties of criticism'. In the recent past, writers like Irving Wardle, Michael Coveney, Paul Taylor, Michael Billington and Lyn Gardner have consistently produced highly knowledgeable, thoughtful, engaging and accessible copy. In 2013 the Critics' Circle will celebrate its centenary at a moment when the future of newspaper theatre reviewing is not at all clear or secure. Theatre reviewing sells very little advertising and as such is one of the more expendable components of the postmodern newspaper. It is not impossible that when some of the current cadre of critics retire they will not be replaced. But this crisis of succession is also an opportunity for the range of 'unofficial' citizen critics – the women, students and 'foreigners' so often traduced or ignored in mainstream criticism – to take to the new platforms of the Internet and write for themselves about the Shakespearean performances they have seen, those they want to see and those they wish to memorialise. For much of its history, Shakespearean reviewing has been a homosocial activity, an event between men whose primary spirit has been competition and 'faction' (Macready). Perhaps inspired by the influence of some of the great critics discussed in this book, the next generation of reviewers might adopt a position that is anti-bardolatrous, iconoclastic and fearlessly experimental as they learn to speak of themselves – as we always must – *à propos* of Shakespeare.

Notes

2 TRADITION AND THE INDIVIDUAL TALENT

1 For studies of the performance history of *Macbeth* from the seventeenth century to the mid to late twentieth century, see Bartholomeusz (1969) and Rosenberg (1978); for a consideration of three twentieth-century stage productions – Welles (1936), Byam Shaw (1955) and Nunn (1976) – in relation to television versions and Roman Polanski's film, see Kliman (1992). See also Smith (2000: 150–2) for a brief discussion of masculine ideology and *Macbeth* performance.
2 Unsurprisingly, the most frequently revived Shakespeare plays on the eighteenth-century London stage were (with the exception of the Dryden–Davenant–Shadwell *Tempest*) all star vehicles. In the first half of the century, according to Hogan, the most privileged Shakespearean leads were found, in descending order, in *Hamlet, Macbeth, Othello, 1 Henry IV, The Merry Wives of Windsor* and *Richard III*, to name the six most frequently revived Shakespeare plays of the period. In the second half of the century, *Hamlet* and *Macbeth* remained cornerstones of the repertory; *King Lear* and *The Merchant of Venice* were more frequently revived, and *Romeo and Juliet* became the most popular Shakespeare of the era (Stone 1957: clxii–clxvi; Hogan 1958: clxxi–ii).
3 As G.E. Bentley (1941–68: II 597) has pointed out, this genealogy is highly improbable, given that both Shakespeare and Burbage were dead before Joseph Taylor joined the King's Men in 1619. Downes's other invocation of Shakespearean authority ('The part of the King [Henry VIII] was so right and justly done by Mr. *Betterton*, he being Instructed in it by Sir *William*, who had it from Old Mr. *Lowen*, that had his Instructions from Mr. *Shakespear* himself' (Downes [1708] 1987: 55)) is at least chronologically plausible.
4 See Bruce Smith's account of the importance of the dominance of blood in the masculine body in early modern theories of the humours:

> In voice as well as in visage the warm-bloodedness of masculinity proves to be an advantage. The pseudonymous astrologer 'Arcandam' in a book translated into English in 1592 describes how different humours produce different qualities of voice, phlegm generating a feeble voice, choler a harsh voice. Best of all is a voice dominated by blood . . . 'They therefore that have hot bodies', Leminus observes, 'are also of nature variable, and changeable, ready, prompt, lively, lusty, and applicable: of tongue, trowling, perfect, and persuasive: delivering their words distinctly, plainly, and pleasantly, with a voice thereto not squeaking and slender, but strainable, comely and audible'

> (*Touchstone*, 45 v). The very qualities of body that produce good exemplars of masculinity are those that produce good actors. (Bruce Smith 2000: 35–6)

5 H.N. Hillebrand (1966: 14) describes the anecdote as 'a yarn' that Kean 'was fond of telling'. But veracity is beside the present point; whether apocryphal or not, the story illustrates the competitive atmosphere of theatrical discourse, the way that criticism, anecdote and biography have traditionally found structure in antagonism. See, for example, F.W. Hawkins's use of the story in his *Life of Edmund Kean* ([1869] 1969: 11):

> in the handsome and intelligent boy who had converted the interpolation in *Macbeth* into a burlesque Kemble probably did not recognise the genius who, twenty years later, deposed him from his pre-eminence on the stage, subjected him on almost every hand to a comparison so unfavourable that positive sibilation marked the distinction between the respective antagonists, and whose powers shone forth with a meridian splendour in which the brilliance of the elder actor faded and turned pale.

6 This traffic between courageous manhood, British military triumph and Shakespearean character is anticipated in Morgann's essay on Falstaff. In an effort to illustrate the distinction between 'principled' and 'natural', or acquired and inherent courage, Morgann ([1777] 1963: 215) wrote that principled courage is based on

> the prevailing modes of honour, and the fashions of the age. – But Natural courage is another thing: It is independent of opinion; It adapts itself to occasions, preserves itself under every shape, and can avail itself of flight as well as of action. In the last war, some Indians of America perceiving a line of Highlanders to keep their station under every disadvantage, and under a fire which they could not effectually return, were so miserably mistaken in our points of honour as to conjecture, from observation on the habit and stability of those troops, that they were indeed the women of England, who wanted courage to run away. – That Courage which is founded in nature and constitution, *Falstaff*, as I presume to say, possessed.

Notice the sleight of hand by which Morgann elides natural, instinctive courage with 'our [British] points of honour', despite the opening contrast between acquired courage (based on 'the prevailing modes of honour') and inherent courage. Is it also pertinent to *Macbeth* that Morgann, like Kemble, chooses for his example Scottish soldiers? See Terence Hawkes's essay 'Swisser Swatter: Making a Man of English Letters' (in Hawkes 1986) for an analysis of how manhood is a category that can exclude, when it suits, the Indian or German other through a process of Caliban-isation.

4 THE REVIEWER IN TRANSITION C.1920–1960

1 The bias towards recording Shakespearean tragedy and history for posterity at the expense of comedy that Tynan initiated in *He That Plays the King* is a vital aspect of the construction of Shakespeare in the critic's republished oeuvre. To claim that 'we love the author of *As You Like It*, but we should not honour him unless he had also written *King Lear*' (Kenneth Tynan 1950: 202) may be an uncontroversial value judgement, but it is surprising that there should be such a gaping generic divide in the reviews Tynan decided to republish in

Curtains and *Tynan Right and Left*. Taking the two plays mentioned in Tynan's comparison as convenient test cases: between 1951 and 1963, the years Tynan wrote as a professional newspaper critic, there were in total eleven productions of *As You Like It* in the West End, Regent's Park, the Old Vic, and at Stratford. Of these, only one (Glen Byam Shaw's 1952 Stratford production) is covered in an anthology of his criticism. In the same period and in the same locations there were seven productions of *King Lear*, reviews of four of which can be found in *Curtains* and *Tynan Right and Left*. A similar discrepancy and bias are apparent throughout the canon. From 1951 to 1963 in the locations listed above, there were ninety-nine productions of the comedies, sixty-nine of the tragedies and thirty-eight of the histories (see Trewin 1964: 280–5, 292–5, 304–7). Tynan chose to republish and anthologise reviews of only ten of the comedies, but fourteen of the histories and thirty-two of the tragedies.

2 By the time Olivier made the film of *Henry V*, he was well aware of his ability to render patriotism an emotion about which it was impossible to be cynical. In a 1967 interview with Tynan (subsequently reprinted in *Great Acting*, ed. Hal Burton), Olivier had remembered his stage performance as Henry at the Old Vic thirty years earlier. After one performance, Charles Laughton 'came round to my dressing-room and said "Do you know why you're so good in this part?" And I said, 'No, please tell me." And he said, "You are England, that's all", and so when people came round and said to me, "Tell me how", I said, "It's simple, I am England"' (Burton 1967: 18).

5 NEW CONTEXTS, NEW CRISES (1997–2012)

1 Raphael Samuel offers an instructive example of this pathologisation in his discussion of *Flogging a Dead Horse*, an exhibition of photography held at the Photographer's Gallery and subsequently converted into a coffee-table book (Reas 1993). The exhibition featured images of tourists at various English Heritage sites. In the images various subjects, including obese men and women, a man with a Rottweiler, and a young boy with a Mickey Mouse t-shirt, were all foregrounded in unflattering ways, the strong implication being that they were incompetent and naive readers of these purportedly ersatz sites. Samuel writes: 'Though directed against the packaging of history, *Flogging a Dead Horse* is a slick production, using a series of stratagems to make its images repellent. Angles and frames are so manipulated as to make every picture out of joint; objects and viewers are juxtaposed so as to diminish one and belittle the other. We are never once shown the objects themselves – they exist as a kind of mocking commentary on the sightseers' (Samuel 1994: 264).

2 Quotation taken from 'The Biography of Sam Wanamaker'. Accessed 24 March 2003 at the Shakespeare's Globe website: www.shakespeares-globe.org/navigation/frameset.htm.

Works cited

Some newspaper reviews are taken from the monthly journal *Theatre Record*. A reference in the text of the sort '(*TR* 2002: 191)' means, for example, that the review can be found on p. 191 of the *Theatre Record* for 2002.

References to the texts of Shakespeare's plays are, unless otherwise stated, from *William Shakespeare: The Complete Works*, ed. Stanley Wells and Gary Taylor (Oxford University Press 2005).

Adler, John, ed. 1997. *Responses to Shakespeare*. 8 vols. London: Routledge.
Agate, James 1932. *The English Dramatic Critics: An Anthology*. London: Arthur Baker.
  1943a. *Brief Chronicles: A Survey of the Plays of Shakespeare and the Elizabethans in Actual Performance*. London: Jonathan Cape.
  1943b. *These Were Actors: Extracts from a Newspaper Cutting Book, 1811–1833*. London: Hutchinson.
  1946. *Those Were the Nights*. London: Hutchinson.
  1948. *Ego 9: Concluding the Autobiography of James Agate*. London: George Harrap.
  1961. *James Agate, An Anthology*. Ed. Herbert Van Thal. London: Rupert Hart-Davis.
Anonymous 1933. Review of *Macbeth*. *The Times* 9 April.
Appleton, William W. 1961. *Charles Macklin: An Actor's Life*. Cambridge, MA: Harvard University Press.
Archer, William 1891. 'The Free Stage and the New Drama'. *Fortnightly Review* 50, 664.
  1896. *The Theatrical 'World' for 1895*. London: Walter Scott.
Armstrong, Alan 2008. '*Romeo and Juliet* Academic Theatre Review Kit'. *Shakespeare Bulletin* 26:1, 109–23.
Arnott, J.F. and J.W. Robertson 1970. *English Theatrical Literature 1559–1900: Bibliography Incorporating Robert W. Lowe's 'A Bibliographical Account of English Theatrical Literature' Published in 1888*. London: The Society for Theatre Research.
Baer, Marc 1992. *Theatre and Disorder in Late Georgian London*. Oxford: Clarendon Press.

Baldick, Chris 1983. *The Social Mission of English Criticism 1848–1932*. Oxford University Press.
Bartas 1605. *Bartas: his deuine weekes and workes translated: & dedicated to the Kings most excellent Maiestie*, by Joshua Sylvester. London.
Barthes, Roland 1975. *The Pleasure of the Text*. Trans. Richard Miller. New York: Noonday Press.
Bartholomeusz, Dennis 1969. *Macbeth and the Players*. Cambridge University Press.
Bate, Jonathan 1989. *Shakespearean Constitutions: Politics, Theatre, Criticism 1730–1830*. Oxford University Press.
Beckett, Samuel 1986. *The Complete Dramatic Works*. London: Faber and Faber.
Beerbohm Max 1896a. 'An Unhappy Poet'. *Saturday Review* 82, 282–3, 315–16.
  1896b. 'Hold, Furious Scot!' *Saturday Review* 82, 395–6.
  1953. *Around Theatres*. London: Rupert Hart-Davis.
  1969. *More Theatres: 1898–1903*. London: Rupert Hart-Davis.
Beetham, Margaret 1990. 'Towards a Theory of the Periodical as Publishing Genre' in Brake et al., *Investigating Victorian Journalism*, 19–30.
Bell, A. 1996. 'Texts, Time and Technology in News English' in S. Goodman and D. Graddol, eds. *Redesigning English: New Texts, New Identities*. Milton Keynes: Open University Press. 3–26.
Benedetti, Jean 2001. *David Garrick and the Birth of the Modern Theatre*. London: Methuen.
Benjamin, Walter 1992. 'The Work of Art in the Age of Mechanical Reproduction' in Hannah Arendt, ed. *Illuminations*. London: Fontana. 211–44.
Bennett, Susan 1997. *Theatre Audiences: Theory of Production and Reception*. London and New York: Routledge.
Bentley, Eric 2008. *Bentley on Brecht*. 3rd edn. Evanston, IL: Northwestern University Press.
Bentley, G.E. 1941–68. *The Jacobean and Caroline Stage*. 7 vols. Oxford: Clarendon Press.
Billington, Michael 1993. *One Night Stands: A Critic's view of British Theatre, 1971–91*. London: Nick Hern.
  2000a. Personal interview with author, June.
  2000b. 'We Will Not Be Muzzled'. *Guardian* 28 June. www.guardian.co.uk/culture/2000/jun/28/artsfeatures2. Accessed: 13 December 2012.
  2004. Review of *Tynan*. *Guardian* 7 October. www.guardian.co.uk/stage/2004/oct/07/theatre. Accessed: 13 December 2012.
  2011a. Review of *Much Ado About Nothing*. *Guardian* 27 May. www.guardian.co.uk/stage/2011/may/27/much-ado-about-nothing-globe. Accessed: 13 December 2012.
  2011b. Review of *Hamlet*. *Guardian* 9 November. www.guardian.co.uk/stage/2011/nov/09/hamlet-youngvic-review. Accessed: 13 December 2012.
  2012a. Review of *Hedda Gabler*. *Guardian* 13 September. www.guardian.co.uk/stage/2012/sep/13/hedda-gabler-review. Accessed: 13 December 2012.

2012b. Review of *Macbeth*. *Guardian* 9 May. www.guardian.co.uk/stage/2012/may/09/macbeth-shakespeares-globe-review. Accessed: 13 December 2012.

Blau, Herbert 1987. *The Eye of Prey*. Bloomington: Indiana University Press.

 1990. *The Audience*. Baltimore: Johns Hopkins University Press.

Bloom, Harold 1997. *The Anxiety of Influence: Theory of Poetry*. 2nd edn. Oxford University Press.

Booth, John E. 1991. *The Critic, Power and the Performing Arts*. New York: Columbia University Press, 1991.

Bourdieu, Pierre [1979] 1986. *Distinction: A Social Critique of the Judgement of Taste*. Trans. Richard Nice. London: Routledge and Kegan Paul.

Bradley, A.C. 1909. 'Hegel's Theory of Tragedy' in Bradley, *Oxford Lectures on Poetry*. London: Macmillan.

Brake, Laurel 1988. 'The Old Journalism and the New: Forms of Cultural Production in London in the 1880s' in Wiener, *Papers for the Millions*, 1–24.

Brake, Laurel, Aled Jones and Lionel Madden, eds. 1990. *Investigating Victorian Journalism*. New York: St Martin's Press

Braunmuller, A.R. 1997. *Introduction to* Macbeth *by William Shakespeare*. Cambridge University Press, 1–93.

Brecht, Bertolt 1964. *Brecht on Theatre*. Ed. and trans. John Willett. London: Methuen.

Bristol, Michael D. 1985. *Carnival and Theater: Plebeian Culture and the Structure of Authority in Renaissance England*. London: Methuen.

Brooke, Nicholas, ed. 1990. Macbeth *by William Shakespeare*. Oxford: Clarendon Press.

Brown, Lucy 1985. *Victorian News and Newspapers*. Oxford: Clarendon Press.

Bulman, James, ed. 1996. *Shakespeare, Theory, and Performance*. London: Routledge.

Burke, Seán 1995. 'The Ethics of the Signature' in Seán Burke, ed. *Authorship: From Plato to the Postmodern, A Reader*. Edinburgh University Press. 285–91.

Burton, Hal, ed. 1967. *Great Acting*. London: Hill and Wang.

Carlson, Marvin 1989. 'Theatre Audiences and the Reading of Performance' in Postlewait and McConachie, eds., *Interpreting the Theatrical Past*, 82–98.

 2003. *The Haunted Stage: The Theatre as Memory Machine*. Ann Arbor: University of Michigan Press.

Carroll, Sydney W. 1931. 'Grievances and Disabilities in Criticism'. *Critics' Circular* 5:17 (May), 1–2.

Carson, Christie and Susan Bennett, eds. 2013. *Shakespeare Beyond English. A Global Experiment*. Cambridge University Press.

Cavanagh, John 1989. *British Theatre, A Bibliography 1901 to 1985*. Mottisfont: Motley Press, 1989.

Cecil, David 1964. *Max: Biography*. London: Constable.

Chomsky, Noam 2002. *Understanding Power: The Indispensable Chomsky*. Ed. Peter R. Mitchell and John Schoeffel. New York: The New Press.

Clarke, Bob 2010. *From Grub Street to Fleet Street: An Illustrated History of English Newspapers to 1899*. Brighton: Revel Barker Publishing.

Cliff, Nigel 2007. *The Shakespeare Riots: Revenge, Drama, and Death in Nineteenth-Century America*. New York: Random House.
Collini, Stefan 1988. 'The Critic as Journalist: Leavis after *Scrutiny*' in Treglown and Bennett, eds., *Grub Street and the Ivory Tower*, 51–76.
Conboy, Martin 2010. *The Language of Newspapers: Socio-historical Perspectives*. London: Continuum.
Connolly, Cyril 1961. *Enemies of Promise*. Harmondsworth: Penguin.
Cook, Dutton 1883. *Nights at the Play*. London: Chatto and Windus.
'Craig, Nicholas' (Christopher Douglas and Nigel Planer) 1989. *I, An Actor*. London: Pan Books.
'The Critic's Progress' (Anonymous) 1895. *Saturday Review* 79 (15 June), 796.
Daileader, Celia R. 2000. 'Casting Black Actors: Beyond Othellophilia' in Catherine M.S. Alexander and Stanley Wells, eds. *Shakespeare and Race*. Cambridge University Press. 177–202.
Danson, Lawrence 1989. *Max Beerbohm and the Act of Writing*. Oxford: Clarendon Press.
Diamond, Elin 1995. *Writing Performances*. London: Routledge.
Darlington, W.A. 1924. 'The Producer'. *Critics' Circular* 1:3 (April), 4.
   1942. 'Minutes of the Annual General Meeting'. *Critics' Circular* 8:29 (June), 15.
   1960. *Six Thousand and One Nights, Forty Years a Critic*. London: George G. Harrap.
Davies, Nick 2008. *Flat Earth News*. London: Chatto and Windus.
Davies, Thomas [1784] 1971. *Dramatic Miscellanies: Consisting of Critical Observations on Several Plays*. New York: Benjamin Blom.
Dawson, Anthony B. 1999. 'The Arithmetic of Memory: Shakespeare's Theatre and the National Past'. *Shakespeare Survey* 52, 54–67.
Derrida, Jacques 1988. *Limited Inc*. Evanston, IL: Northwestern University Press.
Dickson, Andrew 2012a. Email to author. 8 November.
   2012b. Review of *Troilus and Cressida*. *Guardian* 24 April. www.guardian.co.uk/stage/2012/apr/24/troilus-cressida-review. Accessed: 13 December 2012.
   2012c. Review of *All's Well that Ends Well*. *Guardian* 1 June. www.guardian.co.uk/stage/2012/jun/01/alls-well-that-ends-well-review. Accessed: 13 December 2012.
   2012d. Review of *Comedy of Errors*. *Guardian* 7 June. www.guardian.co.uk/stage/2012/jun/07/comedy-of-errors-shakespeares-globe. Accessed: 13 December 2012.
Donohue, Joseph 1967–8. 'Kemble and Mrs Siddons in *Macbeth*: The Romantic Approach to Tragic Character'. *Theatre Notebook* 22:2, 65–86.
   1970. *Dramatic Character in the English Romantic Age*. Princeton University Press.
Downes, John [1708] 1987. *Roscius Anglicanus*. Ed. Judith Milhous and Robert D. Hume. London: The Society for Theatre Research.
'Dumb Britain' 2002. *Private Eye* no. 1053 (3–16 May), 8.

Dundy, Elaine 2001. *Life Itself!* London: Virago Press.
Dusinberre, Juliet 1996. 'Squeaking Cleopatras: Gender and Performance in *Antony and Cleopatra*' in Bulman, ed., *Shakespeare, Theory, and Performance*, 46–67.
'Editorial' 1898. *Saturday Review* 85 (11 June), 769.
Edmondson, Paul, Paul Prescott and Peter J. Smith, eds. 2010. *Reviewing Shakespearean Theatre: The State of the Art.* Special issue of the Shakespeare Association's journal *Shakespeare 6.3.* London: Routledge.
Edmondson, Paul, Paul Prescott and Erin Sullivan, eds. 2013. *A Year of Shakespeare: Re-living the World Shakespeare Festival.* London: Arden.
Ehrenreich, Barbara 1989. *Fear of Falling: The Inner Life of the Middle Class.* New York: HarperCollins.
Eliot, T.S. 1964. 'Tradition and the Individual Talent' in Eliot, *Selected Essays*, 3rd edn. London: Faber and Faber.
Evans, Lloyd 2011. 'Classy Act'. *Spectator* 1 January. www.spectator.co.uk/arts/theatre/6576283/classy-act/. Accessed: 13 December 2012.
Evans, Richard J. 1997. *In Defence of History.* London: Granta.
Fletcher, John 1847. *Studies of Shakespeare.* London: Longman, Brown, Green and Longmans.
Forbes-Robertson, Johnston 1925. *A Player under Three Reigns.* London: T. Fisher Unwin.
Franklin, Bob 1997. *Newszak and News Media.* London: Arnold.
Garrick, David 1744. *An Essay on Acting: In which will be consider'd The Mimical Behaviour of Certain fashionable faulty Actor, and the Laudableness of such unmannerly, as well as inhumane Proceedings, To which will be added, A Short Criticism on His acting Macbeth.* London. Extracts repr. in Vickers, ed., *Shakespeare: The Critical Heritage Vol. III 1733–1752.*
　1981. *The Plays of David Garrick. Vol. III: Garrick's Adaptations of Shakespeare 1744–1756.* Ed. Harry William Pedicord and Fredrick Louis Bergmann. Carbondale, IL: Southern Illinois University Press.
Gentleman, Francis [1770] 1969. *The Dramatic Censor; or, Critical Companion Volumes I and II.* Farnborough: Gregg International.
Gilchrist, Andrew 2012. Review of *The Merry Wives of Windsor. Guardian* 27 April. www.guardian.co.uk/stage/2012/apr/27/merry-wives-of-windsor-review. Accessed: 13 December 2012.
Gilmore, David D. 1990. *Manhood in the Making: Cultural Concepts of Masculinity.* New Haven, CT: Yale University Press.
Grady, Hugh 1991. *The Modernist Shakespeare: Critical Texts in a Material World.* Oxford: Clarendon Press.
Gray, C.H. 1931. *Theatrical Criticism in London to 1795.* New York: Benjamin Blom.
Green, L. Dunton 1927. 'The Second International Congress of Critics at Salzburg'. *Critics' Circular* 3:12 (November), 2.
Grein, J.T. 1899. *Dramatic Criticism.* London: J. Long.
Gross, John 2000. Personal interview with author, June.

Gurr, Andrew with John Orrell 1989. *Rebuilding Shakespeare's Globe*. London: Weidenfeld & Nicolson.
Habermas, Jürgen [1962] 1992. *The Structural Transformation of the Public Sphere: An Inquiry into a Category of Bourgeois Society*. Trans. Thomas Burger. Cambridge: Polity Press.
Harding, James 1986. *Agate: A Biography*. London: Methuen.
Hawkes, Terence 1986. *That Shakespeherian Rag: Essays on a Critical Process*. London: Methuen.
　1992. *Meaning by Shakespeare*. London: Routledge.
Hawkins, F.W. [1869] 1969. *The Life of Edmund Kean*. New York: Benjamin Blom.
Hazlitt, William 1854. *Criticisms and Dramatic Essays of the English Stage*. 2nd edn. London: Routledge.
　1930–4. *Complete Works of William Hazlitt*. Ed. P.P. Howe. 21 vols. London: Dent and Co.
Haywood, Charles 1969. 'George Bernard Shaw on Shakespearian Music and the Actor'. *Shakespeare Quarterly* 20, 417–26.
Herbert, Ian 1999. 'Writing in the Dark: Fifty Years of British Theatre Criticism'. *New Theatre Quarterly* 59 (August), 236–42.
Hillebrand, Harold Newcomb 1966. *Edmund Kean*. New York: MS Press.
Hobson, Harold 1978. *Indirect Journey: An Autobiography*. London: Weidenfeld and Nicolson.
Hodgdon, Barbara 1998. *The Shakespeare Trade: Performances and Appropriations*. Philadelphia, PA: University of Pennsylvania Press.
Hogan, Charles Beecher 1958. *The London Stage 1660–1800: Part 5, 1776–1800*. Carbondale, IL: Southern Illinois University Press.
Holden, Anthony 1988. *Olivier*. London: Weidenfeld & Nicolson.
Holderness, Graham, ed. 1988. *The Shakespeare Myth*. Manchester University Press, 1988.
Holland, Peter 1997. *English Shakespeares: Shakespeare on the English Stage in the 1990s*. Cambridge University Press.
Holroyd, Michael 1990. *Bernard Shaw. Vol. 1: 1856–1898, The Search for Love*. London: Penguin.
Hughes, Alan 1981. *Henry Irving, Shakespearean*. Cambridge University Press.
Hume, Robert D. 1999. *Reconstructing Contexts: The Aims and Principles of Archaeo-Historicism*. Oxford University Press.
Hunt, Leigh 1949. *Leigh Hunt's Dramatic Criticism 1808–1831*. Ed. L.H. and C.W. Houtchens. New York: Columbia University Press.
Jackson, Russell 1978. 'J.F. Nisbet of *The Times*: Conservative Critic of the 'Eighties and 'Nineties'. *Theatre Research International* 3, 114–25.
　1985. 'Shakespeare in the Theatrical Criticism of Henry Morley'. *Shakespeare Survey* 38, 187–200.
　1994. 'Shaw's Reviews of Daly's Shakespeare: The Wooing of Ada Rehan'. *Theatre Research International* 19, 203–13.

James, Henry 1948. *The Scenic Art: Notes on Acting and the Drama 1872–1901*. Ed. Allan Wade. New Brunswick, NJ: Rutgers University Press.
Jauss, Hans Robert 1982. *Toward an Aesthetic of Reception*. Trans. Timothy Bahti. Brighton: Harvester.
Johnson, Samuel 1908. *Johnson on Shakespeare*. Ed. Walter Raleigh. Oxford University Press.
Jury, Louise 1997. 'Now Theatre Critics Are Panned'. *Evening Standard* 14 May. www.standard.co.uk/goingout/theatre/now-theatre-critics-are-panned-6582287.html.
Kemble, John Philip [1817] 1997. 'Macbeth and King Richard III: an Essay, in Answer to Remarks on Some Characters of Shakespeare' in Adler, ed., *Responses to Shakespeare. Vol. v: 1808–1825*.
Kennedy, Dennis 1993. *Looking at Shakespeare: A Visual History of Twentieth-Century Performance*. Cambridge University Press.
Kent, Christopher 1980. 'Periodical Critics of Drama, Music and Art, 1830–1914: Preliminary List'. *Victorian Periodicals Review* 13, 31–55.
Kent, Christopher and Tracy C. Davies 1986. 'More Critics of Drama, Music and Art'. *Victorian Periodicals Review* 19, 99–105.
Kliman, Bernice W. 1992. *Shakespeare in Performance: Macbeth*. Manchester University Press.
Knight, Joseph 1893. *Theatrical Notes*. London: Lawrence & Bullen.
Koenig, Rhoda 2002. Review of *Measure for Measure*. *Independent* 12 April.
Larson, Magali Sarfatti 1977. *The Rise of Professionalism: A Sociological Analysis*. Berkeley: University of California Press.
Laycock, Stuart 2012. *All the Countries We've Ever Invaded: And the Few We Never Got Round To*. Stroud: The History Press.
Letts, Quentin 2011. 'Sensual? This Isabella Is As Sexy as a Bar of Soap'. *Daily Mail* 25 November. www.dailymail.co.uk/tvshowbiz/reviews/article-2065963/Measure-For-Measure-review-This-Isabella-sexy-bar-soap.html. Accessed: 13 December 2012.
Littlewood, S.R. 1939. *Dramatic Criticism*. London: Sir Isaac Pitman.
Lloyd Evans, Gareth and Barbara 1985. *Plays in Review 1956–1980: British Drama and the Critics*. London: Batsford Academic and Educational.
Lowe, R.W. and William Archer, eds. 1894. *Leigh Hunt Dramatic Essays*. London: Walter Scott Ltd.
   1895. *William Hazlitt, A View of the English Stage; or, a series of dramatic criticisms*. London: Walter Scott Ltd.
   1896. *John Forster and George Henry Lewes: Dramatic Essays*. London: Walter Scott Ltd.
Macready, W.C. 1875. *Macready's Reminiscences, and Selections from his Diaries and Letters*. Ed. Frederick Pollock. 2 vols. London: Macmillan.
   1912. *The Diaries of William Charles Macready 1833–1851*. Ed. William Toynbee. 2 vols. London: Chapman and Hall.
Manvell, Roger 1968. *Ellen Terry*. London: Heinemann.
'Marie Corelli' 1896. *Saturday Review* 82 (26 September), 337.

Mazer, Cary M. 1985. 'Shakespeare, the Reviewer, and the Theatre Historian'. *Shakespeare Quarterly* 36, 648–61.
McDonald, Rónán 2007. *The Death of the Critic*. London: Continuum.
McNair, Brian 1994. *News and Journalism in the UK*. London: Routledge.
Michael, Chris 2012a. Profile. www.guardian.co.uk/profile/chris-michael. Accessed: 13 December 2012.
  2012b. Review of *Coriolanus. Guardian* 25 May. www.guardian.co.uk/stage/2012/may/25/coriolanus-review. Accessed: 13 December 2012.
Middleton, David and Derek Edwards, eds. 1990. *Collective Remembering*. London: Sage Publications.
Miller, William Ian 2000. *The Mystery of Courage*. Cambridge, MA: Harvard University Press.
Molloy, J. Fitzgerald 1888. *The Life and Adventures of Edmund Kean, Tragedian, 1787–1833*. 2 vols. London: Ward and Downey.
Moore, Edward M. 1972. 'William Poel'. *Shakespeare Quarterly* 23, 21–36.
Morgann, Maurice [1777] 1963. 'Essay on the Dramatic Character of Sir John Falstaff' in D. Nichol Smith, ed. *Eighteenth-Century Essays on Shakespeare*, 2nd edn. Oxford: Clarendon Press. 203–83.
Morison, Stanley 1932. *The English Newspaper: Some Account of the Physical Development of Journals Printed in London Between 1622 and the Present Day*. Cambridge University Press.
Morris, Mowbray 1882. *Essays in Theatrical Criticism*. London: Remington & Co.
'Mr Clement Scott's Ignorance.' 1896. Letter. *Saturday Review* 82 (24 October), 444.
Mulryne, J.R. and Margaret Shewring, eds. 1997. *Shakespeare's Globe Rebuilt*. Cambridge University Press.
Munsil, Janet 2002. *Smoking with Lulu*. London: Oberon Books.
Murphy, Arthur 1801. *The Life of David Garrick*. 2 vols. London: Joseph Wright.
Needham, Alex 2012. 'Stephen Fry's *Twelfth Night*: This All-Male Affair is No One-Man Show'. *Guardian* 1 October. www.guardian.co.uk/stage/2012/oct/01/stephen-fry-twelfth-night-all-male. Accessed: 13 December 2012.
Nelsen, Paul 1995. 'Oaths and Oracles: Will the Globe Spin on an Axis of "Authenticity"?' *Shakespeare Bulletin* 13:3, 27–32.
Nelson, Richard 1990. *Two Shakespearean Actors*. London: Faber and Faber.
  2004. *Tynan: Based on the Book* The Diaries of Kenneth Tynan, *edited by John Lahr*. London: Faber and Faber.
Nord, Paul David 2006. *Communities of Journalism: A History of American Newspapers and their Readers*. Champaign: University of Illinois Press.
O'Connor, T.P. 1889. 'The New Journalism'. *The New Review* 1, 423.
Orgel, Stephen 2002. *The Authentic Shakespeare, and Other Problems of the Early Modern Stage*. London: Routledge.
Osborne, Laurie E. 1996. 'The Rhetoric of Evidence: The Narration and Display of Viola and Olivia in the Nineteenth Century' in Pechter, ed., *Textual and Theatrical Shakespeare*, 124–43.

PCC Code of Practice. www.pcc.org.uk/cop/practice.html. Accessed: 13 December 2012.
Pechter, Edward, ed. 1996. *Textual and Theatrical Shakespeare: Questions of Evidence*. Iowa City, IA: University of Iowa Press.
Postlewait, Thomas and Bruce A. McConachie, eds. 1989. *Interpreting the Theatrical Past: Essays in the Historiography of Performance*. Iowa City, IA: University of Iowa Press.
Pound, Reginald and Geoffrey Harmsworth 1959. *Northcliffe*. London: Cassel.
Prescott, Paul, Peter J. Smith and Janice Valls-Russell, eds. 2012. '*Nothing if not critical': International Perspectives on Shakespearean Theatre Criticism* Special Issue of *Cahiers Élisabéthains*. Montpellier.
Procter, B.W. [1835] 1969. *Life of Edmund Kean*. 2 Vols. New York: Benjamin Blom.
Pykett, Lyn 1990. 'Reading the Periodical Press: Text and Context' in Brake et al., *Investigating Victorian Journalism*, 1–18.
Radley, Alan 1990. 'Artifacts, Memory and a Sense of the Past' in Middleton and Edwards, eds., *Collective Remembering*, 46–59.
Rayner, Jay 2008. 'Is it Curtains for Critics?' *Guardian (Observer)* 13 July. www.guardian.co.uk/artanddesign/2008/jul/13/art.comedy. Accessed: 13 December 2012.
Reas, Paul, ed. 1993. *Flogging a Dead Horse: Heritage Culture and its Role in Postindustrial Britain*. Manchester: Cornerhouse Publications.
Rebellato, Dan 1999. *1956 and All That: The Making of Modern British Drama*. London: Routledge.
'Review of Reviews' 1897. *Saturday Review* 83 (13 March), 279.
Richardson, John E. 2007. *Analysing Newspapers: An Approach from Critical Discourse Analysis*. Basingstoke: Palgrave.
Roach, Joseph 1996. *Cities of the Dead: Circum-Atlantic Performance*. New York: Columbia University Press, 1996.
  2000. 'The Performance' in Deborah Payne Fisk, ed. *The Cambridge Companion to English Restoration Theatre*. Cambridge University Press. 19–39.
Roberts, David 2002. 'Shakespeare, Theatre Criticism, and the Acting Tradition'. *Shakespeare Quarterly* 53:3, 341–61.
Rosenberg, Marvin 1978. *The Masks of Macbeth*. Berkeley: University of California Press.
  1982. 'Macbeth and Lady Macbeth in the Eighteenth and Nineteenth Centuries' in John Russell Brown, ed. *Focus on Macbeth*. London: Routledge and Kegan Paul. 73–86.
Ross, Robert ['R.'] 1896. Review of *The Musketeers*. *Saturday Review* 86 (12 November), 631.
Rowell, George, ed. 1971. *Victorian Dramatic Criticism*. London: Methuen.
Runciman, J.F. 1899. Review of *The Perfect Wagnerite*. *Saturday Review* 87 (4 February), 140.
Rutter, Carol Chillington 2001. *Enter the Body: Women and Representation on Shakespeare's Stage*. London: Routledge.

Rylance, Mark 1997. 'Playing the Globe: Artistic Policy and Practice' in Mulryne and Shewring, eds., *Shakespeare's Globe Rebuilt*, 169–76.
Samuel, Raphael 1994. *Theatres of Memory. Vol. 1: Past and Present in Contemporary Culture*. London: Verso.
Scott, Clement 1896. *From 'The Bells' to 'King Arthur', a Critical Record of the First-Night Productions at the Lyceum Theatre from 1871 to 1895*. London: John Macqueen.
　1899. *The Drama of Yesterday and To-day*. 2 vols. London: Macmillan.
Seymour-Ure, Colin 1991. *The British Press and Broadcasting since 1945*. Oxford: Blackwell.
Shakespeare, William 2005. *The Complete Works*. Ed. Stanley Wells, Gary Taylor, John Jowett and William Montgomery. Oxford University Press.
Shaw, George Bernard [1891] 1971. Appendix to *The Quintessence of Ibsenism* in Rowell, ed., *Victorian Dramatic Criticism*, 361–3.
　1899. 'The Perfect Wagnerite'. Letter. *Saturday Review* 87 (11 February), 177.
　1920. '"The Dying Tongue of Great Elizabeth" by George Bernard Shaw . . . To which is added a Footnote by William Poel. Published by the London Shakespeare League'. London: London Shakespeare League.
　1932. *Our Theatres in the Nineties*. 3 vols. London: Constable.
　[1911] 1934. *Fanny's First Play. The Complete Plays of Bernard Shaw*. London: Odhams Press Limited. 651–83.
　1937. *London Music in 1888–89 as Heard by Corno di Bassetto*. London: Constable.
　1949a. *Ellen Terry and George Bernard Shaw: Correspondence*. Ed. Christopher St John. London: Reinhardt and Evans.
　1949b. *Sixteen Self Sketches*. London: Constable.
　1956. *Advice to a Young Critic, Letters 1894–1928*. London: Peter Owen Ltd.
　1960. *How to Become a Musical Critic*. Ed. Dan H. Laurence. London: Rupert Hart-Davis.
　1961. *Shaw on Shakespeare*. Ed. Edwin Wilson. New York: E.P. Dutton.
　1981. *Shaw's Music: The Complete Musical Criticism in Three Volumes*. Ed. Dan H. Laurence. London: Max Reinhardt.
　[1895] 1986. 'The Sanity of Art: An Exposure of the Current Nonsense about Artists being Degenerate' in Michael Holroyd, ed. *Bernard Shaw: Major Critical Essays*. Harmondsworth: Penguin. 309–60.
Shellard, Dominic 1995. *Harold Hobson: Witness and Judge*. Keele University Press.
　2003. *Kenneth Tynan: A Life*. New Haven, CT: Yale University Press.
Sheridan, Richard Brinsley [1779] 1940. *The Critic*. Ed. G.A. Aitken. London: J.M. Dent.
Shrum, Wesley Monroe 1996. *Fringe and Fortune: The Role of Critics in High and Popular Art*. Princeton University Press.
'Sir Henry Irving' 1895. *Saturday Review* 79 (1 June), 718.
Smialkowska, Monika 2013. 'Julius Caesar' in Edmondson, Prescott and Sullivan, eds., *A Year of Shakespeare*, 91–5.
Smith, Barbara Herrnstein 1988. *Contingencies of Value: Alternative Perspectives for Critical Theory*. Cambridge, MA: Harvard University Press.

Smith, Bruce 2000. *Shakespeare and Masculinity*. Oxford University Press.
Smith, Peter J. 2012. 'Red Velvet'. *Times Higher Education* 1 November. www.timeshighereducation.co.uk/story.asp?storyCode=421626&section code=26. Accessed: 13 December 2012.
Society of Dramatic Critics. 1907. 'Suggested Rules to be Submitted at a General Meeting, January 4th, 1907'. London.
Sondheim, Stephen, Burt Shevelove and Larry Gelbart 1985. *The Frogs and A Funny Thing Happened on the Way to the Forum*. New York: Dodd, Mead and Co.
Spencer, Charles 2000. Personal interview with author, June.
  2012. Review of *King Lear. Daily Telegraph* 12 September. www.telegraph.co.uk/culture/culturereviews/9536939/King-Lear-Almeida-Theatre-review.html. Accessed: 13 December 2012.
Sprague, A.C. 1947. 'Shakespeare and William Poel'. *University of Toronto Quarterly* 17, 29–37.
Stead, W.T. 1902. 'Character Sketch: Mr. T.P. O'Connor, M.P.' *Review of Reviews* 26, 478 9.
Stedman, Jane W. 1995. 'Theatre' in J. Don Vann and Rosemary T. VanArsdel, eds. *Victorian Periodicals and Victorian Society*. University of Toronto Press. 162–76.
Stefanova, Kalina 2000. *Who Keeps the Score on the London Stages?* Amsterdam: Harwood.
Steiner, George 1967. *Language and Silence: Essays 1958–1966*. London: Faber and Faber.
Stokes, John 1972. *Resistible Theatres: Enterprise and Experiment in the Late Nineteenth Century*. London: Paul Elek Books.
Stone, George Winchester, Jr. 1957. *The London Stage 1660–1800: Part 4, 1747–1776*. Carbondale, IL: Southern Illinois University Press.
Stone, George Winchester, Jr. and George M. Kahrl 1979. *David Garrick: Critical Biography*. London: Feffer & Simons.
Stoppard, Tom 1968. *The Real Inspector Hound*. London: Faber.
Stubbes, Philip [1583] 2002. *Anatomy of Abuses*. Ed. M.J. Kidnie. Renaissance English Text Society. Tempe: Arizona Center for Medieval and Renaissance Studies.
Sutton Trust, the 2006. *The Educational Backgrounds of Leading Journalists*. Downloaded from. www.suttontrust.com.
Tardiff, Joseph C., ed. 1993. *Shakespearean Criticism Volume XX: Macbeth and Timon of Athens*. Detroit: Gale Research Inc.
Taylor, Gary 1991. *Reinventing Shakespeare: Cultural History from the Restoration to the Present*. London: Vintage.
  1996. *Cultural Selection*. New York: Basic Books.
Terry, Ellen 1933. *Ellen Terry's Memoirs, with Preface, Notes and Additional Biographical Chapters by Edith Craig and Christopher St. John*. London: Victor Gollancz.
Theatre of Blood 1973. Screenplay by Anthony Greville-Ball. Dir. Douglas Hickox. MGM/UA.

Theatre Record 1981–. 33 vols. London. www.theatrerecord.org
Thomas, David and Arnold Hare 1989. *Theatre in Europe – A Documentary History: Restoration and Georgian England, 1660–1788*. Cambridge University Press.
Thomson, Peter 2000. *On Actors and Acting*. University of Exeter Press.
TR = see Theatre Record.
Treglown, Jeremy and Bridget Bennett, eds. 1988. *Grub Street and the Ivory Tower: Literary Journalism and Literary Scholarship from Fielding to the Internet*. Oxford: Clarendon Press.
Trewin, J.C. 1964. *Shakespeare on the English Stage, 1900–1964*. London: Barrie and Rockliff.
Tynan, Kathleen 1987. *The Life of Kenneth Tynan*. London: Methuen.
Tynan, Kenneth 1950. *He That Plays the King*. London: Longman.
  1953. 'Down with Scarecrows, Snobs and Sniggers!' *Daily Sketch* 2 October. 4.
  1961a. *Curtains*. London: Longman.
  1961b. 'Post-mortem on the Egoist' *Observer*.
  1964. *Tynan on Theatre*. Harmondsworth: Penguin.
  1966. *Bull Fever: New Edition with Some Afterthoughts*. New York: Atheneum.
  1967. *Tynan Right and Left*. London: Longmans.
  1971. 'The Critic Comes Full Circle'. *Theatre Quarterly* 1, 37–48.
  1975a. *A View of the English Stage*. London: Davis-Poynter.
  1975b. *The Sound of Two Hands Clapping*. London: Jonathan Cape.
  1994. *The Letters of Kenneth Tynan*. Ed. Kathleen Tynan. London: Weidenfeld & Nicolson.
  2001. *The Diaries of Kenneth Tynan*. Ed. John Lahr. London: Bloomsbury.
Van Dijk, Marteen 1982. 'John Philip Kemble and the Critics'. *Theatre Notebook* 36, 110–18.
Van Dijk, T.A. 1988. *News Analysis*. New Jersey: L.E.A.
Vickers, Brian, ed. 1975. *Shakespeare: The Critical Heritage. Vol. III: 1733–1752*. London: Routledge and Kegan Paul.
Walkley, Arthur Bingham 1892. *Playhouse Impressions*. London: Fisher Unwin.
  1903. *Dramatic Criticism*. London: John Murray.
Wardle, Irving 1980. Review of *Macbeth. The Times* 5 September.
  1992. *Theatre Criticism*. London: Routledge and Kegan Paul.
  1997. 'Thieves and Parasites: On Forty Years of Theatre Reviewing in England'. *New Theatre Quarterly* 13:50 (May), 119–32.
Webb, Kaye, ed. 1952. *An Experience of Critics and The Approach to Dramatic Criticism*. London: Perpetua.
Weimann, Robert 1988. 'Bifold Authority in Shakespeare's Theater'. *Shakespeare Quarterly* 39:4, 401–17.
Weller, Bernard 1923. 'Probation for Critics'. *Critics' Circular* 1:1 (November), 5.
Wells, Stanley 1976. 'Shakespeare in Max Beerbohm's Theatre Criticism'. *Shakespeare Survey* 29, 132–44.
  1980. 'Shakespeare in Leigh Hunt's Theatre Criticism'. *Essays and Studies*, 119–38.
  1982. 'Shakespeare in Hazlitt's Theatre Criticism'. *Shakespeare Survey* 35, 43–55.

ed. 1997. *Shakespeare in the Theatre: An Anthology of Criticism.* Oxford University Press.
Werner, Sarah 2001. *Shakespeare and Feminist Performance: Ideology on Stage.* London: Routledge.
Whately, Thomas [1785] 1997. 'Remarks on Some of the Characters of Shakespeare' in Adler, ed., *Responses to Shakespeare. Vol. III: 1783–1791*, n.p.
Wiener, Joel H., ed. 1988. *Papers for the Millions: The New Journalism in Britain, 1850s to 1914.* London: Greenwood Press.
Wilde, Oscar [1890] 1950. 'The Critic as Artist, with Some Remarks upon the Importance of Doing Nothing' in Hesketh Pearson, ed. *Essays by Oscar Wilde.* London: Methuen. 100–88.
Williams, Raymond 1961. *The Long Revolution.* London: Chatto and Windus.
Wilson, A.E. 1941. Editorial. *Critics' Circular* 7:28 (June), 1.
Wilson, M. Glen 1975. 'Charles Kean and the Victorian Press'. *Victorian Periodicals Newsletter* 8, 95–108.
Woolf, Virginia 1925. *The Common Reader.* London: Hogarth Press.
Worthen, W.B. 1997. *Shakespeare and the Authority of Performance.* Cambridge University Press.
Yates, Keiran 2012. Review of *Othello. Guardian* 7 May. www.guardian.co.uk/stage/2012/may/07/othello-review. Accessed: 13 December 2012.

Index

Aberg, Maria 178
academic reviewing 6, 10, 15–17, 135, 149
Addison, Joseph 154
Agate, James 2, 25, 27, 28, 32, 66, 96, 97, 116, 118, 131, 143, 147, 150, 151, 152, 176, 185
Albery, Tim 146
Alexander, Bill 146
Alfreds, Mike 170
Allen, Woody 193
anthologies, anthologisation 64–7, 99, 108, 111, 112, 115
anxiety 27, 84, 89, 97, 148, 155, 175, 193
Archer, William 57, 59, 66, 85, 86, 108, 116
Armstrong, Alan 149
Astor Place Riots 50
Attenborough, Michael 3, 146

Baldick, Chris 10, 19, 20
Baer, Marc 42
Barthes, Roland 153
Barton, John 131
Bassett, Kate 139
Baxter, Beverley 108
Beckett, Samuel 7
Beetham, Margaret 63
Behan, Brendan 9
Beerbohm, Max 3, 5, 12, 25, 27, 28, 34, 59, 61, 65–6, 70–2, 84, 92, 94, 99, 101, 108, 114, 116, 137, 168, 169, 178
Beerbohm Tree, Herbert 85, 87, 101
Benjamin, Walter 60, 79
Bennett, Susan 166
Benthall, Michael 103, 121
Bernhardt, Sarah 97
Betts, Hannah 160, 168, 170
Billington, Michael 3, 19, 109, 137, 141, 142, 143, 146, 150–1, 152, 153, 154, 157, 158, 159, 160, 165, 167, 172, 174, 175–7, 178, 180, 194, 195
Blau, Herbert 5, 33
Boaden, James 43
Bogdanov, Michael 19

Booth, John E. 21, 140, 144
Bourdieu, Pierre 26, 45, 135, 170
Boyd, Michael 187
Bradley, A.C. 39
Brake, Laurel 59
Braunmuller, A.R. 32
Brecht, Bertolt 9, 27, 116, 118, 122, 126, 127–30, 153, 164
Bridges-Adams, William 102
Bristol, Michael D. 155
Brome, Richard 168
Brooke, Nicholas 32
Brown, Georgina 157
Browne Report into Higher Education 192
Burke, Seán 64, 69
Butler, Robert 147, 156, 161

Cahiers Élisabéthains 16
Cameron, David 186
Carlson, Marvin 5, 22–3
Carnegy, Patrick 187
Carr, J. Comyns 53
Carroll, Sydney W. 14, 59
Cass, Henry 102
Cavendish, Dominic 179, 185
Chekhov, Anton 98
Chomsky, Noam 22, 25
Clapp, Susannah 190
comparative criticism 3, 27, 85, 110, 146
competition 17–18, 29, 31, 34, 35, 49, 92–3, 137, 138, 184, 187, 195 (*see also:* masculinity; substitution; succession)
Conboy, Martin 174
Connolly, Cyril 114
Costa, Maddy 161, 180
Coveney, Michael 137, 138, 151, 157, 178, 195
Craig, Edward Gordon 24, 102
Craig, Nicholas 8
Crisp, Clement 174
critics – *see* reviewers
Critics Circle, The 12–15, 91, 142, 174, 195

212

Crowley, John 151
Curtis, Nick 149, 154

Daileader, Celia R. 23, 25
Darlington, W.A. 15, 102, 118, 131
Davenant, William 31, 36, 37
Davies, Thomas 38
Davis, Tracy D. 61
Dawson, Anthony B. 169
de Jongh, Nicholas 139, 154
Dent, Alan 99, 112, 113
Derrida, Jacques 108
Diamond, Erin 4
Dickson, Andrew 173, 180, 181, 194
Doran, Gregory 187, 188, 190, 191
Douchez, George 1, 2, 5
Downes, John 37
Dromgoole, Dominic 185
Dundy, Elaine 94, 123, 136
Dusinberre, Juliet 124

Edwardes, Jane 151, 163, 168
Edwards, Derek 150
Edwards, Gale 24
Ehrenreich, Barbara 192
Eliot, George 19
Eliot, T.S. 19, 107, 110, 161
Elizabethan Stage Society 67, 78, 79, 90, 91, 168, 169
Evans, Lloyd 192
Evans, Richard J. 26
Eyre, Peter 136

Fay, Stephen 159
Fiennes, Ralph 153
Forbes, Bryan 149
Foss, Roger 159
Forbes-Robertson, Johnston 81, 86
Forrest, Edwin 49–50
Forster, John 55, 67, 99
Foss, Roger 156
Foucault, Michel 63, 64
Franklin, Bob 139, 140, 145

Gardner, Lyn 142, 180, 187, 195
Garland, Patrick 131
Garrick, David 27, 31, 36–9, 40–3, 53, 148
Gentleman, Francis 39
Gielgud, John 120
Gilchrist, Andrew 182
Gilmore, David D. 36
Globe to Globe festival (part of the World Shakespeare Festival 2012) 177, 179, 194
Gore-Langton, Robert 9, 160, 168

Gosse, Edmund 89
Grady, Hugh 11
Grandage, Michael 193
Granville Barker, Harley 102
Gray, Charles 21, 43
Green, L. Dunton 14
Gross, John 143, 153, 156, 163
Guinness, Alec 98
Gurr, Andrew 164
Guthrie, Tyrone 101, 102, 103

Habermas, Jürgen 18
Hagerty, Bill 148, 164
Hampton, Christopher 9
Harmsworth, Alfred (Lord Northcliffe) 141
Hart, Christopher 189, 191
Hawkes, Terence 104
Hazlitt, William 1, 5, 11, 20, 22, 29, 44–5, 67, 83, 85, 99, 109, 110–11, 112, 113, 120, 122, 143
Helpmann, Robert 103, 176
Herbert, Ian 144
heroic acting 95, 116, 137
Heron, Gil Scott 180
Hewison, Robert 143, 158
Higgins, Paul 151, 178
Hildy, Franklin 164
Hobson, Harold 112, 138
Hodgdon, Barbara 23, 25
Holderness, Graham 170
Holland, Peter 152
Holm, Ian 178
Holroyd, Michael 76, 82
Horrocks, Jane 148
Hume, Robert D. 58
Hunt, James Leigh 20, 24, 45, 67, 99, 110
Hytner, Nicholas 174

Ibsen, Henrik 98, 108
impressionist criticism 70, 85, 87
Internet, the 133, 135, 139, 182, 193, 195
Iqbal, Nosheen 181
Irving, Sir Henry 2, 27, 33, 49, 51–4, 55, 56, 75, 76–7, 82, 92, 97, 103, 112, 118, 148

Jackson, Russell 22, 25, 76
James, Henry 52
Jauss, Hans Robert 165
Johnson, Samuel 38
Jonson, Ben 66, 109

Kean, Charles 18, 22
Kean, Edmund 1–2, 5, 33, 34, 38, 43, 44–5, 49, 55, 83, 120, 122, 125
Kellaway, Kate 167, 180
Kemble, John Phillip 22, 38, 43–7

Kennedy, Dennis 24
Kent, Christopher 61
Kent, Jonathan 134
Kent, Nicholas 146
Kissoon, Jeffery 178
Koenig, Rhoda 159, 191
Komisarjevsky, Theodore 102, 104–5

Lahr, John 136
Lamb, Charles 85
Larson, Magali Sarfatti 12, 142
Laycock, Stuart 189
Leavis, F.R. 161
Leigh, Vivien 121, 122–5
Letts, Quentin 190, 191
Leveson Inquiry 190
Lewes, George Henry 18, 67, 74, 85, 99, 103, 110, 194
literary criticism 6, 10, 11, 19
Littlewood, Joan 127
Littlewood, S.R. 193
Lloyd Evans, Gareth and Barbara 21
Logan, Brian 181
Lowe, Robert William 66, 85

Macaulay, Alistair 159, 160, 163, 166, 167
Macklin, Charles 33, 39, 42
Macready, William Charles 45, 47–51, 55, 151, 186–7, 195
Marmion, Patrick 164
masculinity 5–6, 9–10, 28–9, 36, 38, 40, 44–7, 53–6, 119, 124, 132, 146, 178, 193, 195 (*see also:* anxiety; competition)
Maxwell, Dominic 186
Mazer, Cary 16
McCrum, Robert 188
McDonald, Rónán 133
McKay, Malcolm 167
McKellen, Ian 151
McNair, Brian 25
McNee, Jodie 191
McWhinnie, Donald 125
memory 5, 33–5, 56, 64, 66, 95, 96, 99, 130, 134, 146, 147, 150, 194 (*see also:* nostalgia)
Michael, Chris 181, 182
Middleton, David 150
Middleton, Thomas 167, 168
Miles, Bernard 120
Miller, Arthur 115, 126, 128
Miller, William Ian 38
Moore, William M. 78
Montague, C.E. 143
Morley, Sheridan 137, 167
Morrison, John 171, 177
Mountford, Fiona 158, 161, 185

Munsil, Janet 136
Murphy, Arthur 37

Nathan, David 149, 159
Nelson, Richard 50, 136
New Journalism, the 63, 73–5, 83, 96, 141
Nightingale, Benedict 137, 146, 151, 159, 161, 166
Ninagawa, Yukio 150
Noble, Adrian 109, 150, 154
Nord, David Paul 173
Norman, Neil 177, 178, 190
North, Madelaine 158
nostalgia 2–3, 125, 134, 138, 193 (*see also:* memory)
Nunn, Trevor 150, 152

O'Connor, T.P. 63, 73
Old Vic Theatre 101, 102, 106, 121, 124, 127, 149, 178
Olivier, Laurence 27, 32, 109, 110, 116, 119, 127, 130, 132, 150, 151, 162
O'Neill, Jonjo 178
Open Air Theatre, Regent's Park 158
Orgel, Stephen 31, 37
Osborne, George 186
Osborne, Laurie E. 24, 36
O'Toole, Peter 149, 178

Parker, Jamie 186, 187
Patterson, Joseph 'JP' 174
Peter, John 151, 153, 157
Pimlott, Stephen 143, 153
Planchon, Roger 129
Poel, William 76, 78–80, 88, 90, 91, 168, 169
Polanski, Roman 126
Porter, Eric 125
Powell, Dilys 15
Proctor, Bryan Waller 45
Pryce, Jonathan 3
Purves, Libby 178, 188
Pykett, Lyn 64

Quayle, Anthony 119, 121

Raleigh, Walter 9
Rebellato, Dan 95, 96
Redgrave, Corin 136
Redgrave, Michael 49, 119
reviewers
  fictional representations 7–9
  historical reputation 7
  parody, pastiche, use of 86, 116, 137, 140
  professionalism 11, 61–2, 73–4, 92, 133, 142, 173
  quotation, use of 3, 32, 106, 107–12, 113, 117, 132, 194

Index

Rice, Emma 174
Richardson, John E. 173
Richardson, Ralph 120
Rickson, Ian 175
Roach, Joseph 5, 28, 33, 34, 40
Roberts, David 108–9
Rosenberg, Marvin 34, 54
Ross, Olivia 186
Royal Shakespeare Company 19, 24, 131, 143, 154, 177, 180, 187, 190, 191, 194
Runciman, J.F. 91
Rutter, Carol Chillington 23
Rylance, Mark 146, 147–50, 164, 165, 187

Samuel, Raphael 162
Schall, Ekkehard 130
Scott, Clement 3, 20, 51, 55, 59, 62, 65, 68, 70–2, 92, 98
Seale, Douglas 126
Sellars, Peter 169
Sewell, Rufus 151
Shakespeare Bulletin 16
Shakespeare Quarterly 16
Shakespeare Survey 15
Shakespeare, William
  All's Well that Ends Well 101, 108, 194
  Antony and Cleopatra 24, 104, 124
  As You Like It 88, 101
  Comedy of Errors, The 80, 101, 177, 194
  Coriolanus 45, 124, 129–30, 181, 182
  Cymbeline 77, 81, 83, 101, 156, 160, 161, 163, 170, 180
  Hamlet 3, 26, 35, 81, 86, 88, 91, 103, 110, 129, 138, 160, 163, 169, 175, 183
  I and II, Henry IV 101, 126
  Henry V 89, 106, 119, 127, 156, 160, 162, 163, 164, 180, 183–7
  Julius Caesar 101, 156, 160, 164, 183, 187–90, 191
  King John 87, 101, 177, 178, 179–87
  King Lear 3, 35, 101, 103, 160, 161, 163
  Love's Labour's Lost 6, 15, 78, 108, 158, 180
  Macbeth 6, 18, 27, 28, 31, 86, 101, 102, 103, 106, 109, 116, 119–26, 129, 134, 145–54, 160, 166, 187, 194
  Measure for Measure 100, 190, 191, 192
  Merchant of Venice, The 100, 101, 109, 159, 167, 169, 180
  Merry Wives of Windsor, The 89, 106, 182, 188
  Midsummer Night's Dream, A 23, 88, 89, 102, 158, 164, 181, 194
  Much Ado about Nothing 76, 78, 102, 105, 171, 175, 194
  Othello 1, 23, 78, 109, 110, 111, 113, 119, 120, 152, 179, 181, 182

Richard II 131, 143, 153
Richard III 74, 77, 83, 120, 177, 180
Romeo and Juliet 40
Taming of the Shrew, The 19, 24, 89, 107, 181
Tempest, The 101, 159, 177
Troilus and Cressida 158, 180, 181
Twelfth Night 67, 80, 87, 89, 90, 107, 121, 131, 169, 177, 192
Winter's Tale, The 166
Shakespeare's Globe Theatre 27, 28, 89, 90, 134, 148, 152, 154–72, 177
Shatner, William 181
Shaw, George Bernard 2, 7, 12, 19, 20, 25, 27, 28, 59, 67, 72, 85, 88, 89, 91, 92, 94, 96, 98, 99, 100, 101, 105, 108, 114, 124, 143, 186
Shaw, Glen Byam 24, 121, 150
Sheen, Michael 175
Shellard, Dominic 21, 25
Sher, Antony 178
Sheridan, Richard Brinsley 7, 42
Shuttleworth, Ian 138, 154, 156, 189
Siddons, Sarah 44
Sierz, Aleks 164
signed article, the 27, 57, 58–67, 75, 92, 96, 173
Smialkowska, Monika 188
Smith, Barbara Herrnstein 162
Smith, Bruce 29
Smith, Peter J. 188
Smith, William 'Gentleman' 40
Society of Dramatic Critics 12, 15 (*see also:* Critics' Circle)
Sofaer, Abraham 109
Sondheim, Stephen 92
Spacey, Kevin 178
Spencer, Charles 3, 136, 138, 146, 153, 156, 157, 160, 161, 164, 168, 178, 189
Sprague, A.C. 79
Stanislavsky, Konstantin 24
Stead, W.T. 73
Stedman, Jane 61
Steele, Richard 154
Stefanova, Kalina 137
Steiner, George 9
Stokes, John 57
Stoppard, Tom 7, 125, 136
Stubbes, George 157
substitution 5, 28, 33, 40, 77, 93, 94, 95, 132, 148, 187 (*see also:* anxiety; competition; succession)
succession 17, 84, 94, 96, 114, 132, 148, 177, 187, 190, 195 (*see also:* anxiety; competition; substitution)
Supple, Tim 194
Sutherland, Donald 141
Szalwinska, Maxie 179

Taylor, Gary 56, 147
Taylor, Paul 146, 160, 166, 169, 179, 195
Terry, Ellen 2, 5, 53, 54, 55, 64, 72, 77, 81, 82, 103
Theatre of Blood 8
Thomas, Stephen 103
Thomson, Peter 45
Tinker, Jack 147, 149
Tynan, Kenneth 24, 25, 27, 28, 32, 48, 56, 94, 113, 134, 136–9, 143, 145, 186
  He That Plays the King (1950) 116–19, 120, 129

Unwin, Stephen 146

Valk, Frederick 111, 113, 119
Van Dijk, T.A. 25
Van Dijk, Marteen 22

Walker, Tim 185
Walkley, A.B. 30, 69–70, 74, 85, 89
Wanamaker, Sam 170–1
'Wapping Revolution', the 139

Wardle, Irving 21, 95, 118, 124, 138, 195
Weimann, Robert 155
Weller, Bernard 13–14
Wells, Stanley 16, 22, 25, 86, 88
Werner, Sarah 24, 25
Whately, Thomas 45, 55
Whiting, John 193
Wilde, Oscar 62, 69, 90
Williams, Tennessee 115
Wilson, A.E. 193
Wilson, Edwin 79
Wilson, Glen M. 22
Woddis, Carole 160
Wolfit, Donald 103, 113
Woolf, Virginia 71
Worthen, W.B. 147, 156, 165, 169
World Shakespeare Festival (2012) 27, 135, 177–90

xenophobia 105, 169, 186

Yates, Kieran 181, 182